# THE
# PACIFIC WAR
## COMPANION
From Pearl Harbor to Hiroshima

OSPREY
PUBLISHING

# THE
# PACIFIC WAR
## COMPANION
From Pearl Harbor to Hiroshima

EDITOR
# DANIEL MARSTON

First published in Great Britain in 2005 by Osprey Publishing,
Midland House, West Way, Botley, Oxford OX2 0PH, United Kingdom.
443 Park Avenue South, New York, NY 10016, USA.
Email: info@ospreypublishing.com
This paperback edition published 2007 by Osprey Publishing Ltd.

A CIP catalog record for this book is available from the British Library

ISBN 978 1 84603 212 7

The authors, Joseph H. Alexander, Raymond Callahan, Richard B. Frank, Theodore
Gatchel, Bruce Gudmundsson, David Horner, Tomoyuki Ishizu, Ken Kotani, Robert
Love, Daniel Marston, Dennis Showalter and H. P. Willmott, have asserted their rights
under the Copyright, Designs and Patents Act, 1988, to be identified as the Authors
of this Work.

Editor: Dr Daniel Marston
Design: Ken Vail Graphic Design, Cambridge, UK
Index by Alison Worthington
Maps by The Map Studio
Originated by PDQ Digital Media Solutions
Printed in China through World Print Ltd

07 08 09 10 11    10 9 8 7 6 5 4 3 2 1

FOR A CATALOG OF ALL BOOKS PUBLISHED BY OSPREY MILITARY
AND AVIATION PLEASE CONTACT:

NORTH AMERICA
Osprey Direct c/o Random House Distribution Center,
400 Hahn Road, Westminster, MD 21157, USA
E-mail: info@ospreydirect.com

ALL OTHER REGIONS
Osprey Direct UK, P.O. Box 140 Wellingborough, Northants, NN8 2FA, UK
E-mail: info@ospreydirect.co.uk

www.ospreypublishing.com

Cover photo: Marine assault troop advancing on Peleliu. (© Corbis)

In memory of my grandfather, Robert Bachelder,
veteran of the USS *Claxton*, "Little Beaver Squadron,"
US Navy, 1943–45

*DPM*

# Contents

# Contributors

**Colonel Joseph H. Alexander** (ret.) served 28 years as an assault amphibian officer in the US Marine Corps, including two combat tours in Vietnam and more than five years at sea. As a colonel, he served as Chief of Staff, 3d Marine Division, in the western Pacific. As a military historian subsequent to his retirement, Col. Alexander has written five books and six monographs, including *Utmost Savagery: The 3 Days of Tarawa*, winner of the Roosevelt Naval History Prize. He has helped produce 28 documentaries for The History Channel, the Arts and Entertainment Network and Fox News. He is chief historian of the exhibit design team for the National Museum of the Marine Corps and makes his home in the mountains of western North Carolina.

**Professor Raymond Callahan** is Professor of History at the University of Delaware, where he has also served as Associate Dean of Arts & Sciences. Previously he held the John F. Morrison Chair of Military History at the US Army's Command and General Staff College and he is a Fellow of the Royal Historical Society. Professor Callahan has written several books and articles, including *The Worst Disaster: The Fall of Singapore* (2001) and *Burma: 1942–1945* (1978) and has also contributed articles to the *New Dictionary of National Biography* (2004).

**Richard B. Frank**'s first book, *Guadalcanal* (1990) won the General William Greene Award from the Marine Corps. His second work, *Downfall: The End of the Imperial Japanese Empire* (1999) won The Harry S. Truman Book Award. Richard Frank has acted as consultant to Dr Robert Ballard for the documentary and book *The Lost Ships of Guadalcanal*, and has appeared on The History Channel many times, as well as on ABC, NPR and Fox.

**Professor Theodore Gatchel** rejoined the Joint Military Operations faculty of the Naval War College in 1998, having taught in the department twice while on active duty. He retired from the US Marine Corps in 1991 as a colonel after a 30-year career that included a wide variety of staff and command assignments and two combat tours in Vietnam. He holds degrees from Oklahoma and the Naval Postgraduate School, and is a graduate of the Naval War College, Marine Corps Command and Staff College and the US Army's Infantry Officers Advanced Course. He is the author of *At the Water's Edge: Defending against the Modern Amphibious Assault* (1996) and *Eagles and Alligators* (1997) in addition to numerous articles, and a monthly newspaper column on military affairs.

**Major Bruce Gudmundsson** (ret.) is an historian who specializes in tactical innovation – the way that military organizations respond to radical change. The author of four major books and several hundred articles, he has taught at the Marine Corps Command and Staff College, the Royal Military Academy Sandhurst, and Oxford University.

**Professor David Horner** is the Professor of Australian Defence History at the Strategic and Defence Studies Centre, Australian National University, Canberra. A graduate of the Royal Military College, Duntroon, who served as an infantry platoon commander in Vietnam, he was later, as a colonel, head of the Australian Army's Land Warfare Studies Centre. He is the author of more than 24 books on military history and defense, including *High Command* (1982) and *Blamey: The Commander-in-Chief* (1992). In 2004 he was appointed Official Historian of Australian Peacekeeping and Post-Cold War Operations.

**Professor Tomoyuki Ishizu**, is currently Professor of the Military History Department at the National Institute for Defense Studies, Defense Agency of Japan. His major fields of study are military history and strategic thought. He has organized several international conferences, including ones on "War and Peace in the 21st Century" and "Leadership in the Anglo-Japanese War of 1941–45." He has published various books and articles in Japanese and English including *Liddell Hart* (2002), and *Essence of War, and Myriad Faces of Military Power* (2003) and is editor-in-chief of the Journal of Strategic Studies in Japan. He is currently co-editing the forthcoming *Making of US–Japanese Strategy* with Professor Williamson Murray.

**Dr Ken Kotani** is Junior Research Fellow in Military History at the National Institute for Defense Studies, Tokyo. He received a BA from Ritsumeikan University, an MA from King's College London and a Ph.D from Kyoto University. He specializes in intelligence history and has been involved as a co-writer of *Encyclopedia of World War II* (2004), and has also written articles for a variety of journals.

**Professor Robert Love** earned his Ph.D at the University of California, Davis, and has taught military and naval history at the United States Naval Academy since 1975. He is the author of the two-volume *History of the US Navy* (1992), a dozen articles on diplomatic and naval history, and the editor and co-author of *Pearl Harbor Revisited* (1995), *The Year of D-Day: The 1944 Diary of Admiral Bertram H. Ramsay* (1994), and *The Chiefs of Naval Operations* (1980). His monograph, *Cold War and New World Order: America and the Powers since 1945*, will be published next year.

**Dr Daniel Marston** is Senior Lecturer at the Royal Military Academy Sandhurst, UK. He completed both his BA and MA in History at McGill University, Montreal, Canada and his DPhil in the History of War at Balliol College, Oxford. Previous publications include *Phoenix from the Ashes: The Indian Army in the Burma Campaign* (2003) which won the 2003 Templer Medal.

**Professor Dennis Showalter** is Professor of History at Colorado College, and past President of the Society for Military History. Dennis Showalter specializes in the military history of modern Germany and the World Wars. Among his books are *Railroads and Rifles: Soldiers, Technology and the Unification of Germany* (1976); *Tannenberg: Clash of Empires* (1991); *The Wars of Frederick the Great* (1995), and *The Wars of German Unification* (2004). He is completing a book on *Patton and Rommel: Men of War in the Twentieth Century*.

**Professor H. P. Willmott** currently holds the Mark W. Clark chair of Military History at The Citadel, Charleston, South Carolina, is a research fellow with Greenwich Maritime Institute, University of Greenwich and Fellow of the Royal Historical Society. Formerly with reserve airborne forces, he has written extensively on modern naval and military subjects. His books include *Empires in the Balance* (1982), *The Barrier and the Javelin* (1983), *The War with Japan: The Period of Balance* (2002), the critically acclaimed *The Great Crusade: A New Complete History of the Second World War* (1990), and the forthcoming *The Last Fleet Action, The Battle of Leyte Gulf, 22–28 October 1944*.

# Chronology

**1931–32** Japan establishes puppet state of Manchuria

**1933**     **March 25** Japan leaves League of Nations

**1936**     **November 25** Japan signs Anti–Comintern Pact with Germany

**1937**     **July 7** Beginning of general attack by Japanese forces on China (China Incident)

**1939**     **July 2** Japanese forces in Manchuria cross into Outer Mongolia (Nomonhan Incident)

    **September 16** Ceasefire with Soviet forces in Manchuria

**1940**     **September 22** Japan granted bases in Indo-China

    **September 27** Tripartite Pact between Germany, Italy, and Japan

**1941**     **July 26** American government freezes Japanese assets in the USA; General MacArthur appointed to command US Army in Far East

    **October 17** General Tojo becomes Prime Minister of Japan

    **December 7–8** Japanese attack Malaya, Pearl Harbor, and the Philippines

    **December 10** *Prince of Wales* and *Repulse* sunk; main Japanese landing in the Philippines

    **December 14** Japanese start invasion of Burma

    **December 24** Wake Island captured by Japanese

    **December 26** Surrender of Hong Kong

**1942**     **January 23** Japanese forces attack Rabaul

    **January 30** Japanese forces attack Ambon

    **February 15** Singapore Island surrenders

    **February 19** Japanese bomb Darwin

    **February 19–20** Japanese forces land on Timor

**February 27** Naval battle of Java Sea

**February 28** Japanese forces land in Java

**March 8** Japanese troops enter Rangoon; Japanese land in New Guinea

**March 17** MacArthur appointed to command Southwest Pacific Area

**April 9** American forces on Bataan surrender

**April 18** Doolittle raid on Tokyo

**May 5–8** Battle of the Coral Sea

**May 6** American forces on Corregidor surrender

**May 20** Allied forces withdraw from Burma

**May 31** Attack on Sydney Harbour

**June 4–6** Battle of Midway Island

**June 7** Japanese land in Aleutian Islands

**July 21** Japanese land at Gona area, Papua

**August 7** Americans land in Solomons

**August 8–9** Naval battle of Savo Island

**August 25–26** Japanese land at Milne Bay

**Late September** Japanese drive over Owen Stanley Range halted

**November 12–15** Naval battle of Guadalcanal

**December** First Arakan offensive begins

1943     **January 23** Organized Japanese resistance in Papua ends

**February 7** Last Japanese withdraw from Guadalcanal

**February 13** First Chindit operation into Burma

**March 2–4** Battle of the Bismarck Sea

**April 18** Death of Admiral Yamamoto

**May** End of the First Arakan offensive

**May 11** American forces land on Attu in Aleutian Islands

**June 30** Americans land on New Georgia

**September 4** Australians land near Lae, New Guinea

**November** Second Arakan offensive begins

**November 1** American troops land on Bougainville, northern Solomons

**November 15** Mountbatten takes command of South-East Asia Command

**November 20** American forces invade Makin and Tarawa in Gilberts

**December 15** Americans land on New Britain

**1944**    **January 31** Americans invade Marshall Islands

**February 4** Japanese Arakan offensive, *Ha-Go*, begins

**February 15** New Zealand forces invade Green Island

**February 29** Americans invade Admiralty Islands

**March 2** Second Chindit operation launched into Burma

**March 15** Japanese Imphal offensive, *U-Go*, begins

**April 22** Americans land at Hollandia and Aitape

**May 27** Americans land on Biak Island

**June 15** Americans invade Saipan in the Marianas; American strategic air offensive against Japan begins from China

**June 19–20** Battle of the Philippine Sea

**June 22** Siege of Imphal is broken

**July 2** Americans land on Noemfoor

**July 18** General Tojo falls from power as Japanese Prime Minister

**July 21** Americans invade Guam

**September 15** Americans land in Palau Islands (Peleliu) and on Morotai in the Halmaheras

**October 10** US Third Fleet attacks Okinawa

**October 20** Americans land on Leyte

**October 23–26** Naval battle of Leyte Gulf

**November 24** Superfortresses attack Japan from bases in the Marianas

**December** Final Arakan offensive begins

**December** Operation *Extended Capital* begins in Burma

**1945**     **January 9** American forces land on Luzon

**February 19** American forces land on Iwo Jima

**March 9–10** First fire-bomb attack on Tokyo

**March 10** American forces land on Mindanao

**March 20** British capture Mandalay

**April 1** American forces land on Okinawa

**May 1** Australians invade Tarakan

**May 3** British troops capture Rangoon

**August 6** Atomic bomb dropped on Hiroshima

**August 9** Atomic bomb dropped on Nagasaki; Soviet troops invade Manchuria

**August 14** Emperor Hirohito announces Japanese forces' unconditional surrender

**August 15** VJ-Day; all offensive action against Japan comes to an end

**August 17** Sukarno announces Indonesia independent

**September 2** Japanese sign instrument of surrender in Tokyo Bay

# Chapter 1

# Storm over the Pacific
## Japan's road to empire and war

*Professor Dennis Showalter*

## INTRODUCTION AND BACKGROUND

The long-term catalyst for the outbreak of the Pacific War of 1941–45 was the penetration of the Far East in the nineteenth century by an alien culture exponentially superior in military and technological contexts. The Russians, Americans, French, Dutch, and British confronted social and political systems incapable of offering effective, long-term, direct resistance to their power. At the same time, the Western intruders, in venturing into the region, were at the outer limits of their own respective capacities. Russia, even after beginning construction of the Trans-Siberian Railway in 1891, was able to do no more than extend its fingertips into Manchuria and China proper. The European maritime powers possessed neither the regional naval base facilities nor the disposable land power to plant more than outposts in peripheral areas like Indo-China and Indonesia. In the aftermath of the Civil War, the Reunited States concentrated on consolidating its own trans-Mississippi territories.

The result was an attenuated imperialism that depended on pressure and cooption rather than force, and was most successful when the Westerners acted in something approaching concert, as opposed to the confrontational patterns manifested in Africa and Latin America. Local systems had corresponding opportunities for proactive response. In the Philippines, Indo-China, and Indonesia, these responses amounted to cutting deals with newcomers that were in positions to provide significant benefits to mediators at the expense of intransigents. In China, an eroding Imperial political order and a moribund Confucian social ethic made farcical the ongoing effort to ignore the underlying realities of western power while seeking episodically to adopt such of its particular features as a modern navy.

# JAPANESE EXCEPTIONALISM

Japan was another story. Its systematic involvement with the West had begun early in the sixteenth century, and ended in 1598 as Western missionaries and Western firearms threatened permanent entropy to a Japan already destabilized by 150 years of civil war among equally balanced feudal lords. Japan's isolation had never been absolute; the Dutch trading center at Nagasaki served as a conduit for scientific knowledge and political intelligence. By the 1840s, the example of China suggested that Japan would be well advised to begin negotiating with the West while it could still partially control the terms. The US naval mission of 1852 has been widely credited with forcing Japan to open its doors. In fact, the "Black Ships" of Commodore Matthew Perry were as much an excuse as a compulsion to recognize the inevitable.

The next quarter-century was an era of comprehensive change. It was a time in which a samurai might carry the traditional two swords and supplement them with a pair of six-shooters. Adopting Western methods, particularly in military and naval spheres, was seen as the way to escape Western domination. At the same time, an emerging generation of diplomats and theorists argued that to survive in its new environment Japan must develop its own imperium. An island state poor in raw materials needed secure sources of the imports on which its industrialization and prosperity depended. Commerce and colonization, underwritten by armed force, were the prerequisites of national identity and national greatness. A restored imperial government initially sought control of Taiwan, which lay across the southern sea route to Japan, and a sphere of influence in Korea, the strategic bridge to an Asian mainland that seemed wide open to Japanese influence.

More was involved here than simply copying Western examples. The control of Korea, in particular, had been the first stage of de facto shogun Toyotomi Hideyoshi's grandiose plan for the conquest of all China in the late sixteenth century. Thousands of Japanese had fallen before the peninsula was evacuated and Korea absorbed as a vassal state of the Manchu Empire. That status still obtained in 1894. By then, Japan possessed a national conscript army organized and trained on German lines. The Navy, originally linked closely to Britain and still prone to place orders in British shipyards, had increasingly developed its own approaches to doctrine and training, regarding British approaches as too haphazard. Seeking both the specific advantage of control over Korea and the general status of Asia's leading power, Japan forced a quarrel with China and won a quick, comprehensive victory.

The Treaty of Shimonoseki, signed in April 1895, conceded Korea's independence – an obvious preliminary to a Japanese takeover. It also gave Japan Taiwan and the nearby Pescadores, and, as a strategic bonus, the Liaotung Peninsula and the fortress of Port Arthur on the Manchurian mainland. For the Western powers it was too much, too soon. France, Russia, and Germany combined to encourage Japan to reconsider its terms for the sake of regional peace. Under the gun, Japan turned over its Manchurian acquisitions to Russia, while the other European powers – Britain included – established lesser footholds along the north China coast, a region Japan increasingly considered in its sphere of vital interest.

Beginning in the 1870s, nationalist poets and writers developed Hideyoshi's vision of a Japanese Asian empire in the context of an updated version of a cult of the Emperor that proclaimed him a direct descendant of the sun goddess Amaterasu, founder of the dynasty. In its original form, this had the virtue of removing the Emperor from such mundane realities as governance, leaving power in the hands of the samurai warlords. The new version left effective power in the hands of a military/economic oligarchy, but made the Emperor the focal point of an ethos of service and sacrifice that, instead of being applicable only to a limited warrior class, extended to every Japanese, however humble his place in society.

This populist *bushido* (warrior's path) differed essentially from the chauvinistic, militaristic nationalism that developed simultaneously in contemporary Europe. A French or German mother whose son was found unfit for military service might entertain private feelings of relief. Her Japanese counterpart might kill herself from shame. A general, forbidden by the Emperor to atone by suicide for the high casualties his men suffered, took his life as soon as his lord's ended. His wife joined him in ritual death. It was a mentality that increasingly fostered a uniquely belligerent national spirit.

The principal focus of this belligerence was Russia, the only state with the strength and location not only to challenge Japan's developing expansionist aspirations, but also to threaten Japan itself. Mutual suspicion of Russian intentions led to the Anglo-Japanese Alliance of 1902, which confirmed Japan's self-image as a dominant regional power and encouraged standing firm against Russian pressure in Manchuria and Korea. The outbreak of war in 1904 came as no surprise to the world's diplomats, generals, and admirals. The surprise came when Japan defeated, on both land and sea, a Western power arrogantly confident in its superiority over the "little yellow monkeys" – at the immediate cost of exhausting its manpower, economic, and industrial resources. By mid-1905, the island empire's need for peace was so desperate that it approached the United States as a mediator. The moderate terms of the resulting Treaty of Portsmouth conceded to Japan a sphere of influence in Manchuria. They nevertheless outraged a Japanese public opinion unaware of the country's inability to continue the war against a Russia only beginning to deploy its immense military strength in the Far East.

## FRUSTRATED ASPIRATIONS

The Russo-Japanese War established Japan as a major power, but its gains proved marginal compared to the requirements for sustaining Japanese greatness. An economy strained to the limit was further burdened by large foreign loans. The ships that won Tsushima had been largely constructed in foreign yards. Ten years later, Japan was constructing its own dreadnoughts, but the kind of navy required to maintain great-power status in the Pacific did not come cheaply. Taxes became increasingly oppressive on a still largely agricultural population. An expanding army found its new units committed to expensive overseas garrison duty. The Western powers continued to compete financially in Manchuria. China remained nearly immune to Japanese economic penetration.

In both China and Russia, Japan had confronted adversaries willing to negotiate settlements rather than fight to a finish against a determined adversary that had seized its main objectives in the war's early stages. That pattern of limitation persisted when, in 1914, Japan entered the Great War on the Allied side. Its government resisted pressure to send troops to the Western Front and make its new battle cruisers available to the Royal Navy; Japan's only direct contribution to the war in Europe was a few small destroyers sent to the Mediterranean. But Japan's warships patrolled Pacific trade routes and occupied German island possessions. Its soldiers overran the German sphere of influence on the Chinese mainland. Its diplomats put increasing pressure on a Chinese government that was the unstable creation of recent revolution. In 1918, Japan sent troops into Siberia as part of the anti-Bolshevik initiative undertaken by the Western powers. By the time the peace conference assembled at Versailles, Japan was recognized as a major player in the Asian power game. Whether the Empire could sustain its gains, and what domestic and international prices must be paid for them, were other stories.

The war had strengthened in Japan a concept of Asian regionalism. Far from diminishing in the twentieth century, differences in ethnic and cultural patterns between Japan and the West had been revitalized by American and Australian hostility to Japanese immigration. Increasing numbers of Japan's political leaders across the ideological spectrum saw 1914–18 as merely the first stage of a long-term, ethnically-based Darwinian struggle, with the winners eventually turning on the peoples of Asia. Woodrow Wilson's issuing of the Fourteen Points was widely interpreted in Japanese decision-making circles as rhetorical camouflage for an American-led Western conspiracy against the only non-Caucasian world power.

Against the background of this apocalyptic vision developed the concept of what was often called an "Asian Monroe Doctrine," based on "coexistence and co-prosperity," with Japan playing the role that the US assumed in the Western hemisphere. Culturally based prewar concepts of a pan-Asian order based on a common Sinic heritage began sharing space with concrete, pragmatic visions of regionalism that assigned to China the role of providing raw materials and labor, to Manchuria the mission of furnishing living space to an overcrowded Japan, and to Japan itself the provision of leadership and protection.

In the aftermath of the Great War, proponents of moderation gained enough influence in Japan's parliament and administration to secure withdrawal of troops from Siberia, and from the old German concessions on the Shandong Peninsula. The Army was reduced by four divisions, and the Navy scaled back, in accordance with the Washington Treaty of 1922. Successive party-based cabinets pursued cooperative diplomacy with the Western powers in China. This challenge to the link between expansionism and national identity continued, however, to confront two other prewar mentalities significantly weakened in the West by the events of 1914–18, but still vital in Japan. One was the continued acceptance of war as a normal continuation of state policy. The other was a definition of war as an affirmative experience.

Japan began its modern existence by modeling itself on Great Britain: an island empire that used a judicious blend of manufacture, commerce, and violence to achieve power beyond what its own resources could support. The national challenge became creating an industrial apparatus that would enable Japan to function as an independent actor. The government's response was "circumstantial adaptability": making the best possible use of an economy still based heavily on subsistence peasant farming to develop crucial industrial sectors.

This policy was successful enough by the 1920s to make Japan a major exporter to Asian markets. It also generated significant imbalances, with the armaments industry at a state-of-the-art level while other sectors of manufacturing lagged behind. And it rendered Japan heavily – indeed almost totally – dependent on imported raw materials. During the Great War, though some areas profited in the short term by filling Allied orders for munitions, the economy as a whole missed the synergies of stimuli that had transformed the Western states into advanced industrial powers.

During the 1920s it became clear that Japan's industrialization, rapid and comprehensive though it was, could not secure a firm footing in a tightening global market. Heavy industry remained domestically focused, in particular on meeting the demands of the Navy. The export products that defined the Japanese economy were significantly vulnerable to external shocks and disturbances. Increasing numbers of economists argued that, if Japan were to advance to the next stage of growth, a broad-based structure of high-quality production combined with cutting-edge innovation, the country must be in a position to control raw materials and influence markets directly.

That line of argument resonated with conservatives increasingly convinced that Japan needed space for its surplus agrarian population and opportunities for its growing supply of managers and engineers. After World War I, France and Britain, the major Asian colonial powers, were concentrating on domestic recovery. Soviet Russia was even more preoccupied with its own affairs. The United States was far away, and historically more interested in trade than in governance. The way seemed open for Japan to develop an imperium in a region offering both markets and resources: China.

# GREATER EAST ASIA

Initially, there were elements of altruism in Japan's policies. Japan owed its written language and much of its culture to its larger neighbor. With China apparently dissolving into chaos as warlord armies vied for control, the time seemed right for Japan to assume the "yellow man's burden": the younger brother coming to the elder brother's aid for their mutual benefit. A burgeoning Chinese nationalism, however, wanted nothing to do with the concept. At the same time, it proved increasingly difficult for Japanese commercial interests to establish functioning connections in a China where private economy was as fragmented as it was underdeveloped, and whose central government, when finally established, exercised at best tenuous control and tended to seek legitimacy by Japan-bashing. The result, in the 1930s, was an increasing congruence of attitudes in Japan between advocates of economic expansion and the growing body of officials and army officers who had talked one another into believing that Japan had its own Asian version of a "civilizing mission."

Rhetoric shifted into action as a consequence of Chinese behavior. Since the Russo-Japanese War, the nominally Chinese province of Manchuria had been a Japanese sphere of influence. It was a low-rent sphere – some financial investment, a monopoly of railway transportation, a few thousand guard and security troops grandiloquently christened the Kwantung Army. However when China's Kuomintang government began directly challenging Japan's position, in an effort to reassert long-lapsed sovereignty, army officers on the spot defied orders to proceed with caution and patience. Instead they responded by armed action in the Mukden Incident of September 18, 1931, overrunning the province and confronting the Japanese government with a fait accompli.

A long-standing Japanese tradition was *gekokujo*: the open, ceremonial challenge of superiors by juniors for reasons of principle. It was kept alive in the Imperial Japanese Army as a manifestation of that fighting spirit considered necessary for victory – and frequently because the senior officers agreed with their subordinates. In September 1932, the Army established a puppet state in Manchuria. In May 1933, a reinforced Kwantung Army invaded north China, forcing economic and administrative concessions from a nationalist government more concerned with destroying its Communist rival. When China called on the League of Nations for help, that body took the matter under consideration. When the League finally got around to censuring Japan, Japan withdrew – accompanied by the applause of Asian nationalists like Indonesia's Mohammed Hatta, who denounced the League as a front for Western imperialism.

The domestic popularity of this initiative was facilitated significantly by a Great Depression that hit hard at exports concentrated at the extremes of Japan's economic spectrum. Luxury goods on one hand, cut-price textiles on the other, lost customers more rapidly than mid-market items. The Western powers cut off trade with their Asian possessions. Japan's initial response was to make such drastic cuts in its domestic economy that total collapse seemed the next probable stage. More and more Japanese, from high officials to ordinary citizens, listened when the imperialists argued that Japan had only one choice: between being hammer or anvil, windshield or bug.

Japan had always taken seriously the military challenge presumably posed to Asia by the West. The Navy's basic plan for war against the United States dated back to 1907. During the Great War, it began a naval construction program designed to provide, by 1927, a fleet of 16 capital ships, with cruisers and destroyers in proportion – a fleet not only strong enough to guarantee Japan's regional position, but if necessary to challenge for mastery of the Pacific an America increasingly critical of Japanese policies and behaviors in China. The admirals were correspondingly bitter as the Washington Treaty and later disarmament agreements left the fleet in a position of permanent inferiority to those of the US and Britain. It made no difference that the agreed-upon force ratios guaranteed Japan virtual hegemony in the northwest Pacific quadrant. What the Navy sought was a power-projection capacity. To that end, it concentrated on building warships individually larger and better armed than their western counterparts. To that end as well, the Navy paid attention to air power, both land-based and in the developing seagoing version of the aircraft carrier. And finally, the planners counted on the physical and moral toughness, the fighting spirit, of their men.

Japan's army fell increasingly behind the technological curve established on the Western Front, remaining a horse-powered, infantry-based force in an era of industrialized war. That fact led, in turn, to a decision that Japan must emphasize moral elements. The experience of World War I, as processed in the Japanese Imperial Army, was that hardness was a prerequisite for survival and success in modern high-tech combat. Discipline, already harsh by Western standards, was tightened to the limit of everyday endurance. The random physical brutality so often noted by interwar Western observers was considered as prefiguring the even greater and more random brutality of the battlefield.

Surrender had not been considered as inherently shameful in Japan's previous wars, nor in the civil wars that had shaped the Empire's earlier history. After the Great War, it was presented as an unthinkable social and military disgrace, permanently dishonoring the captive and his family. Cold steel was emphasized to the point that light machine guns were given bayonet attachments. Soldiers were not actually expected to use bulky automatic weapons weighing almost thirty pounds in hand-to-hand combat: the design symbolized the Army's priorities.

*Bushido*, an aristocratic warrior creed with its roots in Japan's middle ages, originally prescribed correct and honorable behavior towards enemies as a manifestation of one's own honor. Increasingly it became a synonym for a way of war rather than a way of life. The soldiers and sailors of Japan were expected to show concern for nothing but their duty and their mission. This ethos can be a recipe for trouble away from the front lines in any army. Its effect was exacerbated, as Japan's military involvement in China increased, by a sense of being hopelessly outnumbered in a sea of hostile and inscrutable aliens. The infamous Nanjing Massacre was, in good part, sparked by Japanese fear of "plainclothesmen": Chinese soldiers who shed their uniforms to act as snipers and saboteurs. The only time that Chinese could be trusted was at bayonet point, and in the end "stone dead had no fellow."

The armed forces' institutionalization of hardness had other negative manifestations as well. Logistics were a secondary concern for a fleet and an army obsessed with maximizing combat power. Troops were expected to supplement their rations by requisition and foraging. From the plains of China to the jungles of the South Pacific, that became an entering wedge for brutality in subsistence economies. From using a rifle butt on a recalcitrant peasant, it was a short step to teaching the women who their new masters were, and to destroying what could not be carried away.

It was not an environment encouraging altruism or moderation. In July 1937, a skirmish outside Beijing provided an excuse for resuming hostilities with China. Though the Japanese government did not want a full-scale conflict, the renewed Sino-Japanese War was, from its first days, a total war in terms of its conduct. Japanese behavior at all levels was that of conquerors. Businessmen treated the Chinese with the kind of ruthlessness that discouraged even instrumental cooperation. Exploitation increasingly took second place to destruction. Nevertheless, with a solipsism that can only be described as breathtaking, Japan began making plans for a new Asian order.

The Greater East Asia Co-Prosperity Sphere, as initially described, was based on a concept of economic self-sufficiency among Japan, China, and what would become the former Dutch, British, and French colonial possessions. Never precisely defined, the concept of the Co-Prosperity Sphere was intended as much for domestic as external consumption. It provided a set of aims for what was increasingly becoming a "forever war" against China. It appealed to a xenophobia significantly exacerbated both by what seemed the sanctimony of Western attitudes towards Japan's policies, and by the growing economic pressure the US and Britain were turning against Japan. In an Asian context, the Co-Prosperity Sphere's appeal was essentially political, inviting nationalist movements and Chinese progressives disgusted with the existing gridlock of Communists and Kuomintang to consider the alternative of mutual cooperation. Accompanying it were promises of political independence and economic development – both under Japanese auspices, to be sure, but both also preferable to existing circumstances.

Unfortunately for Japan's purposes, China proved both refractory and retrograde. Within eighteen months of the first efforts at "coordination," it was clear that far from finding China a springboard to modernization, the Army was de-modernizing to meet the demands of even minimal control of the parts of China it occupied. Any doubts on that score were eliminated during a series of border clashes with the USSR in 1939, in which bayonets proved no match for medium tanks. The Navy's new construction programs, including the Yamato class battleships, the most powerful of their kind ever built, made increasing demands on scant reserves of fuel.

For all the traditional hostility that existed between the Army and the Navy, the two services increasingly agreed in principle that Japan still confronted a bleak choice between further enhancing the resources under its control, and resigning itself to second-rank status. The Navy favored a southern initiative against the Dutch and French colonial holdings. The Army, despite its rough treatment at Soviet hands, retained its continental ambitions. The government compromised by supporting both. Emperor Hirohito, despite his personal preference for cooperation rather than confrontation with the US and Britain, refused to interfere – neither deities nor constitutional monarchs comment on details of policy and strategy.

## PATHS TO WAR

The image of a Japan backed into a corner by American boycotts and sanctions during the 1930s, finally lashing out in desperation to begin a war with few chances of winning it, was a staple of anti-Roosevelt politics and revisionist historiography for a quarter-century after 1945. In recent years a more sophisticated understanding of Japan's internal dynamics has diminished the intellectual appeal of what is at bottom a fairly crude economic-determinist interpretation of the island empire's behavior in the decade preceding Pearl Harbor. America's use of its economic strength to create diplomatic leverage may not by itself have impelled Japan to war. It added, however, to the negative synergy that was transforming an ambitious, authoritarian, imperialist power into an ideologically-centered would-be Pacific hegemony.

A generalized public sympathy for China in no way carried over into willingness to risk war. Nevertheless, the increasingly internationally-minded administration of Franklin Roosevelt had no intention of seeing Asia slide into chaos as a consequence of Japan's imperial ambitions combined with an imperial overstretch that rendered Britain less and less capable of influencing Asian affairs decisively. And as the US took a hand, by Japanese standards it took sides as well. Its criticism of Japanese initiatives, whether publicly or through diplomatic channels, rekindled a hostility dating to the turn of the century, when American policy had been widely perceived as committed to frustrating Japan's ambitions – not from its own greed, which would be understandable, but from a sense of moral and racial superiority.

In practical terms at least, the antagonism was one-sided. American public opinion, racist though it might have been, considered the Japanese more a joke than a foe. The two navies had long been each other's principal adversaries in terms of planning and construction, but American senior officers drank no toasts to an inevitable confrontation. There was still room for accommodation when war broke out in Europe in 1939. Nor did Japan take immediate direct advantage of the discomfiture of its European rivals eight months later. Instead it used the new situation to increase China's international isolation – a policy that drew the US correspondingly closer to Chiang Kai-Shek's increasingly ramshackle government.

The next stage in the progress of hostility to war was taken by the US. The massive naval construction program of July 1940, while not aimed at Japan, when completed, would create such an imbalance of forces that the Japanese Imperial Navy had no chance of waging even a defensive campaign in its own waters. Any attempts to minimize that fact seemed refuted in September, when an administration still seeking to avoid war – at least in the Pacific and at least temporarily – began imposing restrictions on its trade with Japan. Intended to send a message, the sanctions were initially minimal, involving items like scrap metal rather than essential raw material like oil. The questions in Tokyo were whether they would remain so benign, and what right the US had to impose them in the first place.

Japan had entered into the Anti-Comintern Pact with Germany in November 1936. Germany's continued attempts to make this a first step to inveigling Japan into an anti-European alliance proved failures. Only after the fall of France did support for a German connection develop. Even then, the Hitler-Stalin Nonaggression Pact of August 1939, which had left Japan twisting in the wind, was not entirely obscured by the German victories of 1940. The armed forces and the foreign office nevertheless agreed that the new circumstances obtaining in Europe uniquely favored a south Asian initiative.

War with the United States was an acceptable, though not necessarily a desirable, side effect. The Tripartite Pact of September 1940 bound Germany, Japan, and Italy to assist each other in case of attack by any power not presently involved in the European war or the Sino-Japanese conflict. Japan hoped this show of unity would encourage the US to modify its position, and was privately willing to abandon the Pact as a negotiating chip. The Roosevelt administration refused to be intimidated by what it interpreted as crude saber-rattling.

In the first months of 1941, Japan increased its pressure on the Netherlands East Indies and French Indo-China, establishing a "protectorate" over the latter colony in July. The US initially protested, then on July 25 announced the limitation of oil exports to Japan and the freezing of Japanese assets in the US. The new policy was intended neither to drive Japan into collapse nor to force it over the brink. In a very real sense, however, the US had no idea how fine-tuned Japan's economy really was. After July 25, the Imperial Navy in particular could calculate almost to the barrel and the date the point when its ships would be unable to operate. Japan needed rubber, tin, and iron from Malaya, the Philippines, and the Netherlands East Indies. Japan could no longer clothe or feed its expanding population from its own resources. Not a thumb, but a beam now rested on Japan's windpipe. The alternatives were conquer, negotiate, or starve.

Apart from the fact that with its funds blocked Japan could not even buy oil on the international market – which by 1941 in any case meant the US – nothing in Japan's past history or recent experience suggested it was likely to accept passively the kind of demeaning insult the US sanctions seemed to offer. After the July embargoes, the question of whether to go to war gave way, in Japanese planning circles, to three lesser ones: when, where, and how.

Japanese planners never envisaged a total defeat of the Western powers. Their intention was to strike a series of coordinated blows securing the resources of south Asia and establishing a defensive perimeter around them. This perimeter, extending well into the western Pacific Ocean, would be developed into a barrier of bases and fortifications impregnable to amphibious assault. Behind that shield, the Imperial Navy would wait to launch javelin thrusts at counterattacks from any direction, making up for inferior numbers by interior lines and superior ships.

Japan, in short, proposed to fight the Pacific War as it had fought China and Russia: limiting the conflict by escalating its material and moral costs beyond what the Western powers, America in particular, were willing to pay. The strategy was predicated not on American effeteness, but on American rationality. Americans were businessmen, not samurai. Eventually they would calculate costs and benefits, and come to terms with the realities created by Japanese arms.

Meanwhile, a US increasingly focused on the threat from Germany, still unaware of what it had done in the Pacific, charted its own course towards Pearl Harbor. That course was not unreflective. American strategic planners were absolutely convinced of their country's ultimate ability to defeat Japan. Chief of Naval Operations Admiral Harold Stark spelled it out to the Japanese ambassador: "While you may have your initial successes, due to timing and surprise, the time will come when you too will have your losses, but there will be this great difference. You will not only be unable to make up your losses but will grow weaker as time goes on, while on the other hand we will not only make up our losses but will grow stronger as time goes on. It is inevitable that we will crush you before we are through with you."[1]

Admiral William Halsey put it more bluntly on December 7, 1941: "When this war is over, the Japanese language will be spoken only in Hell."[2]

# Chapter 2

# Pearl Harbor

## Japanese planning and command structure

*Dr Ken Kotani*

"Pearl Harbor" remains a vivid memory in both the US and Japan, despite the fact that it happened more than 60 years ago. As recently as 1998, the families of Admiral Kimmel and Lieutenant-General Short were lobbying the US Congress and President Clinton to exonerate Kimmel and Short of responsibility for Pearl Harbor.[1] President Bush described the attacks of September 11, 2001 as "a new Pearl Harbor." Robert Stinnett's *Day of Deceit* was translated into Japanese in 2001, and was a best seller in Japan. The Hollywood movie, *Pearl Harbor*, was also very popular in Japan, demonstrating that the event remains significant not only for historians, but also for people in both countries.

From a tactical point of view, the Japanese attack on Pearl Harbor was one of the most brilliant operations in naval history. In December 1941, the Japanese carrier task force silently moved 3,300 sea miles from Hitokkapu bay, Etorohu island to the north of Oahu island. At dawn on December 7, 350 Japanese aircraft attacked Pearl Harbor and the military bases on Oahu. Over the next few hours, the United States Navy (USN) lost four battleships, 180 aircraft, and 2,400 sailors, while the Imperial Japanese Navy (IJN) lost only 29 aircraft and 55 pilots. The Japanese operation was a surprise attack, without declaration of war, and US battleships in the harbor were easy targets for the Japanese pilots.

However, it is also said that no USN commander quite believed that a Japanese attack on Hawaii was feasible. Such an operation might be plausible as an armchair theory, but it was quite difficult for the IJN to practice the attack and anticipate logistical and functional problems. Therefore, this chapter will focus on Japanese planning behind the attack, what the Japanese hoped to achieve and how they hoped to achieve it.

# FROM TSUSHIMA TO THE INTERWAR PERIOD

Before Pearl Harbor, it was the battle of Tsushima (May 27–28, 1905) that exercised the greatest influence on Japanese naval strategy.[2] Tsushima was a decisive naval battle of the Russo–Japanese War. Admiral Heihachiro Togo, leading the Japanese Combined Fleet, had fought against the Russian Baltic fleet in the Sea of Japan. The Russians had lost 28 battleships and 4,800 dead, while the Japanese lost only three torpedo boats and 110 dead. This triumph provided not only a legacy but also a naval doctrine for the IJN, known as *Taikan Kyohosyugi*, the principles of big ships and big guns.[3] The IJN's operational plan was dominated by Tsushima, which focused on a counterattack against an enemy fleet off the Japanese mainland.

After the Russo–Japanese War ended, the IJN came to regard the USN as its hypothetical enemy. The Imperial National Defense Plan in 1907 outlined Japanese naval strategy accordingly; prior to any USN advance into the western Pacific, the IJN was to prepare to counterattack the USN's fleet off the coast of Japan, and thus secure command of the sea.[4] Staff officers imagined that the USN was far superior to the IJN, and that the IJN had no option but to choose the passive and defensive strategy and to rely on the Anglo-Japanese alliance.

This situation changed when, in 1922, Japan joined the Washington Naval Limitation Treaty and the Anglo-Japanese alliance was dissolved. The treaty forced the IJN to limit her battleship tonnage to a ratio of 60 percent of that of the British Royal Navy and USN, and thus to scrap 48,000 tons' worth of battleships.[5] The Navy General Staff (*Gunreibu*) opposed this limitation on the grounds that the IJN needed a ratio of at least 70 percent in order to effectively engage the US fleet in combat. In reality, the treaty was advantageous for the IJN, since even without any limitation treaties she could not keep up a battleship complement equaling 60 percent of the USN's tonnage. As late as March 1934, the Japanese Navy Ministry (*Kaigunsho*) Armament Limitation Research Committee estimated that Japanese shipbuilding capacity was 45,000 tons per year, compared to 80,000 tons in the US. In other words, Japan could match only 55 percent of US shipbuilding output.[6] When considered in this context, the treaty era (1922–36) could constitute a strategic break for the IJN.

# AFTER THE TREATY: BIG GUNS OR AIR POWERS

In 1937, Japan seceded from the treaty system. In doing so, she challenged both her Anglo–American rivals and the status quo in the Pacific. The principles of big ships and big guns were still influential dogma in the IJN, and had evolved into the super-battleship strategy. During the treaty era, the IJN's concern had shifted from quantitative ratio to qualitative superiority, and energy had been directed toward planning the biggest and most powerful battleships ever built: the *Yamato* and the *Musashi*. These battleships, weighing 65,000 tons and carrying nine 18-inch guns, were laid down in 1937 at Kure and Nagasaki dockyards and launched in 1940. They were believed to be unsinkable, and to outstrip the USN's Iowa class, which weighed in at 45,000 tons and carried nine 16-inch guns. The IJN's strategy was to wait and react, forcing a decisive battle with the USN in the Mariana and Marshall Islands (western Pacific), and to beat the American fleet with superior ships and guns.

There were some high-ranking officers among the Navy General Staff who doubted the "big ships" dogma. Both Vice-Admiral Shigeyoshi Inoue, the Chief of the Naval Air Department, and Admiral Isoroku Yamamoto, the Commander-in-Chief of the Combined Fleet, believed in the superiority of naval air power over super-battleships. In January 1941, Inoue submitted a long report to the Navy minister, Koshiro Oikawa, which argued against possessing big ships, and advocated the usefulness of air power and submarines in the coming war with the US.[7]

Yamamoto also doubted the Navy's orthodoxy; he had believed in the potential of naval aviation since the 1930s. In spring 1940, he observed naval air grand maneuvers, which convinced him of their superiority to battleships and gave him the idea for an air raid on Hawaii. He immediately proposed this idea to Chief of Staff Vice-Admiral Shigeru Fukutome who wholeheartedly endorsed it.[8] In January 1941, Yamamoto tried to urge the Navy Minister to reconsider the principle of big ships and big guns, and abandon the old dogma for a new focus on air power.

Was it a coincidence that both Inoue and Yamamoto suggested their new idea to the Navy Minister in January 1941? Undoubtedly the British raid on Taranto in November 1940 had some influence;

three other factors also exercised an influence on the IJN's strategy in 1941.

The first of these factors was the signing of the Tripartite Pact with Germany and Italy on September 27, 1940, which caused a serious deterioration in US–Japanese relations. The pact allowed the Japanese to advance into Southeast Asia and confront Anglo-American powers in the region. Admiral Yamamoto gave the order to increase the production of the plane that was to be the centerpiece of naval aviation, the Zero fighter.

The second factor, in June 1940, was the passage by the US Congress of the naval expansion bill. Known as the Vinson Act, the bill provided for an 11 percent increase in naval tonnage and 4,500 naval aircraft and helped to replace the aging US fleet with new ships. A month later, Congress authorized the Two-Ocean Navy Act, which planned to produce 1,325,000 tons of shipping,[9] a goal far beyond Japanese industrial capacity. As Table 1 indicates, the gap between the two navies was considerable in 1941, and was only expected to increase over time. It was therefore in Japan's interests, if war with the US was inevitable, to engage in combat as soon as possible, and for the IJN to reconsider its war plan accordingly.

**TABLE 1:**
**ANTICIPATED RATIO OF IJN TO USN TONNAGE** [10]

| End of 1941 | 1942 | 1943 | 1944 |
| --- | --- | --- | --- |
| 70.6% | 65% | 50% | 30% |

The third factor was an incident in December 1940 in which the IJN obtained top secret British documents: the capture of the *Automedon*. The *Automedon* was a British Blue Funnel cargo liner which was attacked by a German raider, *Atlantis*, in the Indian Ocean on November 11, 1940.[11] *Automedon* possessed a secret copy of the British War Cabinet Minutes for August 1940 which was being sent to Singapore from Liverpool. These documents, which showed a blueprint of the British Far Eastern strategy, were en route to Britain's Commander-in-Chief, Far East, Air Marshal Robert Brooke-Popham.[12] This document indicated that Britain would not go to war against Japan, even if Japan invaded French Indo-China, and revealed that British chiefs of staff regarded Thailand and Hong Kong as indefensible against Japanese attack.

Bernhard Rogge, captain of the *Atlantis*, recognized the significance of the documents and sent them to the German Naval Attaché in Tokyo, Rear Admiral Paul Wenneker. On December 12, 1940, Wenneker handed the documents to the Vice-Chief of the IJN General Staff, Admiral Nobutake Kondo. There is no doubt that these documents encouraged Japan to wage a war against the Anglo-American powers, and attack not only Singapore, but also Pearl Harbor.

## HAWAII OR PHILIPPINES?

Planning for the Pearl Harbor attack was initiated by Admiral Yamamoto, with his challenge to the principles of big ships and big guns. Practicing the plan involved myriad tactical and technical difficulties. In January 1941, Yamamoto secretly ordered Rear Admiral Takijiro Onishi, Chief of Staff of the 11th Air Fleet, to research a plan of attack.[13] Onishi was one of the IJN's pioneers of both naval aviation and the suicide bomb attack known as *kamikaze*. Onishi invited commander Minoru Genda, a famous airman of the Yokosuka air group, to study and comment on Yamamoto's design. In April 1941, Genda provided a draft to Onishi, which summarized the plan as follows:

1. The attack must catch the enemy completely by surprise.
2. The main objective of the attack should be US carriers.
3. Another priority target should be US land-based planes on Oahu.
4. Every available carrier should participate in the operation.
5. The attack should utilize all types of bombing – torpedo, dive and high-level.
6. Fighter planes should play an active part in the attack.
7. The attack should be made in daylight in the early morning.
8. Refueling at sea would be necessary.
9. All planning must be done in strict secrecy.[14]

Genda stressed the IJN's superiority of aircraft carriers and the necessity of the task force for the operation. He also addressed technical problems, such as the fact that Pearl Harbor was too shallow to permit the use of torpedoes. Yamamoto read the draft, and realized that it would be necessary to modify torpedoes for Pearl Harbor.[15]

However, Captain Sadatoshi Tomioka, the Chief of Staff's operation section, Navy General Staff, objected to Genda's plan. He pointed out the risks of the operation, including the necessity for secrecy, as well as the difficulties of staging an air raid on Hawaii and undertaking operations in the south, Malaya, and the Philippines. Tomioka considered southern operations particularly significant because the Navy needed oil in the region and the Hawaii operation would undermine the southern operations, especially aircraft carriers. Yamamoto's staff officer, Captain Kameto Kuroshima, disputed Tominaga, creating a controversy that lasted through the summer of 1941.[16]

Despite the Navy General Staff's disagreement, Yamamoto and the staff officers of the Combined Fleet continued to study the possibilities of the Pearl Harbor operation. From September 11–20, the Combined Fleet exercised a simulated attack on Hawaii, which resulted in four battleships, two aircraft carriers, three cruisers, and 180 aircraft lost for the USN, compared with two aircraft carriers and 127 aircraft lost for the IJN.[17]

Heartened by these results, the Navy General Staff, the Combined Fleet, and the First Air Fleet carried out joint discussion of the potential for a Hawaii operation on September 24. The discussion focused principally on carrying out parallel operations in the south and Hawaii. The Navy General Staff required aircraft carriers for its southern operation because its latest aircraft, the Zero fighters, could not fly from air bases in Taiwan to the Philippines. Two new aircraft carriers, the *Zuikaku* and *Shokaku*, had been launched on September 1 and the Navy General Staff was assured that these two craft could support the southern operation. According to the Navy General Staff's plan, four aircraft carriers could be allocated to the Hawaii operation and two to the south. Finally, after extensive discussion, Admiral Osami Nagano, the Chief of the Navy General Staff, agreed to Yamamoto's plan.[18] Nagano was not reluctant to fight against the US, but he had no grand strategy in case of war, and was more or less persuaded by Yamamoto.[19]

Having accomplished this, Yamamoto still had to tackle the problem that, according to Genda's draft, he actually needed six aircraft carriers for Hawaii, not four as he had promised. The Navy General Staff, not surprisingly, unequivocally rejected the six-carrier plan. Yamamoto, undaunted, sent Kuroshima to the Navy General Staff with the message that he would resign his position if the plan was not accepted. Nagano, thus compelled, officially approved the Hawaii operation on October 19, and the Combined Fleet was allowed to proceed with the use of six aircraft carriers.[20]

We have already seen examples of Admiral Yamamoto's persistence in pursuing his plan for a speculative air raid on Hawaii, despite the IJN's preference for defensive strategy. Yamamoto, an adherent of "Lanchester's Theory of Warfare,"[21] had already realized that Japanese traditional naval power – big ships and big guns – would be no match for the US fleet in a pitched battle. This insurmountable tactical obstacle had compelled him to abandon the Navy's traditional dogma in an attempt to find a way to take the initiative in a battle between an inferior power and a superior one. Yamamoto was conscious of the comparative weakness of the IJN, and had once told Prime Minister Fumimaro Konoe, "If I am ordered to fight against US, I will make a good job for a half[-year] or year. But I cannot do it for a few years."[22] Yamamoto assumed that the IJN could fight against the USN for, at the longest, one year.

Yamamoto believed that the task force could beat the US Pacific fleet and her aircraft carriers with a surprise attack. His plan was that the IJN should physically damage the USN's ships in an attempt to neutralize the USN's material advantage. Before the USN could repair the initial damage, Japan would construct the *Daitoa Kyoueiken* (Great East Asian Co-Prosperity Sphere) in Southeast Asia, secure necessary natural resources, especially oil in the Netherlands East Indies, and exclude the US fleet from the western Pacific. This maneuver would provide the IJN with sufficient resources to fight against the USN for a few years.[23] Yamamoto believed that if the IJN could succeed in controlling the western Pacific as a Japanese strategic sphere, a significant strategic victory would be achieved.

Yamamoto also expected that a successful surprise attack would damage the USN's morale and enthusiasm to engage in a long-term war with Japan. Therefore, one of the vital aims of the Pearl Harbor attack was to undermine the USN's morale from the very beginning. (In reality, of course, the attack would have the opposite effect on both the USN and the people of the United States, and in this sense Yamamoto's perspective was irrelevant.)

# PREPARATIONS FOR PEARL HARBOR

The staff officers chose fast, long-ranging ships to form a task force for the surprise attack. Yamamoto supervised the entire operation from the Combined Fleet's HQ, the flagship *Nagato*, which stayed in Hashirajima, Japan. Vice-Admiral Chuichi Nagumo commanded the task force from the aircraft carrier *Akagi*. The task force consisted of the First Air Fleet, the First Torpedo Flotilla, the Third and Eighth fleets, the Second Submarine Squadron, the Seventh Destroyer Fleet, and the First and Second supply ship squadrons. The First Air Fleet, the main fleet to strike Pearl Harbor, possessed six aircraft carriers (the *Akagi*, *Kaga*, *Soryu*, *Hiryu*, *Zuikaku*, and *Shokaku*) and 350 aircraft. The First Torpedo Flotilla (one light cruiser, the *Abukuma*, and nine destroyers) and the Second Submarine Squadron (three submarines, the I-19, I-21, and I-23) were for reconnaissance and the Third and Eighth fleets (two battleships, the *Kirishima* and *Hiei*, and two heavy cruisers, the *Tone* and *Chikuma*) providing support to the First Air Fleet. The Seventh Destroyer Fleet (two destroyers and one tanker) had a mission to attack Midway as a demonstration. On the other side, the US had four aircraft carriers, nine battleships, four heavy cruisers, and seven light cruisers in Pearl Harbor, plus around 500 aircraft on the ground bases.

One of the principal difficulties for the task force was deciding a route to Hawaii. The staff officers had researched ten years' worth of weather data for the northern Pacific and merchant shipping routes. The northern Pacific in winter was generally considered too rough to sail, but the deciding factor was keeping the task force's passage secret. As a result, the commanders chose a route that would depart from Etorohu (at latitude 45 degrees north and 148 degrees east), travel at 42 degrees north and terminate at latitude 33 degrees north and 147 degrees west, north of Hawaii.

Another difficulty was re-fueling en route to Hawaii. Only seven ships included in the task force could make the long voyage to Hawaii; the remainder needed re-fueling. Since the IJN's traditional strategy was to fight in Japanese home waters, they had little experience in replenishing big ships in mid-ocean. The task force gathered oil tankers and aircraft carriers in Kyushu for re-fueling training in early November; the exercise was successfully completed by the end of the month.

Air squadrons also began practicing high-level and dive bombing, targeting a California class battleship painted on the ground. The hitting ratio of level bombing on the moving target was about 10 percent; dive bombing on moving targets was 40 percent, while dive bombing on fixed targets was approximately 80 percent.[24] The modified torpedo (Type-91 version 2), which could perform in shallow water, reached the task force at the end of October. Pilots of the squadron practiced continuously, not even breaking for weekends; they described their week as "Monday, Monday, Tuesday, Wednesday, Thursday, Friday and Friday."

By the middle of November 1941, the task force had substantially completed training and awaited a sortie. Their destination had been kept secret throughout the training period, and most officers speculated that it would be either the Philippines or Southeast Asia. The possibility of Hawaii was inconceivable.

## THE ROAD TO PEARL HARBOR

On November 5, 1941, the Japanese government decided, at *Gozenkaigi* (the government's supreme decision-making conference with the Emperor Hirohito), to declare war on the US (and by default the UK and the Netherlands) in early December, if US-Japanese negotiations in Washington had not concluded satisfactorily by December 1. After the conference, Nagano, the Chief of Navy General Staff, gave Yamamoto the order known as *Daikairei Ichi-go* (Great Naval Order No.1): in the expectation of going to war with the US, the UK, and the Netherlands in early December, the Commander-in-Chief of the Combined Fleet was to begin operational preparations.[25]

Three days after the conference ended, the IJN and IJA (Imperial Japanese Army) began coordinating initial operations in the south and Hawaii, and the IJN revealed the Hawaii operation to the IJA. On November 13, Yamamoto gathered the commanders of the Combined Fleet at Iwakuni air base to discuss a concrete plan to attack Pearl Harbor. On November 17, Yamamoto advised Navy officers of the plan to attack Pearl Harbor. Their response was generally one of excitement. One officer wrote in his diary that "It has been 20 years since the Navy signed the humiliating Washington Naval Treaty. During [that] time we have whetted our swords to stab [the] US."[26]

On November 23, the task force convened at Hitokkapu Bay; three days later, they set sail for Hawaii. A few hours after the sortie began, Cordell Hull, the US Secretary of State, presented the Japanese ambassador in Washington with the Hull Note. The Note urged the Japanese government to withdraw forces from China and renounce the Tripartite Pact, requests which Japan could never accept. The Japanese Foreign Minister, Shigetoku Togo wrote that he was greatly disappointed with the note, and that it constituted an ultimatum for Japan.[27] Once the voyage had begun, the task force regularly received radio information from the Navy General Staff. In the event that the US–Japanese negotiations had concluded successfully, the fleet would have stopped its advance and returned to Japan, but once they knew of the receipt and contents of the Hull Note, they realized that war was inevitable.

The task force was strictly prohibited from using radiotelegraph communication, in order to keep the voyage silent. Radio communication would have alerted the USN to the IJN fleet's approach to Hawaii, and so the fleet was limited to receiving radio waves from Tokyo during the advance.

On November 28 and 29, the fleet, aided by calm weather, successfully re-fueled its aircraft carriers without being noticed by US patrols, and continued the advance to Hawaii. At 20:00, on December 2, the fleet received a coded message from HQ, "Nii Taka Yama Nobore 1208," which meant "Execute the Hawaii operation on December 8 (Japanese time)." On December 4, the Navy General Staff provided the task force with military intelligence on Pearl Harbor and the weather forecast for Honolulu. Two days later the fleet reach its rendezvous point at 34 degrees north and 158 degrees west, north of Hawaii. The task force gathered information on Pearl Harbor from radio traffic interception and reconnaissance by submarines. They judged that the USN did not appear to be on the lookout for a Japanese attack, and that nine battleships and three cruisers were in Pearl Harbor.

## ATTACK PEARL HARBOR!

At 06:00 on December 7, Admiral Yamamoto sent a telegram order to aircraft carrier *Akagi*, stationed 230 sea miles north of Oahu island. This was the signal to begin the operation. The first air attack, consisting of 183 aircraft led by commander Mitsuo Fuchida, sortied from *Akagi* to carry out air raids on Pearl Harbor naval base and Ford and Hickam air bases. Yamamoto sent his telegram believing that Kichisaburo Nomura, the Japanese ambassador in Washington, had already handed the US government a declaration of war. However, Nomura handed Hull the declaration 50 minutes after the operation had begun, which meant that the attack was in violation of international law and was characterized as a "sneak attack" in the US.

Yamamoto had certainly intended the attack on Hawaii to be a surprise, but also that it should follow a formal declaration of war. There were several reasons for the delay in delivering the declaration; the primary reason was an ongoing estrangement between the Navy and the Japanese Ministry of Foreign Affairs. The IJN had expended a great deal of energy to keep the operation secret, and as a result the Ministry of Foreign Affairs was not provided with a detailed plan of the operation until early December. This estrangement was compounded by another, between the Ministry of Foreign Affairs in Tokyo and the Japanese embassy in Washington. Tokyo sent the ultimatum, divided into 14 parts, to Washington 26 hours before the Pearl Harbor attack began, assuming it would take no more than eight hours for the Japanese embassy to deal with the documents. The Japanese embassy, however, was not advised of the urgent nature of the situation, and was slow in translating and typing the documents, which resulted in the late delivery of the final draft.

By the time Nomura handed the documents to Hull, the first air attack had almost completed its raid. Fuchida telegraphed the task force and the HQ in Nagato with the words "*Tora Tora Tora*" (I have attacked successfully) at 07:53 Hawaiian time.[28] An hour and a half later, the second Japanese attack, under Lieutenant-Commander Shigekazu Shimazaki, bombed Pearl Harbor. This attack was confronted by antiaircraft fire, and by clouds of black smoke from damaged ships. The first attack lost nine aircraft, while the second lost 20. The two attacks sank four US battleships, and damaged another two battleships, as well as two cruisers and two destroyers. The air raids were unquestionably a great success – but the US aircraft carriers were not in the harbor and had thus not been hit. Neither had naval docks or oil tanks been damaged.

The commander of the second air troop, Rear Admiral Tamon Yamaguchi, along with Genda, expected a third attack on Pearl Harbor, but Nagumo did not order one in. Later, Gordon Prange wrote, "Was Nagumo's decision sound? The question raises a historical controversy which has never been settled and may never be."[29] Nagumo's decision was based on his appraisal of the Pearl Harbor operation as a part of Japanese grand strategy. It would advance Japan's claims in Southeast Asia, and damage the US Pacific Fleet. Balanced against this, he knew it was his duty to keep six aircraft carriers undamaged for the next operation. In other words, the Pearl Harbor operation was a very important, but not the most important, step on a long journey. In addition, Nagumo, who was not a specialist of naval air power, but rather a specialist of torpedoes, judged that the first and second strikes had sufficiently damaged the USN fleet to attain his goal.[30]

Back at HQ, Kuroshima strongly advocated a third attack, but Yamamoto dismissed this plan. Yamamoto probably would have preferred to find a way to attack the missing aircraft carriers, but it became apparent that the task force was ready for withdrawal and Yamamoto missed the opportunity to telegraph further orders to the fleet. Furthermore, Yamamoto shared Nagumo's fear that further strikes would increase the possibility of a US counterattack on the Japanese fleet, perhaps from the missing aircraft carriers.[31]

The task force withdrew from Oahu at dawn on December 8 to a rendezvous 600 sea miles away. During the withdrawal, the task force determined the position of the US aircraft carrier *Enterprise* by radio interception, but too late for effective action. The task force returned to Japan on December 23.

## SIGNIFICANCE OF THE PEARL HARBOR ATTACK

On December 18, the Japanese Navy General Staff of the Imperial Headquarters published the results of the Pearl Harbor Operation as five battleships sunk; three battleships, two cruisers, and two destroyers heavily damaged; one battleship damaged; and 450 aircraft destroyed.[32] Newspapers reported that the "US Pacific fleet was devastated"[33] and Japanese public opinion fanatically endorsed the war.

From a tactical point of view, the Pearl Harbor operation showed the potential of naval aviation and subsequently influenced not only USN strategy but also the IJN's institutional thinking. For the Navy General

Staff, the Pearl Harbor operation was a strategic triumph and the beginning of grand strategy. The Navy General Staff had been unwilling to be caught short by the USN, but after Pearl Harbor, the USN had too little strength in the Pacific to disrupt the Japanese southward advance. As a result, during the first four months of 1942, Japan successfully occupied Singapore, the Philippines, and the Dutch East Indies without any active Allied resistance.

Despite these successes, Yamamoto was not fully satisfied with the result. His goals in striking Pearl Harbor had been to annihilate the US Pacific Fleet, including aircraft carriers, and to damage American morale to continue the war. He knew that the aircraft carriers had escaped, and as far as morale was concerned, the attack had the opposite effect, uniting American citizens against Japan. Yamamoto was also disappointed to discover that the Pearl Harbor attack had been executed before the Japanese declaration of war was issued.

Yamamoto's concern about the escaped aircraft carriers proved to be well founded. On April 18, 1942, the aircraft carrier *Hornet* invaded the western Pacific without alerting Japanese patrols, and bombed Tokyo in what became known as the "Doolittle" air raid. The psychological effect on Yamamoto was so great that he became determined to sink the USN aircraft carriers at Midway, and ironically lost four of his own precious aircraft carriers in the attempt.

## DID ROOSEVELT KNOW ABOUT THE ATTACK?

It is useful to examine revisionist views of Pearl Harbor for a fuller understanding of the context and ramifications of the operation. Simply put, revisionists claim that President Roosevelt knew about the Japanese attack on Hawaii beforehand, but deliberately concealed warnings from the US Pacific Fleet and left them exposed as a decoy. His reason for doing this was that he wanted a reason to declare war against the Axis powers.

Famous conspiracy theories include Charles Beard's *President Roosevelt and the Coming of the War 1941* (1948); George Morgenstern's *Pearl Harbor* (1947); Charles Tansill's *Back Door to War* (1952); Robert Theobald's *The Final Secret of Pearl Harbor* (1954); John Toland's *Infamy* (1982); James Rusbridger's *Betrayal at Pearl Harbor* (1991); and Robert Stinnett's *Day of Deceit* (2000).

Most of these conspiracy theories focus on how Roosevelt obtained the secret intelligence. According to the revisionists' claims, the first source was signal intelligence, which eavesdropped on Japanese signal traffic. The second was RDF (radio direction finding), used to follow the Japanese task force. It is known that the US code-breaking teams (Army's SIS and Navy's OP-20-G) could read Japanese diplomatic ciphers (known as "Red" and "Purple") before the Pacific War. Broken Red and Purple ciphers have been opened in recent years at the National Archives, Washington, DC, and London, but these do not provide any indication of a Japanese attack on Hawaii.[34] As far as Navy cipher (JN series) is concerned, specialists' opinions are still split.

Stinnett contends that the US code-breaking teams had broken JN-25b (one IJN cipher comprising five-digit code, adopted in December 1941) before Pearl Harbor. He quotes a deciphered Japanese naval cipher in his book, which indicated that the IJN task force was in Hitokkapu bay.[35] However, the date of the deciphered code is listed as "6 May 1946" in the document. On the other hand, Ronald Worth, Jr. wrote that "the common view is that it was a far [more] modest 10 percent – which, in all but the most exceptional case, meant that little could be read."[36] Captain Laurance Safford, director of the OP-20-G, also wrote, "On 1 December 1941, the numbers system became unreadable."[37] There has been no clear evidence presented to show that the US could have read JN-25b before the Pearl Harbor attack.

The problem of RDF depends on whether the task force used radiotelegraph or not on the route to Hawaii. If the task force had sent signals during their voyage, the position of the fleet should have been detected by US RDF. Robert Ogg, USN electronics expert, was interviewed by the USN in 1983. He described how he monitored signals from Japanese ships in December 1941, and indicated his belief that the Japanese broke radio silence because of stormy weather.[38] However, there is no record of such weather during the Japanese voyage to Hawaii, nor any IJN veteran who witnessed radio silence broken, nor any record of signals being sent to HQ from the task force. Without any such evidence, it is difficult to imagine that the task force broke the order. They knew that they were under surveillance by US RDF, and that it was for their own safety, as well as for the success of the operation, that the order had been given. They used flag and light signaling for communication.

So what did Ogg monitor? The answer may be the signals from Tokyo to the task force. The HQ regularly sent the task force information on international relations and military intelligence, called "*A Joho* (information)," during the run-up to Pearl Harbor. The strike order, "*Nii Taka Yama Nobore*," was also *A Joho*. From December 1–7, the HQ sent 13 *A Joho*s to the task force; some of them were intercepted by US RDF in San Francisco, where Ogg was working.[39]

It is difficult to assert conclusively that US code-breaking teams were able to read JN-25b, or that US RDF was following the Japanese task force before Pearl Harbor, without any specific documentary evidence in either US and Japanese intelligence records. The only assertion that can be made confidently is that the task force was good at keeping silence during the voyage to Hawaii.

It is possible, however, that the US successfully predicted a Japanese attack on Pearl Harbor by following up on some fragments of information, as Wohlstetter asserts.[40] For instance, US code-breaking teams intercepted IJN messages which discussed the IJN's development of a new torpedo for shallow water, as well as the distribution of oil tankers to the First Air Fleet. In other messages, the Navy General Staff paid close attention to merchant shipping routes and weather conditions in the northern Pacific.[41] If the US had assessed this information carefully, they could have predicted that the Japanese fleet was likely to be in the northern Pacific in December 1941. An imaginative officer could deduce from this that the Japanese target was Hawaii. Such an assumption is a mere historical inference, but we cannot deny the possibility that Roosevelt knew that an attack on Pearl Harbor was at least a risk.

## Chapter 3

# The Rising Sun strikes
## The Japanese invasions

*Professor Tomoyuki Ishizu and*
*Professor Raymond Callahan*

## INTRODUCTION

In the Asia-Pacific theater, one takes it for granted that World War II began on December 7, 1941 (US time) at Pearl Harbor, Hawaii, then the advanced naval base for the US Pacific Fleet, which was taken by surprise when a Japanese strike from aircraft carriers hit soon after dawn. But the landing for the Malaya Campaign at Kota Bharu, northern Malaya, was made one hour and twenty minutes before Pearl Harbor. In the air attack on Pearl Harbor, 18 US warships were sunk or damaged, including eight battleships, of which the *Arizona* and *Oklahoma* were never recovered. Japanese losses from the carrier task force were minimal: some 30 aircraft, and five midget submarines. Militarily, Pearl Harbor represented the largest mass use of aircraft carriers up to that time, the farthest-range conduct of a naval attack, the largest air attack against a naval target up to that time, and one of the most elaborate efforts to coordinate simultaneous attacks by aircraft and submarines.[1] Politically, December 7 was "a date which will live in infamy" to the Americans.

However successful and impressive it may have been, Pearl Harbor must be examined in the wider context of Japanese grand strategy. Admiral Isoroku Yamamoto, Commander-in-Chief of the Combined Fleet, planned this preemptive strike hoping to gain an early advantage and buy time for Japan's southern advance. He never had any illusions that a successful attack might cause the US to give in to Japanese demands. With Yamamoto's strong initiatives, the Imperial Japanese Navy's "classic" strategy of defensive operations against the US was revised to an offensive, the first aberration from the traditional Japanese naval strategy. Pearl Harbor was, in fact, a strategic gamble.

Historians have been debating the pros and cons of the attack on Pearl Harbor since 1941, but from the Japanese point of view there were no alternatives. The Pearl Harbor attack was the only way to secure the flank of the main Japanese thrust into Southeast Asia to capture its raw materials. If the attack had not been carried out, the Japanese would have found themselves fighting a two-front war in the Pacific, a continuation of their offensive in Southeast Asia coupled with defensive operations in the Central Pacific. Japan's operational plan at Pearl Harbor was only designed to "buy time," time to construct a defensive zone and to negotiate a settlement of hostilities favorable to Japan. The Japanese grand strategy in the Pacific War was to fight a "limited war." Tokyo had prepared no alternative strategy; it lacked the resources to wage a "total war" against the US. Japan's grand strategy provided for a negotiated settlement with the US after Southeast Asia was secured, and after German victory in Europe strengthened its bargaining position vis-à-vis the US. However, the treacherous nature of the surprise attack at Pearl Harbor so inflamed the American public that later negotiations became impossible.

Japanese grand strategy in 1941 called for the capture of the Southern Resources Area and the establishment of a defense perimeter through the Pacific islands on its eastern flank. The Japanese calculated that a year or so would be necessary for the US to mobilize its economic potentials fully, and that by that time, the Japanese defense perimeter in the West Pacific would be strong enough to deter or repel any US attempts at penetration. Pearl Harbor was to secure Japan's "left flank" to the south. The main thrust of the Japanese advance was to be towards Malaya and Singapore.

## THE MALAYA/SINGAPORE CAMPAIGN

On February 15, 1942, the "impregnable" Singapore was surrendered into the hands of the Japanese, only 70 days after the start of the Malaya Campaign. This was a month less than General Hajime Sugiyama, the Chief of the General Staff of the Imperial Japanese Army, had predicted during the Imperial Conference on November 5, 1941.[2] Since landing in southern Thailand and northern Malaya barely 55 days before, the Imperial Japanese Army had advanced some 1,100 kilometers to Johore, fighting 95 large and small engagements and repairing more than 250 bridges.[3] To many commentators, the fall of Singapore marked one of the worst disasters and largest capitulations in British military history.

While it may be true that the Japanese had complete air and naval superiority and also had the initiative on when and where to attack, this alone cannot explain the magnitude and speed of their victory. The responsibility for the outcome of the Malaya/Singapore Campaign, both Japanese success and British failure, lies primarily with British defense policy, dating back to the 1920s and 1930s.[4] There were some, if not many, in both London and Singapore, who had recognized that the defense of Singapore was inadequate. However, they also knew that it could be improved only by taking risks elsewhere. As a result, throughout the Malaya Campaign, Britain had no choice but to take the military strategy of fighting in constant retreat to delay the Japanese advance. Since these were not planned and coordinated withdrawals, they resulted in total confusion. Fearful at all times of being surrounded and cut off by the Japanese Army, the British were liable to retreat before it became absolutely imperative to do so. It can be said that this psychological collapse on the part of the British soldiers was a crucial factor of the Japanese success in this campaign.

The first and most important question concerning the campaign is whether the Imperial Japanese Army was really as formidable as its reputation indicates. Its victory in the Malaya/Singapore Campaign can be attributed, as is often argued, to its speed and efficiency, as well as to prewar preparations, the intelligence service, and the morale of well-trained individual soldiers. Compared with their British counterparts, this may well be true. However, the Japanese were in reality far from being ready for war.

The Japanese did not take the possible capture of Malaya/Singapore under serious consideration until the latter half of 1940.[5] In fact, Japan did not possess even one accurate and detailed map of the area. True, the study of jungle warfare had been set down as one of the responsibilities of the Research Department of the Taiwan Army. (The Research Department was established in December 1940.) Practically speaking, however, very little work could be done on the subject, as there was no suitable jungle in Taiwan.[6] Also, military maneuvers had been carried out in February 1941 in Taiwan and Kyushu (in the southern part of Japan), and on Hainan Island in June 1941, as part of the preparations for the

Malaya Campaign, but these were far from satisfactory.[7] In fact, it was only in September 1941 that Japan began active and detailed preparations for the military operations to the south.

Strictly speaking, the Malaya/Singapore Campaign consisted of two separate campaigns: one to conquer the Malaya peninsula and the other to conquer Singapore Island. The respective plans were not simultaneously prepared. In organizing both campaigns, General Yamashita greatly underestimated British military strength in Malaya and Singapore. At the beginning of the Malaya Campaign, both he and his staff inferred that on the British side, there could be "at most fifty thousand soldiers or at the low end about thirty thousand." As we now know, the British had more than double the number that the Japanese estimated – some 88,600.[8] This underestimation was not corrected until the fall of Singapore. As Lieutenant-Colonel Masanobu Tsuji (Chief of Operations and Planning Staff, Twenty-fifth Japanese Army) aptly wrote in his *Singapore*, "ignorance is bliss." Even Yamashita himself remarked later that "our battle in Malaya was successful because we took the enemy lightly."[9]

In principle, three divisions, the 5th, 18th, and the Imperial Guards, took part in the campaign. In reality, however, they were not so strong. As late as December 26, 1941 for example, one of the infantry regiments of the 5th Division was still in Shanghai; barely one-third of the strength of the Imperial Guards Division had reached the front; and the 18th Division Headquarters and two of its infantry regiments were still waiting at Canton. Including the Takumi Detachment on the east coast of the Malaya peninsula with its numerically weak regiments, Japan in reality had barely two divisions available. The Imperial Guards Division had had no actual battle experience since the Russo-Japanese War of 1904–05, and had long been regarded in the Japanese Army as, although the smartest division, notorious for a lack of fighting spirit. The 5th and 18th divisions had had abundant battle experience on the Chinese front, but only in the cold climate of northern China. They lacked tropical and jungle experience. In fact, most of the Japanese soldiers involved in the campaign did not even know the meaning of the word "jungle."[10] Most of them saw jungle for the first time when they commenced the landing in Malaya. The pamphlet entitled, *Read This Alone: And the War Can Be Won*, written chiefly by Tsuji and the primary form of information distributed to the Japanese soldiers prior to the campaign by Imperial Army Headquarters, is surprisingly elementary in its content.[11]

It is a fact that the 5th Division and the Imperial Guards Division had been comparatively "motorized." It is also true that the 5th Division had been trained for amphibious operations. Perhaps most important, the Twenty-fifth Army and the Malaya/Singapore Campaign had been given priority over Burma, the Philippines, and the Dutch East Indies in the provision of both personnel and equipment. As a result of this favor, the Malaya/Singapore Campaign can be characterized by firepower and speed. There were some 400 guns including trench mortars, and some 120 tanks including armored vehicles. Nine companies of engineers were following just behind the advance guard to repair bridges, railways, and airfields. Ground forces were supported by 459 Army and 158 Navy aircraft. Ground forces were dependent upon locals (and sometimes the enemy) for rations. All these considerations aside, however, organization, equipment, and military strategy which had been designed for a war against the Soviet Union had to be radically revised for fighting in tropical conditions.

Furthermore, it should be noted that all military planning relevant to the very beginning of the Pacific War was subordinate to the planning and execution of the surprise attack planned at Pearl Harbor, although it was not supposed to be the main engagement. As a result, the date and time for landings in Thailand/Malaya had to be chosen in accordance with the operational plan in the Pacific, and most of the first-line warships and aircraft were allocated there.[12]

Finally, but most importantly, the conduct of the Malaya/Singapore Campaign is suspect when considered in the wider context of Japanese grand and military strategy in 1941–42. In effect, although Malaya/Singapore was the most important route for Japan's advance to the south for natural resources in Southeast Asia, Japan decided to allocate considerable part of its military power to other campaigns, most notably Pearl Harbor.

Japan's grand strategy on the eve of the Pacific War was encapsulated in a document adopted at the liaison conference between Imperial General Headquarters and the Cabinet three weeks before the fighting commenced. The document, entitled *Tai Bei-Ei-Ran-Shou Senso Shumatsu Sokushin-ni Kansuru Fukuan* (A Plan for Completion of the

War Against the United States, Great Britain, the Netherlands, and Chiang Kai-shek), contained the following passage:

> The Empire will...crush American, British and Dutch strongholds in East Asia and the Western Pacific...and secure major resource areas and lines of communication in order to prepare a posture of long term self-sufficiency. All available methods will be exerted to lure out the main elements of the US fleet at an appropriate time to attack and destroy them.[13]

This document indicates that the official assessment of the prospects for the coming war acknowledged the likelihood that it would be a protracted struggle. This required a swift occupation of the resource-rich areas of Southeast Asia and their integration into an autarchic "Greater East Asia Co-Prosperity Sphere" that could resist the US for an extended period without major defeats. This document clearly stated Japan's strategic position on the eve of the Pacific War: that Japan could not win the war outright, but could take steps to avoid losing it. In this grand strategic environment, Admiral Yamamoto's naval plan to attack Pearl Harbor, an offensive plan predicated on a quick and decisive operational victory, was formulated.[14]

In order to execute this grand strategy, Japan, already embroiled on the Chinese mainland for the previous few years, planned to deploy formidable forces not only to Malaya/Singapore, but also to the Philippines, Hong Kong, Burma, and other strategically important places, including Pearl Harbor, on its way to the Dutch East Indies. In fact, the Japanese Southern Army diverted the Japanese air forces from Singapore to the Sumatra Campaign just before the Singapore Campaign was due to begin – and failed to notify the Twenty-fifth Army of the diversion.[15]

## THE INFLUENCE OF MASANOBU TSUJI ON THE MALAYA/SINGAPORE CAMPAIGN

In examining the Malaya/Singapore Campaign, it is important to consider the role of Lieutenant-Colonel Masanobu Tsuji, Chief of Operations and Planning Staff under General Tomoyuki Yamashita, Commander of the Twenty-fifth Army, and one of the main architects of the Campaign.[16]

Arguably, Tsuji is still regarded as one of the best staff officers ever to serve in the Imperial Japanese Army. Known as an excellent staff officer, he was also notorious for his fanaticism, ruthlessness, and unorthodox methods in conducting military operations. Tsuji was one of the key staff officers who shaped the Imperial Japanese Army's operational plans, both before and during the Pacific War, and he was among the chief architects of the successful Malaya/Singapore Campaign.[17] Although it is debatable whether the campaign can be described as a *blitzkrieg* in East Asia, as it has been in some accounts, advancing some 1,100 kilometers in 70 days was a remarkable military achievement by any standard. In fact, the Malaya/Singapore Campaign was a successful example of a joint operation combining Japanese ground, sea, and air forces.[18] After the failure of the operations against Imphal in 1944, Tsuji was assigned to the Burma theater, and his staff work there for the fighting retreat was excellent. In fact, he received a letter of commendation from the Commander-in-Chief of the Burma Army.[19]

Against these achievements, however, it is important to consider that he was also in Nomonhan in 1939, and in Guadalcanal in 1942. Much of the responsibility for the failure of these campaigns lies with Tsuji's narrow-minded approach. He was also too obsessed with the "cult of the initiative and offensive" to take the steps necessary to minimize casualties. Some 9,600 casualties – 3,500 dead and 6,100 wounded – in the Malaya/Singapore Campaign were not insignificant, particularly given the total manpower available for the Japanese Army.[20]

Furthermore, the scale of his brutal activities cannot be justified in the name of military effectiveness. It is critical to remember that it was Tsuji who ordered the massacre of thousands of Chinese civilians in Singapore, and that it was Tsuji who was primarily responsible for the slaughter of thousands more US and Filipino soldiers in the Philippines.[21] Diaries and memoirs of the Japanese soldiers now available for historians have revealed various inhumane activities conducted or ordered by Tsuji.[22]

Tsuji was not a man of generalship. He was a ruthless and sinister professional soldier whose sole objective was to win a campaign. He was not trained to see the campaign in a wider political and strategic context. To put it simply, he did not care about the casualties suffered by the Japanese Army, much less those inflicted upon enemy soldiers and civilians. Worse, he was notorious for his inhumane treatment of enemy soldiers and POWs. He was, however, comparably harsh to Japanese soldiers and prisoners of war, known, among other things, for forcing Japanese officers (those who had been taken prisoner in Nomonhan in 1939 and sent back to the Japanese side after the armistice) to commit suicide. From Tsuji's point of view, the massacre of Chinese civilians in Singapore was necessary to carry out a "peaceful" occupation of Singapore, and to carry out the next stage of the Japanese advance to the south.[23] Tsuji apparently gave little consideration to the political and moral repercussions of these brutal activities. "Military necessity" was always at the forefront of Tsuji's mind, and he used this phrase to justify everything he did.

## THE END OF THE CAMPAIGN

In examining the Malaya/Singapore Campaign, one could safely conclude that it was the British side, rather than the Japanese, which was responsible for the consequences of the campaign. One could also argue that Japanese soldiers were *relatively* flexible in adapting to a new environment in Malaya. Some sources cite the principal problem as Britain's failure, dating back to the 1920s, to provide in advance balanced naval, land, and air forces adequate to defend the area. In fact, British defense policy in the Far East was not formulated based upon its assessment of Japan's military capabilities and intent. Rather, it was simply a function of the competition among services for more budgets, and of the strategic environment in Europe.

It is interesting to note that Western literature on the Malaya/Singapore Campaign tends to overemphasize the military effectiveness of the Imperial Japanese Army in the same way as it does to the German African Corps under General Erwin Rommel. It seems likely that this is partly due to soldiers' and politicians', and perhaps historians', desire to evade their own responsibility by praising their opponents.

## IMPERIAL TWILIGHT

The Japanese design for the war launched against the Western empires on December 7/8, 1941 was extraordinarily complex, ranging from the massive carrier air assault on Pearl Harbor to the seizure by a small infantry detachment of Victoria Point, at the southernmost tip of Burma, the loss of whose airfield cut Malaya's air reinforcement link to India. The essence of this sprawling assault can however be summed up easily: seize the "Southern Resource Area," whose oil, tin, rubber, and rice would enable Japan to construct an autarchic economy. This, in turn, would sustain Japan until the Anglo–Americans were constrained, by a German victory in Europe or the cost of retaking their lost territories, to accept a peace on Japanese terms.

The seizure of the Southern Resource Area in turn required assured command of the sea and air, something the Japanese accomplished in the first 48 hours of the war. The American Pacific Fleet was shattered at Pearl Harbor (although its carriers survived, a fact whose importance was only clear in retrospect); Britain's belated attempt to redeem a generation of promises ("main fleet to Singapore") with a token force ended with the destruction of *Prince of Wales* and *Repulse* on December 10 off Kuantan in Malaya. Japanese success in the air was equally rapid and complete. The RAF in Malaya, whose largely obsolete aircraft were posted on exposed fields with inadequate warning systems, was crippled in the first few days of fighting. The US Army Air Force in the Philippines, upon whose new B-17 heavy bombers much hope rested, was mostly based at Clark Field near Manila. Caught on the ground, parked wingtip-to-wingtip some *10 hours* after word of the Pearl Harbor attack reached Manila, the force was decimated (three dozen B-17s and some 200 other aircraft destroyed). The surviving B-17s rapidly withdrew, first to the southernmost island of Mindinao and then to Australia. It was a worse blunder than any committed by Admiral Husband Kimmel at Pearl Harbor or Lieutenant-General A. E. Percival in Malaya – and one, astonishingly, for which General Douglas MacArthur, the American commander, was never called to account.

Secure in command of the sea and air – and enjoying the psychological edge that their successful opening attacks and their possession of the initiative gave them – the Japanese promptly moved on to develop a vast pincer movement on the Southern Resource Area. Under the overall control of General Count Terauchi's Southern Army, Lieutenant-General Tomoyuki Yamashita's three-division Twenty-fifth Army drove down the Malayan peninsula, planning to take Singapore in 100 days. (The Imperial Japanese Army did not have corps headquarters

– its "armies" were, in effect, corps formations.) An initially faulty disposition of his forces by Percival (most of whose troops were new, inexperienced and, often, inadequately commanded by equally raw officers), control of the air, and the unfailing tactical aggressiveness of Japanese infantry carried Yamashita to victory in two-thirds of the time budgeted. The surrender of Singapore on Sunday, February 15, 1942, was a blow to British imperial prestige in Asia from which, despite Winston Churchill's best efforts, it never recovered.

The other arm of the pincers, Lieutenant-General Masaharu Homma's two-division Fourteenth Army, secured its principal objectives even more rapidly. The Philippine Commonwealth was in transition to independence. The Tydings-McDuffie Act, signed by Franklin Roosevelt in 1934, set 1944 as the date for Philippine independence. A quasi-autonomous Philippine administration began to build up its own armed forces, advised by Douglas MacArthur after his retirement in 1935 as US Army Chief of Staff (Roosevelt regarded MacArthur as the most dangerous man in the country during his tenure). In 1941 MacArthur, recalled to active service by Roosevelt in July, commanded both the small American force in the Philippines and the fledgling Philippine Army (one regular and 10 reserve divisions, none fully trained or completely equipped). On the main island of Luzon he had about 20,000 American regulars, the 12,000 strong Philippine Scouts and the bulk of the Philippine Army – some 65,000–70,000 men in total. The war opened with the Clark Field disaster ("On the ground! On the ground!" said the incredulous Roosevelt when the news reached him).[24] MacArthur's plan for the defense of Luzon was based on holding the beaches, a plan abandoned almost as soon as a reinforced division of Homma's army came ashore at Lingayen Gulf on December 22. Telling US Army Chief of Staff General George C. Marshall that Homma's force numbered 80,000–100,000 (the correct figure was 40,000) while he himself had only 40,000 (a very considerable underestimate), he retreated rapidly, declaring Manila an open city on December 26 and withdrawing into the mountainous Bataan peninsula. The US Army's official historian later admitted that "no evidence has come to hand" to explain the discrepancy between the actual size of MacArthur's force and the one he reported to Washington in justifying his retreat.[25] The fact is that Homma, following MacArthur's own Pearl Harbor at Clark Field, had won an even more startling victory than Yamashita in Malaya. In a few days he had eliminated the American forces in the Philippines as a threat on the flank of the drive toward the Southern Resource Area.

Much has been made of the subsequent months-long siege of Bataan (surrendered April 9, 1942) and the island fortress of Corregidor at its tip (surrendered May 6). This stubborn defense, it is claimed, denied the Japanese the use of Manila Bay and tied up Homma's troops. Heroic the defense certainly was. It was also strategically irrelevant. The Japanese plan for the next phase – the assault on the Netherlands East Indies (NEI) – did not depend on the use of Manila Bay. Davao on Mindinao was the key point, and it was taken by a reinforced Japanese regiment on December 20, 1941 against slight opposition. The continued employment of Homma's forces on Luzon made no difference either (the one division scheduled to move on to join the assault on Java duly did so). The Japanese did not, in any case, lack for infantry at any point in their drive south.

Long before Bataan fell, MacArthur had left, at Roosevelt's orders, for Australia. He was awarded the Congressional Medal of Honor for his defense of the Philippines, a tribute less to the military skills he had demonstrated than to the careful treatment he always received from Roosevelt and Marshall (who had been a colonel when MacArthur was Chief of Staff), both conscious of his strong support among American politicians on the right. By the time MacArthur left on March 12, 1942, the Japanese had completed their conquest of the Southern Resource Area. Java had surrendered on March 8, 1942.

Of all Japan's targets, the Netherlands East Indies were the weakest. The sprawling Dutch empire, built by a great trading concern in the 17th century, had two great vulnerabilities: its political situation and its military forces. The British and Americans had made concessions in the interwar years to rising Asian nationalism and had some support (although less than they thought) in Malaya and the Philippines. The Dutch – like the French in Indo-China – had made none. That in turn affected the archipelago's defensibility. Dependent on their home country for personnel and equipment, the NEI were severed from their military base in May 1940. A handful of cruisers, destroyers, and submarines, based on Java, and 144 aircraft (almost as many – or as few – as the British had in Malaya) constituted a first line of defense that would be a rapidly wasting asset once combat was joined. The Royal Netherlands East Indian Army (Dutch-officered local troops) was impressive numerically but in no other way. Designed for internal security, it had neither the training and equipment nor the doctrine and leadership to confront the Imperial Japanese Army. Moreover, the unpopularity of Dutch rule on Java, the core of the NEI, meant that the Dutch would fight among an indifferent or even hostile population, and that prolonged resistance to the Japanese might put the large Dutch civilian population at risk. This knowledge weighed heavily on Dutch officers and civil administrators. If Allied air and sea power could not keep the Japanese from landing in Java, Dutch resistance was unlikely to last long.

To coordinate the defense of what was dubbed the "Malay Barrier," Churchill and Roosevelt, at the post-Pearl Harbor "Arcadia" conference in Washington, set up the war's first integrated Allied theater command, christened "ABDACOM" (American-British-Dutch-Australian Command). The Americans nominated General Sir Archibald Wavell, the Commander-in-Chief, India, as the supreme Allied commander. Fired more frequently than any other senior British general by Churchill, Wavell's greatest weakness in 1942 was his consistent underestimation of Japanese capacity. Even had Wavell enjoyed Churchill's enthusiastic backing and properly appreciated Japanese skills and aggressiveness, ABDACOM was a hopeless proposition. Cobbled together to meet the political imperative of being seen to be doing something, Wavell's headquarters at a Dutch "hill station" in Java had a small, improvised staff, poor communications, and no reserves to commit in any direction – yet responsibility for everything from Burma to New Guinea. (MacArthur's crumbling fiefdom was excluded from ABDACOM but Wavell was instructed to "support" him – no one explained how.)

With Malaya and Singapore in their hands and American resistance in the Philippines confined to the doomed Bataan-Corregidor enclave, the Japanese began to close in on Java in February. In fact, success in Malaya and the Philippines had led them to begin operations against the NEI in December, first seizing key points in Borneo, the Celebes, and other outlying islands, and then, coincidentally with Singapore's fall, taking the oilfields around Palembang in southern Sumatra. The Japanese Sixteenth Army, three divisions and a reinforced regiment commanded by Lieutenant-General Imamura, had responsibility for this final phase of the assault on the Southern Resource Area. As the Japanese closed in on Java, island by island, the mixed force of British, American, Dutch, and Australian warships struck repeatedly at Japanese landings. Although they inflicted some damage, they could do little to stop the Japanese and, lacking both air cover and secure bases, were steadily worn down. As the assault on Java approached, ABDACOM, its futility obvious, was dissolved on February 25, 1942. In its last weeks, there had been vigorous discussions among Wavell, the Australian government in Canberra, and London about the destination of the 1st Australian Corps, whose two divisions, returning from the Middle East, were spread across the Indian Ocean in a series of convoys. These Australian troops represented a reserve that Wavell could use, and Churchill pressed the Australian government of John Curtin to make it available. Having lost a division at Singapore and all too aware of the speed with which the Japanese were approaching Australia, Canberra demurred, thus saving their divisions from involvement in the debacle.

Two days after ABDACOM dissolved, Japanese invasion convoys were sighted approaching Java. The remaining Allied warships, five cruisers and nine destroyers under the Dutch Rear Admiral K. W. F. M. Doorman, sortied to meet them. After the ensuing battle of the Java Sea (February 27), only four American destroyers survived (Admiral Doorman did not). The Sixteenth Army landed at both ends of Java on March 1. The 65,000 Dutch-officered local troops began to disintegrate immediately. The token British and Australian contingents could do little but retreat. On March 5, the Dutch commander-in-chief, Lieutenant-General Hein ter Poorten, warned the senior British officer, Major-General H. D. W. Sitwell, that Dutch headquarters were not designed for mobile operations and that the end was near. On March 8, citing the danger to Dutch civilians from a hostile population, the NEI capitulated. The Japanese owned the Southern Resource Area, purchased at a trifling cost in three astounding months.

In 60 years' retrospect, some aspects of the fall of the Philippines and the NEI are less astounding than they seemed at the time. The Americans had decided long before December 7, 1941, to stand initially on the defensive in the Pacific – that, in effect, wrote the Philippines off. Churchill had in fact made a similar decision about Malaya/Singapore, giving priority to the war against Germany.[26] Neither of Japan's major

Western opponents wanted a war with Japan in 1941; both hoped it would not happen. Neither was ready when it started. This explains much of Japan's startling success. MacArthur's inept handling of his command certainly gave the Japanese what they needed in the Philippines quickly, but the islands were outposts that America could lose and reclaim later. The NEI was very important to the Dutch, but they lacked the capacity to defend it, however gallantly their small naval forces performed. The Japanese certainly did an excellent job of planning and coordinating their operations, and within 48 hours were supreme at sea and in the sky. Because they had been so badly underestimated by most Western military men and nearly all Western civilians, their swift, nearly cost-free victories over weak opponents produced a near-panic among Westerners and a corresponding overestimation of Japanese abilities.

The dramatic opening of the Pacific War tended to mask the serious weaknesses in the Japanese military machine: its weak industrial base, its dependence on a body of highly trained but hard to replace naval airmen, and the logistic recklessness and tactical obtuseness of the Imperial Japanese Army. All this would begin to reveal itself within months of Java's fall, but for a moment, Japan reigned supreme over an immense empire, created in the twinkling of an eye. Japan's Western opponents had been not just beaten, but humiliated. The curtain was coming down on what a shrewd Indian writer would later christen the "Vasco da Gama" age in Asian history.

## Chapter 4

# Coping with Disaster
### Allied strategy and command in the Pacific 1941–42

*Professor Raymond Callahan*

They had all long expected war with Japan – and yet they were all surprised when the attack came, and they all suffered immediate tactical disaster. The US Navy had planned for a war with Japan for two decades, yet were blindsided at Pearl Harbor. Hours later the US Army had a still inexplicable Pearl Harbor of its own at Clark Field in the Philippines, where the opening Japanese raid destroyed half its bombers, still parked wingtip to wingtip. The British, who had also viewed Japan as a potential enemy for 20 years, saw the war open with the bombing of Singapore, whose lights no one could manage to turn off despite an hour's advanced warning. This was swiftly followed by the loss of their two available capital ships and the crippling of both the RAF and the Indian Army divisions deployed to defend northern Malaya by Japanese air and army units whose skill and efficiency the British, despite available evidence, had grossly underrated. The Australians, expecting an Anglo-American shield between them and Japan, quickly came close to panic. The Dutch, weakest of all, could only grit their teeth and await their turn.

The disasters of the war's first week set the tone for the next six months. Prewar plans were revealed either as hopelessly flawed or irrelevant, while Allied military, naval, and air units were shown to be either insufficiently strong or, more commonly, ill-equipped, ill-trained, and ill-led for the war to which they were committed. Amidst the cataract of disaster, the first Allied experiment of the war with a theater supreme commander – an initiative strongly influenced by alliance politics untrammeled by operational reality – was predictably futile. The Japanese quickly swept to the borders of India; made the Indian Ocean temporarily a "no go" area for the Royal Navy; and menaced Australia. War is the ultimate test of military organizations, their strategic and operational concepts as well as their tactical competence. By May 1942, there seemed little reason to feel much confidence about Anglo-American proficiency in any of these areas.

Since the late 1930s, neither British nor American planners had projected offensive operations against Japan at the outbreak of a Pacific war. The British strategy had been, since the early 1920s, "main fleet to Singapore." A one-ocean navy, all that the British could build after the 1922 Washington Naval Conference – and all that their finances could, in any case, support – still could sustain a global empire if two conditions were present: an appropriate fleet base in the Far East, and tranquility in Europe allowing the eastward deployment of the fleet. The first condition had been fulfilled by building the great base on the north shore of Singapore Island, which opened in February 1938. By that time, however, the second condition had already evaporated. There had always been an element of fantasy about the Singapore strategy, of course. Japan was most likely to move against the British when European distractions left their eastern empire exposed – something that had been repeatedly pointed out by critics of the strategy. But it was a necessary fantasy. After 1918, sustaining Britain's global position against simultaneous threats in both hemispheres was simply beyond its powers. The Singapore strategy was a bluff, designed to sustain Australia and New Zealand in their all-too-willing belief that they were still protected by the mantle of British sea power. In reality, by 1939, the British knew that they could not send a fleet to the Far East, and hoped that American pressure would keep Japan in check. This British hope was something that Winston Churchill had made very clear in his first message to Franklin Roosevelt after becoming prime minister in May 1940.

Over the next 18 months, the British situation in the Far East worsened. To reassure Britain's Pacific dominions, a new strategy was devised in the summer of 1940 that substituted air power for a fleet. The RAF would defend Malaya and Singapore. Unfortunately the RAF was no more able to spare squadrons than the Admiralty was to provide carriers and battleships. The airfields to support those unavailable squadrons, however, were built the length and breadth of Malaya, thereby distorting the dispositions of the Army, which had to choose not the optimal defensive positions but those necessary to defend the airfields, about whose siting they had not been consulted. The Army was slowly increased in size, but most of its formations – and all of those that would meet the initial Japanese attack – were from the Indian Army, which was being expanded at a breakneck pace. As a result these new units were, in many cases, incompletely trained and equipped, and led by officers as inexperienced as the men they commanded.

British planning for a Pacific war was therefore based on inexperienced troops holding air bases, for which there were not enough planes, in order to defend an empty naval base. Of course there were comforting misperceptions about the ability of the Japanese and the hope, which lay behind Churchill's repeated invitations to Roosevelt to base American warships at Singapore, that American pressure would restrain the Japanese. At bottom, however, the British were in an impossible situation. Their position as an imperial power and good faith with their Pacific dominions required them to mount a defense against Japan, but by 1941 it was an improvised and incoherent defensive structure to which, it is clear, no one in London was paying very close attention. If the American deterrent failed, the hope was that irreparable damage could be averted until victory in the West freed resources for a Pacific counteroffensive. The British scenario for a Pacific war thus anticipated a very long conflict.

British plans, such as they were, rested on the expectation of American involvement. American plans on the eve of war, however, assumed an initial defensive posture in the Pacific, which precluded much support for the British in Southeast Asia. It was in fact Britain's worsening situation that refocused American attention upon the Atlantic and Europe, a development the British were aware of, and that Churchill actively campaigned for. The ultimate incoherence in British plans for a Pacific war was that they depended on a degree of American commitment there which, had it come about, Churchill himself would have deplored and fought to reverse.

The American interwar plans for a conflict with Japan – the "Orange" series – did envision a trans-Pacific projection of American power, with Manila serving as the base of operations in the Far East (an American version of "main fleet to Singapore"). It also foresaw a long war, as the US Navy fought its way slowly across the Pacific to Manila. While war gaming a totally unlikely Anglo-Japanese war with the United States, however, American planners rapidly concluded that the Atlantic theater was the more significant by far for American security. Once the growth of German power substituted a real menace for the sand-table fantasy of an Anglo-Japanese coalition, the planners' conclusion was powerfully strengthened. By 1941 the basic American war plan, "Plan Dog," foresaw a concentration on defeating Germany first, with a strategic defensive in the Pacific for a prolonged period. The Philippines and island outposts like Guam and Wake would of course be defended, but their eventual loss was foreseen and accepted. Thus American and British plans by early 1941 were similar: Germany was the priority; a Pacific war, if it could not be averted, would have to be a lengthy holding operation with losses expected, but also expected ultimately to be made good. The Anglo-American staff talks that opened in Washington in January 1941 wrote this into the basic strategy document of the emerging alliance – "ABC-1," the "Germany first" strategy from which the alliance never wavered, although considerable, if unofficial, exceptions would be conceded. This would be necessary because there was one powerful dissenter to the "Germany first" strategy: the US Navy.

While the British had no difficulty maintaining a united front on strategy – they had an effectively integrated system of war direction produced by the Chiefs of Staff committee and its network of sub-committees, the whole presided over by the powerful, articulate, and ruthlessly single-minded Prime Minister and Minister of Defence – things were otherwise in Washington. The "Germany first" strategy had the support of the US Army and its formidable Chief of Staff, General George C. Marshall. It was a strategy that called for a large army. The Navy, however, understood that it was a strategy that they could not dominate. It also called for intimate cooperation with the British, and many of the Navy's senior officers were deeply Anglophobe. It called, as well, for a degree of inter-service cooperation that they were uneasy about. British officers, not unaccustomed to inter-service rivalry, were shocked at the level of Army–Navy hostility in Washington. Roosevelt did not play a continuously active role in enforcing service unity. As a consequence, the US Navy was prone to place a much higher emphasis on Pacific operations – which would be their war – than did the US Army, the British, or official Allied strategy. The worst complications from this state of affairs lay in the future, beyond the confines of this chapter, but it added an additional dimension to the situation on the eve of Pearl Harbor: the British hoped for American help, but American strategy in the Pacific was defensive, and the dominant American service there had little interest, in any case, in cooperation with the British.

Despite all this, there were eve-of-war gestures, part deterrent aimed at Japan, part reassurance for the increasingly anxious Australians and Dutch. A new British battleship, HMS *Prince of Wales*, accompanied by an elderly battlecruiser, HMS *Repulse*, arrived at Singapore. Churchill was the driving force in sending them, but he realized as he did so that, should war come, "Force Z" could only survive by making itself scarce. Unfortunately its commander, Vice-Admiral Sir Tom Phillips, a former Vice Chief of the Naval Staff and much liked by the Prime Minister, remained convinced of the viability of the capital ship in the age of air power. Meanwhile in Manila, General Douglas MacArthur, a former US Army Chief of Staff, received some of the new B-17 "Flying Fortress" heavy bombers. Based at Clark Field north of Manila, their supposedly great accuracy as well as considerable bomb load promised formidable offensive action against any Japanese attack. Of course, at Pearl Harbor the powerful American Pacific Fleet had to be of major concern to the Japanese, everyone assured themselves.

After the Pacific War's calamitous opening week, it was painfully obvious that a damage limitation strategy was needed, lest the expected initial setbacks mushroom into irrecoverable losses. If the Americans were momentarily stunned by the cascade of calamity, Churchill was perhaps no less shaken, especially by the loss of Force Z (he was still writing notes defending Tom Phillips, and himself, nine years later while drafting his memoirs). ABC-1 was fundamental to how the British believed the European war would be – indeed, the only way it could be – won. If the impact of Pearl Harbor on American opinion led to a reversal of Washington's priorities, it would be a devastating blow to the British. To preempt this possibility, Churchill invited himself to Washington, overriding Roosevelt's obvious reluctance to host a summit at that moment, and set out on a stormy voyage westward. During the trip, he produced three lengthy memoranda to guide the British delegation at the upcoming talks, christened the "Arcadia" conference. His object was to win a reaffirmation of ABC-1 from the Americans, while constructing a damage limitation strategy for the Pacific that would prevent large diversions to that theater. The official British position paper for the conference reflected this, although cast in much blander language than Churchill's. The crucial opening paragraphs reaffirmed ABC-1. At this point, however, Churchill still expected Singapore to hold out, as did his military advisors. (These included Admiral Sir Dudley Pound, the Chief of the Naval Staff; Air Chief Marshal Sir Charles Portal, the Chief of the Air Staff; and Field Marshal Sir John Dill, recently deposed by Churchill as Chief of the Imperial General Staff, but brought along by the Prime Minister because his successor, General Sir Alan Brooke, was just settling into office.)

The ensuing meetings with the Americans went very well, from the British perspective. (Some of this was doubtless owing to superior British organization, something the Americans came to resent but could never fully emulate.) The British draft on alliance strategy was accepted by the Americans with little argument or amendment. The key words were in the opening sentence: "Germany is the predominant member of the Axis Powers, and, consequently, the Atlantic and European area is considered to be the decisive theatre." Christened "WW1," it became the basic constitutional document of the Anglo-American partnership, although like all constitutions it would spawn numerous arguments over interpretation. The Pacific War got only a few brief sentences at the end: Australia and New Zealand must be safeguarded, along with India, and the Japanese advance held along a line stretching from Rangoon through Singapore and the island chain of the Netherlands East Indies (the "Malay Barrier," now Indonesia) to the Philippines. How exactly this was to be done was left to the first of the conference's two great innovations – the war's first integrated Allied supreme command. Christened "ABDA" (American-British-Dutch-Australian), it would be responsible for the vast area from Burma to northern Australia (the Philippines were not included, although ABDA was to "support" their defense). The ABDA commander would report to the President and Prime Minister through the second innovation, an Anglo-American Combined Chiefs of Staff Committee. (Dill would stay in Washington as the British representative on the committee, building a rapport with Marshall that was to be of immense value to Britain.) There had been an Anglo-French Supreme Command in 1918 and again in 1939–40, of course, but these had been exercises in high-level coordination, with limited powers. ABDA was to pioneer an Allied theater command that would have an integrated staff and continuous supervision by a combined Allied military high command. The road to Eisenhower's SHAEF headquarters, and later to NATO command arrangements, began at Arcadia with ABDA.

A felt need for alliance integration and coherent command and control arrangements at the theater level were not, however, the only, or even the most immediately significant, of the factors that called ABDA into being. A thick fog of alliance politics enveloped the venture from the beginning. Who would be the Allied supreme commander? The Americans quickly nominated General Sir Archibald Wavell, then Commander-in-Chief, India. Churchill was not excited by the prospect. Underwhelmed by the famously inarticulate Wavell from the moment they had first met in the summer of 1940, the Prime Minister had removed him as Commander-in-Chief, Middle East, in June 1941 and sent him to India to get him off stage. Churchill could not easily refuse, however, although he and others on the British side suspected that the Americans preferred that the defeats they saw coming – US planners had, of course, written off the Philippines well before Pearl Harbor – take place under a British supreme commander.

Then there was the question of what would be included in Wavell's new command. Burma had just been moved from Far East Command at Singapore – which had never paid it any heed – to India Command, from which its supplies and reinforcements had to come. Now the Americans insisted it be included in ABDA, whose headquarters were to be in Java, a thousand miles away (a distance that, in those days, made even radio contact occasionally difficult). The reason was that Rangoon was the port of entry for Lend-Lease supplies carried to China by the long rail-and-road link known as the Burma Road. If Burma was in ABDA, the Americans, working through the Combined Chiefs of Staff, could keep British attention focused on American's primary interest in Southeast Asia: sustaining its link with the China that so beguiled American policymakers' dreams. (Churchill would tell Wavell, in exasperation, after his return to London from Arcadia, that he could sum up what he had learned in Washington in one word: China.) Moreover, General Douglas MacArthur was left out of ABDA, although Wavell was to "support" his defense of the Philippines. It is not surprising that, reviewing the creation of ABDA, British official historians would later dub its structure "artificial."

Finally, there were the Australians. Three of Australia's four available divisions were serving in the Middle East; the fourth in Malaya, where it would soon be lost. Disagreements over the employment of Australian troops in the desert campaign against Rommel already had Churchill telling his staff before Pearl Harbor that the Australian government caused difficulties out of proportion to the help it gave. However unfair this may have been, it was the background to the Anglo-Australian crisis that unfolded in December 1941. Seeing their cherished security blanket disintegrating as the British lost control of the seas around Malaya and the air over it, and warned by their representative in Singapore that a comparable debacle was unfolding on land, the Australian Labor government of John Curtin began to panic. While Churchill was in Washington, Curtin published an open letter in the *Melbourne Herald*, in which he threatened to put his country under American protection, since Britain could not fulfill its commitment to Australia's security. (His government also, however, rushed its last available troops, largely untrained recruits, to Malaya.) Churchill was embarrassed and enraged – but also aware that Commonwealth solidarity required a British effort to reassure the Australians. This too was something Wavell was supposed to produce. Rangoon, Singapore, and Manila, widely separated from each other, and from ABDA headquarters in Java – somehow all were to be defended, thus stemming the Japanese onrush and alleviating a number of tensions in alliance politics. While the US Navy, its vital carriers still intact, caught its breath after Pearl Harbor, the problems of strategy and command in the Pacific War revolved about ABDA's attempt to achieve the impossible tasks set for it at Arcadia.

Wavell's staff looked like the integrated Allied staffs that operated in Europe and Southeast Asia later in the war, but appearances were all they had in common. Wavell had an excellent Chief of Staff in Lieutenant-General Sir Henry Pownall (no stranger to desperate situations – he had been Chief of Staff to the British Expeditionary Force during its withdrawal to Dunkirk), but the rest of his hastily improvised team was weak. Wavell's American deputy was Lieutenant-General George H. Brett. The others were Admiral Thomas Hart, the commander of the tiny US Asiatic Fleet; Lieutenant-General H. ter Poorten, commander of the Royal

Netherlands East Indian Army (some 195,000 strong but, in the eyes of its own officers, of dubious reliability); and Air Chief Marshal Richard Pierse (available because he had recently been removed as head of Bomber Command, in the United Kingdom, after a run of disappointing operations). Wavell's improvised headquarters at Lembang in Java, a Dutch colonial "hill station" with inadequate communications, lacked the troops, ships, and planes to stabilize the situation. He could only preside grimly over rapidly accelerating disintegration. The "Malay Barrier" he was bidden to defend was not, of course, an organized defensive position, but merely an evocative slogan. The long chain of Dutch islands from Sumatra to New Guinea were indefensible without ships and planes in numbers and of a quality far greater than anything ABDA had available – or in prospect. The two defensive anchors of the system, Singapore and Manila (1,400 miles apart, and the later not even included in ABDA), were already hopelessly compromised before Wavell even reached Java.

MacArthur's war began badly at Clark Field and rapidly got worse. That the Japanese force that took Malaya and Singapore was smaller than the total of British defenders has often been noted; less frequently remarked upon is the fact that MacArthur's forces enjoyed an even larger numerical superiority over the attacking Japanese. Some of his troops were prewar American regulars, but most were from the infant army of the prospective Philippine republic. The collapse of Manila's defenses, however, was even more rapid than the pace of defeat in Malaya. By Christmas Eve, Manila had been declared an open city and abandoned, the American and Filipino forces falling back into the Bataan peninsula and the island fortress of Corregidor at its tip. The subsequent stubborn (but strategically irrelevant) five-month defense of those besieged positions, a defense celebrated in inimitable Hollywood style, has tended to overshadow both the Clark Field debacle and the speed with which MacArthur's forces were routed in the field.

Singapore lasted two months longer than Manila, but its defense too had been fatally compromised by the time ABDA came into existence. The two inexperienced and under-strength Indian divisions defending up-country Malaya had been beaten in detail, their initial dispositions fatally flawed by the need to defend airfields that the undermanned RAF rapidly abandoned. By the time Wavell came on the scene, northern and central Malaya had been lost. Lieutenant-General A. E. Percival (who impressed neither Wavell nor Pownall) was preparing to defend southern Malaya with the remnants of his Indian divisions and an as yet uncommitted Australian division, also under strength and without combat experience. The Australians quickly vindicated Pownall's observation that they would be the most difficult of the allies with whom he and Wavell would deal.

Wavell had only two options: try to slow down the pace of withdrawal in Malaya, and find reinforcements that he could commit to influence the battle there. To effect the former, he intervened in Percival's conduct of the fighting, demonstrating a lack of confidence in him, while leaving him in command – a poor combination. Moreover, Wavell's interventions failed to slow the Japanese advance. Reinforcements ready to hand were two Indian infantry brigades, little better than raw recruits, one of which was shredded by the Japanese within days of its arrival. There was, however, a full-strength British infantry division available, the 18th. Originally bound for the Middle East and diverted to India after Pearl Harbor, it remained at Wavell's disposal. Its fate became bound up in the politics of ABDA and the deepening Anglo-Australian crisis.

In mid-January Wavell told Churchill that the "Singapore Fortress" (like the "Malay Barrier" a resounding phrase that masked reality) did not, in fact, exist. A chain of decisions, or failures to make decisions, going back years, had left Singapore Island without defenses against an attack from the north. Though appalled and furious both at the situation and (more understandably) at the failure of anyone in London to warn him of the true state of affairs, Churchill quickly adjusted and, mindful of American concerns with China, suggested to Wavell that the 18th Division should go not to Singapore but to Rangoon, where it might yet save America's prized link with Chiang Kai-Shek. Wavell, however, who still felt that committing a reserve would influence the Malayan battle (and, moreover, consistently underestimated the Japanese) was unresponsive. The whole discussion almost immediately became moot when what the Prime Minister intended as a British discussion was leaked to the Australians. Their pent-up anger, building since well before the Japanese attack and sharpened by their mounting sense of vulnerability, finally exploded. Curtin, with a division at risk in Malaya, sent Churchill a message that characterized the idea as an "inexcusable betrayal." Faced with this, Churchill again reversed course. The luckless

18th Division went to its doom, two of its brigades disembarking barely two weeks before Singapore fell.

With Manila lost and Singapore doomed, there remained only Rangoon of the strategic anchors ABDA had been conjured into existence to hold. Two of the three Australian divisions on their way home from the Middle East were then crossing the Indian Ocean in a series of convoys. Wavell wanted them diverted to Rangoon. Churchill agreed and ordered the leading convoy to alter course toward Rangoon without waiting for the Australian government's response to his request. It was an astoundingly inept move. Curtin immediately refused, angrily pointing out to Churchill that if any losses were sustained because of the convoy's diversion, the responsibility would be Churchill's alone. Churchill then tried emotional blackmail, reminding Curtin that the 18th Division had gone to Singapore at Australia's insistence; he also invoked Roosevelt, reminding Curtin that US divisions were being committed to Australia's defense. It was all in vain; the Australians would not budge. (In retrospect, it seems clear that, even had Curtin agreed, the Australians could not have reached Rangoon, disembarked, and been ready to fight in time to hold the city.) The episode, in addition to demonstrating Churchill's obtuseness in dealing with the Australians, also reflected how out of touch Wavell was with reality on the ground in Burma.

Following Pearl Harbor, Burma had bounced from Far East Command to Wavell in India, and then followed him to ABDA. None of this did anything to remedy the total lack of resources on the spot. When the Japanese invaded Burma early in January, it was defended by yet another raw Indian division. Wavell made two very brief visits, during which his interventions paralleled those he made in the Malayan campaign. He pressed the local commander, Lieutenant-General Thomas Hutton, to stand on each successive defense line in front of Rangoon longer than Hutton or his subordinates thought wise or even possible. Wavell lost confidence in Hutton (his former Chief of Staff in India) but did not replace him, just as he had failed to replace Percival in Malaya. He also displayed, once again, an unawareness of just how formidable his opponents were, a curious failure of imagination which would go uncorrected despite his experience at ABDA. (In 1945 he would finally admit – to a golf partner – that he had underestimated the Japanese.)

Wavell's unhelpful interventions made, in fact, little difference to the campaign in Burma. The Japanese pressed steadily closer to Rangoon, maneuvering the 17th Indian Division – which became more worn and ragged with each battle – out of one position after another. Wavell had clearly appreciated the importance of Rangoon, both to holding Burma and to satisfying the Americans, but he simply could not find forces whose numbers and quality might have made a difference. Churchill's attempt to divert the 18th Division was undone by the Australian reaction; the attempt to get an Australian division instead by Canberra's refusal to throw good money after bad. By that point, ABDA itself was disintegrating.

Lacking sea and air power, not to mention first-quality troops, there was nothing Wavell could do to halt the inexorable Japanese advance on Java. On February 25, ABDA was dissolved and command of all Allied forces passed to the Dutch. Wavell returned to India, to become Commander-in-Chief there once again. Only token Allied contingents – including about 5,000 British personnel, two Australian battalions, and a handful of Americans – remained to share the final days with the Dutch (whom Pownall, by now a connoisseur of collapse, found more dignified in the face of catastrophe than the French had been in 1940). On February 27, the small Allied fleet, commanded by a Dutch admiral, was destroyed in the battle of the Java Sea. The next day, the Japanese landed in Java. On March 8, the Dutch surrendered, unwilling to risk the Dutch civilian population and, in any case, uncertain about the loyalty of their locally recruited soldiers. On that same day the Japanese entered Rangoon, whose defense had been fatally weakened on February 23 when the 17th Indian Division had been temporarily erased as a fighting force at the Sittang River east of Rangoon, two-thirds of its personnel being trapped when the bridge that was their only withdrawal route was prematurely demolished.

ABDA had lasted barely six weeks. An attempt to make a rout look more like an organized withdrawal, its history nevertheless highlights some fundamental issues that would shape British and American approaches to the war against Japan until its end.

For the British, the war against Japan was a distraction from the main struggle against Germany. They hoped it would not happen; then that America participation would at least limit the losses. But that there would be losses – to be redeemed after victory in Europe – Churchill always understood and accepted, even though their full calamitous scope was not foreseen. ABDA was both a bow to the American belief in unity of command and a damage-limitation exercise. Even after its speedy dissolution, and with the Japanese on the borders of India, the policy of concentrating on the war in the West was unwavering. In his Secret Session speech to Parliament, explaining the fall of Singapore, Churchill spent comparatively little time (in a very long speech) on the Japanese war before turning, almost with relief, to the war against Germany. During the entire course of the Far Eastern war, the British committed only four British divisions – one of them the 18th – to it. After the dissolution of ABDA and the loss of Java, an American proposal to redefine areas of strategic responsibility so as to leave control of the entire Pacific area, including Australia and New Zealand, to the United States, was accepted in London with little demur; it came into effect on April 4. The British remained responsible for South and Southeast Asia, and Churchill would quickly begin to press Wavell for offensive action – but resources for the amphibious strategy the Prime Minister favored would never be available.

The American position was very different. Committed to "Germany first," the United States had nonetheless the resources to mount a very significant Pacific effort – indeed, it is hard to see that the US war in the Pacific was in any serious way constrained by the primacy of the European theater. Partly this was because the sea and air power requirements were very different from those needed for the Atlantic war, and American productivity could supply both. It was also true that the Pacific's demands on the US Army's manpower were comparatively slight, the Navy having its own private army in the Marine Corps, none of which was used in Europe. The biggest factor, however, was the powerful institutional pressures exerted by the Navy and the MacArthur lobby on the shape of American strategy.

The most insular and xenophobic of the American services, the US Navy had little interest in allies, and its Chief of Staff, Admiral Ernest King, was a very intense Anglophobe. The Central Pacific War waged by carriers and marines across immense distances was the US Navy's private war, and outsiders were unwelcome. The British got only sketchy information, and Churchill had a very difficult fight in late

1944 to push even a token Royal Navy force into the final stages of that conflict.

MacArthur, ordered from the Philippines to Australia by Roosevelt, became a quasi-autonomous warlord in his own Southwest Pacific theater. His manpower was US Army and Australian, and he would acquire his own dedicated naval component (known as "MacArthur's Navy"). His ability to develop and implement his own strategy, aimed at the reconquest of the Philippines, owed much to the uncharacteristic deference shown him by Marshall (who had been a mere colonel when MacArthur was Army Chief of Staff) and Roosevelt, who was well aware of his strong domestic political support in the Republican party. MacArthur, while imperious, was not a King-style Anglophobe, so the British had at least a good sense of what was happening in his fiefdom, even if they had no influence there. Nor, more surprisingly, did the Australians, who provided both his base of operations and much of his military manpower.

The Australians had resented the way in which London treated their contribution to the British war effort, disposing of Australian divisions without sufficient consultation, and from midsummer 1941 on had become increasingly vocal about it. After the Arcadia conference, "Pacific War Councils" were established in both London and Washington to provide forums in which all the Allied powers engaged against Japan could discuss strategy and policy. A bow to minor allies, they remained largely cosmetic exercises. Shortly thereafter, MacArthur set up his headquarters in Australia, and the Anglo-American redivision of strategic responsibility put Australia in the American sphere. If, however, the Australians expected this would finally elevate them to the status of a major ally, they were quickly disillusioned. Washington, the US Navy, and MacArthur ran the Pacific War. Australian troops would be used far more ruthlessly by MacArthur than either Churchill or any British theater commander had ever dared. American Pacific strategy after the Japanese were finally contained would be shaped by American institutional pressures with little real concern for allies, great or small.

Indeed, the British would discover that even in their own sphere, the Americans would exert their powerful influence to bend theater strategy towards the fulfillment of American goals. Churchill had been surprised by the power of the China Lobby in Washington; ABDA's structure had reflected the importance the Americans attached to their link with China. The Americans even set up a theater command – "CBI" (China-Burma-India) – under the rabidly Anglophobe Lieutenant-General Joseph ("Vinegar Joe") Stilwell, based in Delhi and with the dual mission of maintaining an air lift to China and restoring an overland road connection. To do the latter required the reconquest of north Burma, which no one in London or Delhi wanted to undertake. Lacking resources to follow their own preferred amphibious strategy, however, and vulnerable to American pressure because of the need for cooperation in Europe, even theater strategy in Britain's own sphere of the war against Japan ended up being driven by American objectives. The dissolution of ABDA marked the last moment when there was even a pretense that the conflict with Japan was being conducted by an alliance with an agreed-upon strategy. Henceforth, the strategy would be American – or rather there would be several American strategies – with both the British and the Australians cast in supporting roles, if allowed a role at all.

Although no one could know it, April 1942 was the Japanese high-tide mark. Their objectives had been secured with a high speed and a low cost that surprised even them. What to do next? The Imperial Japanese Army and Imperial Japanese Navy, who negotiated strategy much like the American services (but without anyone in the roles of referee, arbitrator, and court of appeal filled by Roosevelt), discussed an invasion of Australia – only to rule it out, both for lack of troops (the Army thought ten divisions would be needed) and because of the problems of logistical support it would create. A further advance southeastward, however, to prevent Australia becoming the base for an American counteroffensive by severing its communications with the United States, was finally agreed. It was this plan that led to the battle of the Coral Sea (May 7–8), the first serious setback inflicted on the Japanese Navy by the US Navy's carriers. Ultimately the Japanese move against Australia would give the Americans the opening for their first, improvised offensive at Guadalcanal in August.

Meanwhile, in the central Pacific, a minor American venture, the famous "Doolittle Raid" on Tokyo (April 18), essentially a morale booster for the American public, inflicted on the Japanese something worse than damage – it embarrassed the high command. Admiral

Isoroku Yamamoto, the architect of Pearl Harbor, had been arguing for an attack on Midway Island to force a final battle with the remnants of American seapower. After the raid on Tokyo, both the Japanese Army and Navy high commands quickly embraced the idea. The ensuing battle crippled the fast carrier attack forces that had been crucial to Japan's six-month run of victories. It was, to borrow a Churchillism, the end of the beginning.

Chapter 5

# The Height of Folly
## The battles of the Coral Sea and Midway

*Professor Robert Love*

The battles of the Coral Sea and Midway concluded a Japanese offensive begun with the invasion of Malaya and the attack on Hawaii on December 7, 1941. Pearl Harbor had transcendent political and strategic importance but was devoid of tactical military significance. The appearance of Japanese planes in Hawaiian airspace constituted an act of war, which in turn brought an American declaration against Japan and retaliatory declarations by the European Axis against the United States. By engaging the United States in the ongoing struggle between the British Empire and the Soviet Union on the one hand, and the European Axis on the other, and the hitherto unrelated Sino-Japanese conflict, the Pearl Harbor attack created World War II. The geopolitics of that struggle involved American power not only in Europe and the Mediterranean, but also in the Middle East, East Asia, and the South Pacific, regions where American force and presence remained beyond the end of the 20th century. And by provoking Japan over China, President Franklin D. Roosevelt thoughtlessly put the United States astride a two-ocean war for which he had refused to prepare and against which the military chiefs had repeatedly warned.[1]

Although the brief action over Hawaii shocked American leaders, the results were unsurprising and produced no military result for Japan. The decision to declare war on the United States and the British Empire, attack Pearl Harbor, and later to enter the Coral Sea and challenge the US Pacific Fleet off Midway mainly demonstrated the utter stupidity of Japan's wartime leaders.

Christmas Day 1941 found President Roosevelt hosting British Prime Minister Winston Churchill at the White House for the second of their 10 wartime summits. The British delegation was relieved that, the situation in the Pacific notwithstanding, the Americans remained committed to a "Europe first" grand strategy. This meant not only that Allied forces in the Pacific and Southeast Asia would not be significantly reinforced, but also that existing theater forces would necessarily cede forward positions to the Japanese onslaught.[2] A series of decisions – "Europe first"; the relief of the witless Commander-in-Chief, Pacific Fleet (CinCPac), Rear Admiral Husband Kimmel; the Japanese invasion of Malaya; and the impending loss of the Philippines – led to a reshuffling of the American higher command and the establishment of new Allied overseas theaters. In March 1942, Admiral Ernest J. King,[3] already in charge of the US Fleet, also became Chief of Naval Operations (CNO), succeeding Admiral Harold R. Stark, who traveled to London to take command of US Naval Forces, Europe. The disestablishment of the Asiatic Fleet and the defeats in the Philippines led the US Joint Chiefs of Staff to negotiate new combined command arrangements with their British counterparts. Admiral Chester Nimitz was named CinC Pacific Ocean Areas (POA), which stretched from the Eastern Pacific north to the Aleutians and south via the Mandates to New Zealand. General Douglas MacArthur, once he escaped the Philippines and reached Australia, assumed command of the South West Pacific Area (SWPA), which encompassed Australia, New Guinea, the Philippines, and the islands in between.[4]

Including Australia and New Zealand in the SWPA reflected the collapse of Britain's military authority east of India and a profound shift in the regional arrangements of power lasting throughout the Cold War and beyond. Assuming responsibility for the defense of Australia combined with participation in a struggle of large coalitions negated all prewar American strategic plans for a war against Japan. The venerable Orange Plan, revised eight times between the Russo-Japanese War of 1904–05 and the eruption of the Sino-Japanese War in 1937, assumed a conflict between the United States and Japan with neither side aided – or impeded – by allies.[5]

Hard upon arriving in Washington in December 1941, Admiral King had to devise a new grand strategy to defeat the Japanese. He wanted to compel Japan to divide its forces to deal with five active opponents: the Red Army on the Manchurian border; the Chinese on the Yangtze; the British in Southeast Asia; and the Americans along two axes in the Central and South Pacific. Considerable intelligence suggested that Japanese resources, especially aircraft production and shipping, could not support such widely separated fronts and that geography would prevent the enemy from quickly moving forces from one threatened front to another. Burdened with the defense of Australia–New Zealand, he set aside the Orange Plan strategy, reasoning that Australia would provide a base for a counteroffensive northward to the Philippines. For this purpose, and for obvious political reasons, the Pacific Fleet would have to defend the sea lines of communication between the Panama Canal–West Coast and Australia–New Zealand. To accomplish this, King created a rear line of island air bases south of the Coral Sea, anchored on Fiji and Samoa. Forward defense of this line would be provided by positioning one or two carrier task forces in or near the Coral Sea, which would also guard the eastern flank of Australia. This was the "blocking" mission of the "block and raid" strategy intended to staunch the enemy offensive.

The raiding strategy was the product of King's assessment of Japan's conduct of operations, which were carefully planned, rigidly implemented, and surprisingly inflexible. By deploying carrier task forces to conduct brief, unexpected raids against unprepared outlying Japanese bases, King hoped to compel his opponents to reinforce all of their many exposed positions, thus reducing their ability to concentrate against a genuine threat and, perhaps, to unhinge them and stimulate them to react rashly. Few commanders in history have devised a strategy which so perfectly exploited the objective and subjective strengths and weaknesses of a powerful enemy.

Having invaded China in 1937 to dismember an alliance of the Nationalists, the Chinese Communists, and the Soviet Union, the Japanese had conducted four offensives over three years but failed to force the Chinese government to surrender or even negotiate. Once Japan joined the Axis in September 1940, German leaders pressed Tokyo to declare war on the English-speaking powers. "A quick attack on Singapore," Foreign Minister Joachim von Ribbentrop told his Japanese counterpart, "would be a very decisive factor in the speedy overthrow of England."[6] Japanese leaders believed this, and also that occupying Burma via Malaya and Thailand would, by isolating China, force her to sue for peace, albeit at the cost to Japan of waging war against the British Empire and the United States. In a rare moment of recognizing the obvious, Admiral Isoroku Yamamoto, the CinC of the Combined Fleet, told a friend in October 1941 that "after more than four exhausting years of operations in China, we are now considering simultaneous operations against the United States, Britain, and China, and then operations against Russia as well. It is the height of folly."[7]

Admiral King's raiding strategy derived not only from geopolitical realities but also from an informed confidence in the superiority of US Navy carrier aviation. Nimitz was uneasy about stationing two carriers in the South Pacific, however, as this exposed the Hawaii–Midway line to another major enemy raid. At the outbreak of the war, the Pacific Fleet included the heavy sister ship carriers the *Saratoga* and *Lexington*, and the *Enterprise*. Her sister ships, the *Yorktown* and *Hornet*, the smaller carriers *Ranger* and *Wasp*, and the escort carrier *Long Island* were deployed with the Atlantic Fleet, until the *Yorktown* was reassigned to the Pacific on December 16 by Admiral Stark. On January 11, the Japanese submarine I-6 torpedoed the *Saratoga* while she was escorting a convoy to reinforce Samoa, forcing her to retire to the Puget Sound shipyard for extensive repairs.

The *Saratoga* was relieved by the *Yorktown*, which joined a task force commanded by Vice-Admiral William "Bull" Halsey. After escorting the Marines to Samoa, they sailed north into the Central Pacific to raid on the Gilberts and Marshalls on February 1.[8] Vice-Admiral Wilson Brown in the *Lexington* was closing on Rabaul on February 20 when Japanese reconnaissance planes discovered his task force, compelling him to withdraw. Four days later, Halsey in the *Enterprise* attacked installations on Wake Island and, on March 4, bombed sites on Marcus Island.

These raids inflicted modest damage, but when King reinforced Brown's *Lexington* task force with the *Yorktown*, they steamed into the Coral Sea and sent bombers escorted by fighters across the Owen Stanley Mountains on the Papuan Peninsula to attack enemy bases at Lae and Salamaua. This devastating raid sank or damaged several transports, disrupted the campaign on Papua, and caused Yamamoto to not only strengthen his base air defenses but also to plan a complex operation to occupy Port Moresby and seize control of the Coral Sea. The strategy culminated with the Doolittle raid on Tokyo on April 18, which did little damage but thoroughly unhinged the Japanese high command, fulfilling King's every expectation.

The most optimistic prewar Japanese policy envisioned a violent series of successful early blows followed by a negotiated compromise with the empire's British and American opponents. By early April 1942, the foreign minister, worried that Japanese forces were overextended, began to urge the Germans to negotiate a settlement with the Soviet Union so as to allow the Axis to concentrate against the English-speaking Allies. The Japanese Army, heavily committed to Manchuria, China, Burma, the Philippines, and the outlying bases in the Central and South Pacific, was incapable of resuming the offensive on mainland Asia. The Naval General Staff was locked in a struggle with Admiral Yamamoto, who proposed another daring thrust by the Combined Fleet into the Eastern Pacific to assault the Hawaii–Midway line. At the height of Japan's power, none of these authorities made a move to exploit their military success and explore a negotiated settlement – one more lapse in Tokyo's conduct of the war.

Rather than exploit strength either via diplomacy or by adopting a more robust defensive strategy, Japan's leaders chose to mount two risky offensives, both "characteristically complex." The first – codenamed MO – aimed at seizing Port Moresby.[9] On May 1, Yamamoto ordered the commander of the Rabaul base, Rear Admiral Shigeyoshi Inoue, to assemble an Assault Force of troop transports escorted by the small carrier *Shoho* and a destroyer screen. Part of this squadron was to steam through the Solomons chain and establish a seaplane base on Tulagi, a small island west of the large island of Guadalcanal. Once reunited, the Assault Force was to cross the Coral Sea and seize Port Moresby, supported by Rear Admiral Takeo Takagi's MO Strike Force, led by the new carriers *Shokaku* and *Zuikaku*.

Yamamoto's order of battle and his plan to seize Port Moresby were known to the US Navy's high command from April 9 onwards, thanks not only to an institutional commitment to signals intelligence, but also to the many inexplicable deficiencies of Japanese communications security. American naval codebreakers began reading Japanese naval message traffic soon after World War I, and continued intermittently for the next two decades.[10] Improvements to the main operational code, JN–25, made it unreadable prior to Pearl Harbor, but work in early 1942 by teams in Washington, Hawaii, and Australia revealed some message fragments in March.[11] Intelligence warnings that Yamamoto intended to position a carrier task force in the Coral Sea to shield an invasion of Port

Moresby not only seemed reasonable to King but also justified the continuance of his blocking strategy. He ordered Nimitz to deploy a powerful task force to check the enemy drive.

The first move in the battle of the Coral Sea came on May 3, when a small Japanese assault force escorted by the *Shoho* occupied Tulagi. The carrier then steamed north to join the Assault Force, which was standing out to sea from Rabaul. To obstruct the invasion of Port Moresby, Nimitz deployed two task forces. Composed of the *Lexington* and *Yorktown* and their screens, TF 17 was commanded by Rear Admiral Frank Jack Fletcher, whose orders were to seek out and sink the opposing carriers.[12] A Cruiser Force composed of the Australian cruisers *Australia* and *Hobart*, the American cruiser *Chicago*, and destroyers under a British commander, Rear Admiral John G. Crace, was to defend Port Moresby by blocking the enemy Assault Force.

Upon learning of the new enemy base on Tulagi, Fletcher ordered the oiler *Neosho* to refuel the *Lexington* while he sailed north in the *Yorktown* to launch an attack on Tulagi. The May 4 attack sank a transport-destroyer and three small craft and told the Japanese that at least one American carrier was nearby.[13] TF 17 was reunited two days later, when Fletcher organized his ships into a single task force defended by one cruiser-destroyer screen. Meanwhile, the Japanese Assault Force was approaching from the Solomon Sea to the northeast and Takagi's MO Strike Force had entered the Coral Sea from the north.

Confusion, mishaps, and bad weather prevented either side from landing a decisive blow on May 7. That morning, Fletcher detached Admiral Crace's Cruiser Force and ordered him to pursue the Japanese transports, which had been sighted steaming through the Jomard Passage. The MO Strike Force, northeast of TF 17, was protected by a storm front, but it was clear to the northwest, where a pilot flying dawn patrol from the American carriers reported sighting two carriers and two cruisers off Misima Island at 08:15. Eager to deliver the first blow, Fletcher ordered the carriers to launch a massive strike of 93 planes. When told that the initial report had mistaken cruisers for carriers and destroyers for cruisers, Fletcher nonetheless allowed the flight to proceed. When another scout, at 10:22, located an enemy carrier task force 35 miles from the original location, he redirected the attacking planes to the new target. At 11:00, the Americans reached the *Shoho*. The

Somewhere in China a Japanese unit cheers a victory with the shout of "Tenno Haika banzai": "May the emperor live ten thousand years!" (Imperial War Museum; HU55367)

Aboard the *Zuikaku* or *Shokaku*, crewmen cheer as a Japanese Navy Type 97 Carrier Attack Plane takes off as part of the second wave attack on Pearl Harbor, December 7, 1941. (US Naval Historical Center)

Pearl Harbor, 0800, December 7, 1941. This photograph, taken from a Japanese aircraft shows "Battleship Row" under attack, and in the distance, white smoke rising from Hickam Field. Grey smoke in the center middle distance is from the torpedoed USS *Helena* (CL-50) at the navy yard's 1010 dock. (US Naval Historical Center)

Rescue operations alongside the sunken USS *West Virginia* during or shortly after the raid on Pearl Harbor. The extensive distortion of the ship's lower midships superstructure was caused by torpedoes which exploded below the area. (US Navy)

Japanese troops mopping up in Kuala Lumpar during their advance through Malaya in 1942. (Imperial War Museum; HU2776)

Lieutenant-General Percival and his party carry the Union Flag on their way to surrender Singapore to the Japanese, February 15, 1942. (Imperial War Museum; HU2781)

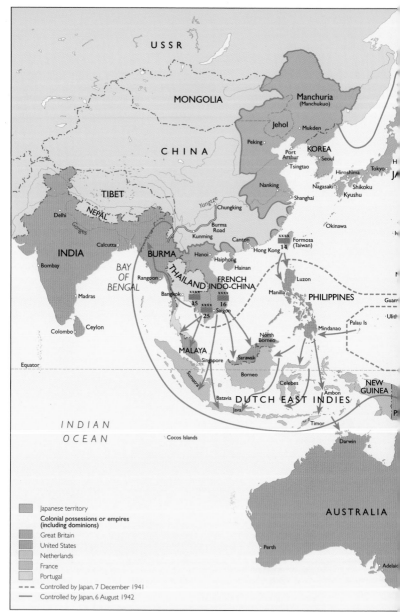

**Japan's conquests December 1941–August 1942**

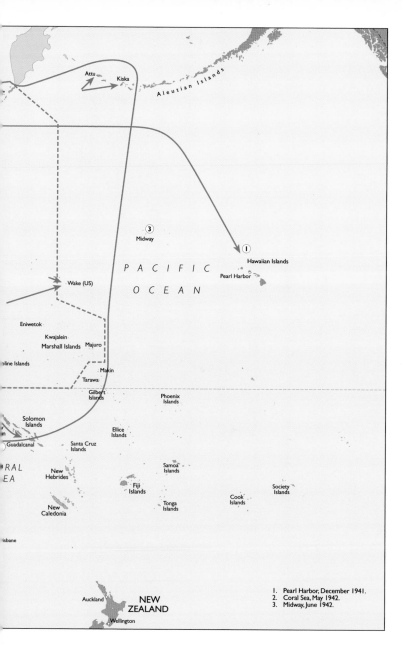

Attu
Kiska
Aleutian Islands

**3** Midway

**1** Hawaiian Islands
Pearl Harbor

P A C I F I C

O C E A N

Wake (US)

Eniwetok

Kwajalein
Marshall Islands  Majuro

oline Islands

Makin
Tarawa
Gilbert
Islands

Phoenix
Islands

Solomon
Islands

Guadalcanal  Santa Cruz
Islands

Ellice
Islands

RAL
EA

New
Hebrides

Samoa
Islands

Fiji
Islands

Tonga
Islands

Cook
Islands

Society
Islands

New
Caledonia

isbane

Auckland  NEW
ZEALAND

1.  Pearl Harbor, December 1941.
2.  Coral Sea, May 1942.
3.  Midway, June 1942.

Wellington

The rear 2-pounder of the 13th Battery, 4th Australian Anti-Tank Regiment near Bakri, Malaya on January 18, 1942. (Australian War Memorial; Neg. No. 001302)

The most lethal naval bomber of WWII, the SBD Douglas Dauntless first joined the US Fleet in 1940. (United States Naval Institute Photo Archive)

Men on the March of Death from Bataan to Cabanatuan in May 1942. (NARA)

American troops surrender at Corregidor, Philippine Islands, May 1942. (NARA)

General Sir Claude Auchinleck, the British commander-in-chief for India Command from July 1943 to the end of the war, inspects Indian troops carrying out jungle warfare training in 1944. (Imperial War Museum; IND 2930)

Indian soldier in a slit trench overlooking the difficult terrain to the east of the Imphal Plain. (Imperial War Museum; IND 3403)

The US aircraft carrier *Hornet* at the battle of Santa Cruz near Guadalcanal, October 24, 1942, seconds before a Japanese aircraft crashed into it. Another Japanese aircraft passes horizontally above the ship. (NARA)

Dauntless dive-bombers nosed over at 15,000 feet and put 13 bombs into the ship, and the low-flying Devastators hit her with seven torpedoes. Within minutes she was going under.

Meanwhile, Admiral Inoue on Rabaul received a floatplane sighting of two enemy carrier forces. A few minutes later, a Tulagi scout reported sighting a third carrier, which was actually the *Neosho* and her escort, the destroyer *Sims*. Rabaul launched two attacks at the first position report, which turned out to be Crace's detached Cruiser Force. Skillful maneuvering and good antiaircraft gunfire allowed the ships to escape unscathed. Inoue ordered Takagi to attack the third sighting and the *Zuikaku* and *Shokaku* launched a massive strike, which sank the *Sims* with three bombs. Despite taking seven hits, the *Neosho* remained afloat for four days. The *Yorktown* was spotted by Japanese reconnaissance at dusk. Takagi, anxious to destroy his main enemy, launched 27 aircraft for a risky night attack, which departed at 16:15. Bad weather now covered TF 17, but shipboard radars located the incoming flight and fighters on Combat Air Patrol (CAP) ambushed the attackers, splashing nine bombers. Other Japanese planes were mauled when they mistakenly joined TF 17 aircraft circling the *Yorktown*. Others ditched. Only six of 27 attackers returned to the Strike Force.[14]

Both admirals expected the main action on May 8. Whereas the Japanese ships were partly covered by the front, TF 17 had withdrawn southward overnight and was exposed by clear skies at dawn. At 06:15, the Japanese carriers launched seven search planes out to 250 miles, then awaited a sighting while the naval bombers were armed. Counting both air groups, 95 of 109 planes were operational. At 07:00, the MO Strike Force turned to the southwest to rendezvous with two heavy cruisers, which reinforced the formation's air defense. Yamamoto intended the seven flying boats on Rabaul and Tulagi to sweep the northern Coral Sea, but wet runways grounded the planes on Rabaul and limited the coverage. TF 17, meanwhile, was steaming westward. With a total of 128 embarked aircraft, 117 were operational. Fletcher's air officer, Rear Admiral Aubrey Fitch, ordered the *Lexington* to launch a 360-degree search with 18 SBD Dauntless dive-bombers.[15] Twelve Dauntlesses searched the northern sector out to 200 miles; six Dauntlesses flew the southern sector out to 150 miles. When the dawn patrol departed at 06:25, the weather was clear.

Each side located the other at about the same time. At 08:20, Lieutenant Joseph Smith, flying a Dauntless, sighted the MO Strike Force carriers. His first message was garbled, so Fitch did not receive a confirming report until 08:38, when he turned the carriers to close the distance to the enemy and readied a deck-load strike. The *Yorktown* launched 33 bombers and six F4F-3 Wildcat fighter escorts at 09:00; the *Lexington* launched 27 bombers with nine escorts at 09:17. Fitch withheld a four-plane fighter CAP from each carrier overhead.

Having no surface search radars, the Japanese depended on their flying boats or cruiser-launched floatplanes to provide air early warning and kept their CAP A6M2 Zero fighters on deck to preserve fuel until an attacker was spotted. As a result, they were overly reliant on close-in interception, always best in clear weather. Since the front covered the MO Strike Force when it was found by the *Yorktown* bombers at 10:32, the planes circled until 10:57, when the Dauntlesses rolled over at 20,000 feet, went into a 70-degree dive at 300 knots, and attacked without scoring a hit. Flying out to 200 miles, the *Lexington* air group did not find the enemy until 11:30, when the Strike Force was sighted 15 miles to the west. The escorting Wildcats absorbed an ambush by the defending CAP, allowing the bombers to penetrate to the ships. Using cloud cover to mask their approach, 11 TBF-1 Devastator torpedo-bombers attacked the *Shokaku* at 11:42, but the nine torpedoes were launched too far from the vessel, which maneuvered sharply and avoided any hits. Of the 13 fighters protecting the MO Strike Force, two were lost, but the defenders splashed two Dauntlesses and three Wildcats in both attacks.[16] The *Shokaku* was burning when the *Yorktown* air group departed. Hidden under a rainstorm, the *Zuikaku* was unmolested.

The Japanese assault on TF 17 developed at roughly the same time. Shipboard radar made contact with the Japanese flight at 09:48, but the defending CAP Wildcats could not see the incomers until 10:03, when they were within 15 miles of the carriers. Fletcher ordered Fitch to put more fighters aloft. In addition, at 10:12, Captain Frederick Sherman in the *Lexington* launched Dauntlesses, which circled the ship as a low-level, anti-torpedo plane defense, although one aviator recalled that this "took away the dive-bombers needed to knock out the two enemy carriers" later.[17] In short order, everyone realized they were reacting to a false alarm. Then, at 10:55, both carriers' radars reported a large incoming flight 68 miles out. Because the planes on CAP lacked enough fuel for a long-distance interception, the preferred American tactic, Fitch ordered the *Lexington* to launch five more Wildcats and five Dauntlesses. Nine defenders were vectored out to 15–20 miles, and six were directed to attack the low-flying Japanese B5N2 Kate torpedo planes.[18] Eight CAP planes circled over the carriers.

The Japanese attack developed within minutes. Eighteen Kates dived from 10,000 to 4,000 feet to make a shallow run; 14 flew against the *Lexington*, four against the *Yorktown*. CAP fighters and Dauntless patrols splashed three of the 18 attackers, and riddled the survivors with antiaircraft gunfire. Steaming at 32 knots by 11:19, Captain Eliot Buckmaster turned the *Yorktown* into the flight, maneuvered sharply, and evaded most of the attackers. When Sherman saw the enemy launching an anvil attack on the *Lexington* at 11:18, he ordered a turn away from the nearest torpedoes, but his ship was the longest in the world and slow to respond to the helm. Sherman was turning again at 11:20 to evade the second spread when the carrier was struck by one torpedo forward and another amidships opposite the island. Within moments "great clouds of smoke were pouring from her funnels," observed Rear Admiral Thomas Kincaid, "and she was listing to port."[19]

The attack by the Val dive-bombers commenced at 11:21, when the Japanese pilots nosed over at 14,000 feet, evaded the *Lexington*'s furious antiaircraft fire, released their armor-piercing bombs at 1,000 feet, and pulled up.[20] One hit the flight deck portside, penetrated the wooden planking, and detonated. Another struck the portside of the smokestack above the deck and the rest surrounded the ship with so many near misses that the sailors "thought that additional torpedoes had struck her."[21] While the Vals were descending on the *Yorktown*, Buckmaster sped south away from the fray, his CAP well-positioned and braced for an assault. The Vals scored their only hit on the *Yorktown* at 11:27, when one 250-kg bomb pierced the center of the *Yorktown*'s flight deck, went down four decks, and detonated in a storeroom. Near misses also did some damage, one exploding underwater amidships and opening a seam in a fuel bunker to the sea. Believing they had sunk both carriers, the Japanese pilots fought their way through the CAP and Dauntless patrol back to the MO Strike Force. The first battle in naval history involving only carriers was over.

Admiral Takagi recovered his aircraft after 12:00 and ordered the Strike Force to retire northward. Japanese aircraft "losses were catastrophic."[22] Only 77 of 108 aircraft were recovered and only 24 fighters, nine Vals, and six Kates were operational, scarcely enough for a second strike, which Takagi wisely ruled out. Although the *Zuikaku* was unharmed, three bomb hits left the *Shokaku* unable to launch aircraft. After shielding the retiring task force, at 15:00 the *Zuikaku*, escorted by two cruisers and a destroyer, steamed to the north to rendezvous with their oiler. Shipboard intelligence told Admiral Yamamoto that the attackers had not only sunk the *Lexington* but also the *Yorktown*.

Admiral Fletcher also decided against a second strike. He shifted the *Lexington*'s planes to the *Yorktown* at 13:52 and ordered her to steam to the south. When a sighting report erroneously suggested that another Japanese carrier, the *Kaga*, was in the area at 14:22, Fletcher assessed his situation. His fighter strength was so depleted that he could not provide the bombers with an escort. No surface attack was possible without CAP, which he could not provide, and the loss of the oiler *Neosho* meant that TF 17 could not risk high-speed operations, so he decided at last to withdraw. Then, at 15:25, the *Lexington* was rocked by another explosion. The fires were out of control by 15:38. Worried that the enemy might return, at 16:00 Fletcher divided TF 17 into two squadrons. Kincaid with two cruisers and three destroyers was to stand by the *Lexington*, while the *Yorktown* group departed. Captain Sherman ordered the 2,770 sailors in the *Lexington* to abandon ship at 17:07 and, when everyone was off at 18:41, the destroyer *Phelps* was ordered to pump five torpedoes into the carrier and the great ship rolled over and sank.

Combined Fleet headquarters was upset with Admiral Inoue for retiring from the Coral Sea, so Admiral Takagi's Strike Force sailed southward after refueling on May 9 in a futile search for the American task force. It was quickly apparent that the aircraft losses meant that the carriers could not provide cover for the invasion force or close ground support after a landing. Yamamoto refused to admit defeat until the 10th, when he recalled Takagi and suspended the invasion of Port Moresby until the summer, after he had dealt with the American carriers.

Admirals King and Nimitz understood that the battle of the Coral Sea caught the Pacific Fleet with its carrier force divided between Halsey's TF 16 retiring from the North Pacific after the Tokyo Raid and

Fletcher's TF 17 in the lower South Pacific. Nimitz ordered the *Hornet* to steam for Pearl Harbor and told Halsey to take the *Enterprise* south with her two oilers, but the Japanese fleet base on Truk blocked the easy junction of the two American forces. On May 9, Nimitz instructed Fletcher to refuel at Tongatabu and return to Pearl Harbor. King wanted Halsey to conduct another raid in the Central Pacific, but Nimitz was anxious that the *Enterprise* also reinforce the Hawaii–Midway line.

The Pacific Fleet scored a strategic victory in the battle of the Coral Sea, not only by thwarting the seizure of Port Moresby, but also by disrupting the timing of Japanese operations. The Combined Fleet scored a tactical victory by sinking the *Lexington*, although at the cost of gutting two frontline air groups, which put *Zuikaku* and *Shokaku* out of action for months. Wildcats splashed three Zeros at the cost of six Wildcats. Wildcat fighters on CAP shot down three Japanese Vals and one Kate and shipboard antiaircraft claimed three Kates and one Val. Other Japanese aircraft ditched in the open sea, and dozens were damaged. Of 23 American planes flying CAP, the Japanese downed three Wildcats and five Dauntlesses. The Navy Department was already working to improve its frontline fighter and, when the fleets next engaged, the F4F-4 had replaced the F4F-3 in all Pacific Fleet squadrons.[23] Dive-bombers scored most of the hits in the Coral Sea, largely because the defending CAP could not follow them once they nosed over and because the descending bombers presented shipboard gunners with a fast-moving, thin profile.

The setback in the Coral Sea caused the Japanese to modify their grand strategy.[24] Having consolidated a perimeter from Burma in the west via New Guinea and the Bismarck Sea in the south to the Gilberts in the east, Yamamoto's first plan was to push southward and sever the sea lines of communication between Australia and the United States. He remained convinced of the need for bold moves because there was "absolutely no prospect of victory through ordinary naval operations."[25] The South Pacific campaign was superseded in mid-May by a risky offensive into the Eastern Pacific, which Yamamoto had devised in April to put an end to King's raiding strategy. In the face of Yamamoto's immense prestige, a product of a commonplace misinterpretation of the Pearl Harbor attack, the Naval General Staff resisted the Midway operation – codenamed MI – until the Tokyo Raid, which shamed the entire high command by endangering the emperor's life. This "ended the debate...as to whether Midway was to be attacked."[26] A reckless gambler with his nation's security, Yamamoto's strategic views reflected a dreary national fatalism. "There is no choice but to force a decisive fleet encounter," he had told the Naval General Staff. "If we set out from here to do that and we go to the bottom of the Pacific in a double suicide, things will be peaceful on the high seas for some time."[27] This was an especially self-defeating attitude when confronting such a calculating, unsentimental opponent as Ernest J. King, once described by an admirer as the "perfect human machine."[28] And what neither the Japanese Naval General Staff nor Combined Fleet headquarters apparently bothered to ask before mounting another major operation was why the American carriers had appeared so unexpectedly in the Coral Sea.

The shortcomings of Japanese communications security allowed US Navy codebreakers to report fragments of Yamamoto's plan to admirals King and Nimitz in early May, when Nimitz's recurrent demand to abandon the blocking and raiding strategy and concentrate the carriers on the Hawaii–Midway line became more insistent. By May 5, King realized that a major offensive was afoot, but he reasoned that Yamamoto would renew the drive against the South Pacific bases and, perhaps, suspected that Nimitz was interpreting vague intelligence to support his conservative strategic instincts. This debate came to a climax on May 16, when Nimitz cancelled a planned raid by Halsey's task force and ordered him to return the *Enterprise* to Pearl Harbor without King's approval. King withheld comment until the 17th, when he deferred to his fleet commander. He was taking a tremendous military and political risk; if the Combined Fleet re-entered the Coral Sea unopposed and descended on the South Pacific bases, Australia would be isolated and exposed.[29] Halsey's ships stood into Pearl Harbor on May 26 and Fletcher in the *Yorktown* followed the next day.[30] For the first time in the war, the Pacific Fleet carriers were concentrated on the Hawaii–Midway line.

Yamamoto's strategy sought two ends. The primary objective was to occupy Midway Atoll and transform it into a base for a renewed assault on Hawaii. Expecting Nimitz to react by deploying the remaining Pacific Fleet carriers and battleships to the waters off Midway, Yamamoto intended to overwhelm them with a Mobile Force composed of four carriers and a Main Body of seven battleships and two light carriers. The secondary objective was to establish bases in the Aleutians to prevent the

US Army Air Force from conducting a strategic bombing campaign across the North Pacific against Japan's home islands. For both operations, 165 ships, the largest fleet yet to appear in the Pacific, was assembled in May. A Northern Area Force, commanded by Vice-Admiral Boshiro Hosogaya, consisting of a light carrier, seven cruisers, and transports, sailed for the Aleutians to establish bases on Attu and Kiska islands after attacking the American base at Dutch Harbor on Unalaska Island. This action intended to divert Nimitz's attention from the primary attack on the Hawaii–Midway line. Yamamoto divided the Combined Fleet into a Main Body of one light carrier, seven battleships, and four cruisers; a Mobile Force of Nagumo's 1st Air Division with the carriers *Akagi*, *Hiryu*, *Kaga*, and *Soryu*, and their screens; Vice-Admiral Nobutake Kondo's Occupation Force of two battleships, two seaplane carriers, seven cruisers, and 29 destroyers escorting 12 transports embarking 5,000 troops. A detached Submarine Force of 18 I-boats was to take station off French Frigate Shoals between Midway and Hawaii, report on Pacific Fleet movements westward, and attack targets of opportunity.

The defects in this strategy were numerous. The Japanese fleet could not reasonably expect either to hold Midway or operate aircraft from its runways inasmuch as the US Seventh Air Force in Hawaii could easily destroy the exposed site with one high-level raid by B-17 Flying Fortresses. And Yamamoto's belief that the Japanese carriers could again close on Hawaii – now defended by constant long-range patrolling, early warning radars, and an immense concentration of land-based fighters and fighter-bombers – betrayed not only another sorry feature of Japanese military intelligence, but also the admiral's inability to make reasoned strategic calculations.[31] Detaching the Northern Area Force diminished the strength of the primary attack and represented an unthinking expectation that Nimitz would divert forces to defend the Aleutians at the expense of exposing both Australia and Hawaii. Yamamoto's tactical organization was equally poor. He put to sea in the superbattleship *Yamato* with the Main Body, intending to coordinate the operation, but he then separated the Main Body from the Mobile Force by 400 miles. He was thus unable to issue orders until late into the action, owing to the need to maintain radio silence. Distancing the Main Body from the Mobile Force also deprived the carriers of additional, impressive antiaircraft defenses. Finally, Japanese naval intelligence possessed a primitive understanding of the American order of battle; among other failings, it underestimated the threat posed either by the US Naval Station (NAS) Midway or the B-17E bombers in Hawaii.

King's orders to Nimitz on the conduct of the battle reflected a shrewd reckoning of the opponent's strengths. He intended to defeat Japan in the Pacific theaters with immense amphibious lunges, led by a heavy carrier-fast battleship fleet of unprecedented size and power, but the 24 Essex class carriers and the 12 South Dakota and Iowa class battleships then building would not begin to join the Pacific Fleet until mid-1943. Until then, he pursued a "defensive-offensive" approach entailing great risks to the afloat carriers; although they would not be needed for the major strategic counteroffensive, until that movement developed they were not wholly expendable. King ordered that "strong attrition tactics, only, be employed and that our carriers and cruisers not be unduly risked."[32]

Nimitz deployed his forces on May 28. To deal with the Alaskan diversion, he ordered Rear Admiral Robert Theobald to take a cruiser–destroyer task force, a third of the Pacific Fleet, sail into the North Pacific, defend Dutch Harbor, and ambush Hosogaya's Northern Force. He positioned Admiral William Pye's task force, consisting of the small escort carrier *Long Island* and the old battleships, between San Francisco and Hawaii, just in case. At King's behest, he had already strengthened NAS Midway and arranged for the Seventh Air Force in Hawaii to fly long-range bomber support for the fleet.

Rear Admiral Raymond Spruance, who had replaced Halsey, took his TF 16, with *Enterprise* and *Hornet*, and stood out to sea on the 28th. The *Yorktown* was sufficiently patched up so that Fletcher could depart with TF 17 on May 30. Steaming to the northwest on parallel courses, the 50 ships avoided the Japanese submarine patrol at French Frigate Shoals, which did not take station until June 1. The Pacific Fleet that rendezvoused on June 2, 325 miles northeast of Midway included eight cruisers, 15 destroyers, and three carriers embarking 221 aircraft, including 79 Wildcat fighters, 101 Dauntless dive-bombers, and 41 Devastator torpedo planes. Nimitz's strategy was to create a "scissor battle" by placing the Japanese carriers between land-based air attacks from Midway and an ambush by the carrier air groups. And "surprise was paramount," recalled Captain Joseph Worthington, captain of the escorting destroyer *Benham*, "because we believed that the Japanese did not know of the presence of our carriers."[33] Unbeknownst to Yamamoto, Nimitz was not surprised to learn that the Northern Force was raiding Dutch Harbor on the 3rd. Admiral Hosogaya's planes returned the next day and his ships landed troops on Kiska Island on June 6 and on Attu Island on the 7th. Hosogaya's movements flummoxed Admiral Theobald, whose error-ridden failure to defend the Aleutians justified his nickname, "Fuzzy." Rather than diverting Nimitz's attention from Midway, however, the secondary North Pacific diversion merely diminished the Japanese forces available to conduct the primary attack.

Yamamoto's main battle strategy began to unfold at this stage. He planned to open the battle of Midway on June 4 by occupying the atoll, establishing Japanese land-based aircraft on the undamaged runways there the next day, and confronting the Americans with a "scissor battle" between land- and sea-based air when they appeared on or after the 6th. So, at first light on the 4th, Admiral Nagumo in the flagship *Akagi* launched half of his carrier air strength – 36 Zero fighters, 36 Val dive-bombers, and 36 Kate torpedo-bombers, a total of 108 planes. Expecting to destroy the NAS Midway aircraft on the ground with this powerful attack, he wisely held half of his planes in reserve, armed and on the deck, to react to an emergency. As a precaution, he also sent floatplanes from his cruisers to search out to 300 miles east of Midway.

At 05:34, search planes from Midway reported that an incoming Japanese flight was heading for the air station. Despite little warning, before the enemy approached every operational aircraft – divided into two groups – was aloft. The attack group – six TBF-1 Avengers, 16 Marine SB2C Dauntless dive-bombers, 11 SB2U-3 Vindicator dive-bombers, and four B-26 Marauder medium bombers – made altitude and flew toward the enemy carriers, without fighter escort. And 14 of 18 B-17E Flying Forts heading from Hawaii toward the Transport Force were diverted to attack the Mobile Force. The Midway defenders – 18 F2A-3 Buffalo fighters and six F4F-3 Wildcat fighters – were on CAP protecting the station. When the Marine fighters met the incoming Japanese flight 30 miles out at 06:20, they were overwhelmed by the escorting Zeros. The attackers lost one Zero and two Vals, but claimed 13 Avengers and two Wildcats, leaving NAS Midway with only two fighters. At 06:30, the Japanese broke through the defending CAP. Midway gun crews claimed four Japanese aircraft and others were badly shot up, but the attackers destroyed or damaged every structure at the station except the runways, which they intended to use the next day. However, the failure to destroy the Midway aircraft on the ground and the station's stiff resistance caused the flight leader, Lieutenant Joichi Tomonaga, to report to the flagship that "there is need for a second attack wave."[34]

Nagumo was upset by having to delay the landing by the Invasion Force. Still, his reconnaissance had not located the Pacific Fleet, so he decided to commit his reserve bombers in a massive strike, despite Yamamoto's orders to withhold some planes to defend against and attack any American ships which unexpectedly appeared. At 07:15, he ordered that 36 Kates from *Kaga* and *Akagi* be rearmed with 800kg high explosive (HE) bombs instead of torpedoes, and that armor piercing (AP) bombs be replaced with HE bombs on the 36 Vals on the *Soryu* and *Hiryu*. Twelve Zeros were flying CAP at the moment and Nagumo intended to hold the remainder in reserve. All four carriers had to clear their decks anyway to recover the returning Midway strike, recover the CAP, and refuel the Zeros to provide an escort for the second strike.

Nagumo's plan began to unravel at 07:28, when a sighting of 10 American ships 235 miles northwest of Midway was reported. Confused by the message, which made no mention of carriers, Nagumo dithered. He decided at 07:45 that the enemy formation had the highest priority, so he halted the rearming of the bombers and ordered that they be rearmed with AP bombs and torpedoes for an attack. He attached little urgency to the order, however, as he failed to reason that such a large opposing body was likely to include aircraft carriers.

Moreover, Nagumo was aware that the enemy knew his strength and location because the first strike from Midway attacked at 07:00, when six Avengers and four B-26 Marauders bearing torpedoes approached at low level. At 08:00 the second Midway strike, led by sixteen Marine Dauntlesses, approached. Owing to the inexperience of his pilots, the flight leader organized a low-level glide attack on the *Hiryu*, but the dive-bombers were met by 19 Zeros on CAP, which shot down eight of them at the cost of only one fighter and no damage to the carrier. Then 14 Flying Forts flew a high-level run over the *Soryu* and *Hiryu*. Nine Zeros rose to defend the ships. None of them reached the bombers, but bomb loads failed to hit the maneuvering ships below. Finally, 11 Marine Vindicators attacked the screening battleship *Haruna*. None scored a hit and 12 defending Zeros splashed three dive-bombers before the survivors escaped. On the one hand, not only did the Midway strikes fail to damage to the Japanese ships, but their appearance also provided Nagumo with priceless tactical intelligence, which he disregarded. On the other, the Midway strikes kept the enemy admirals and their ships busy and off balance for several crucial moments.

Pleased with the defeat of the Midway strikes, Nagumo was shocked to receive another report at 08:20 warning that the American formation included at least one carrier. At that point, the bombers on *Akagi* and *Kaga* were only partly rearmed with torpedoes and were on the hanger decks. Thirty-six Vals were ready on the *Soryu* and *Hiryu*, although few of them were appropriately rearmed. However, only six Zeros were ready to escort a strike against the enemy ships; the rest had to be recovered and refueled. Moreover, the Midway strike group was overhead, low on fuel, and awaiting recovery. Nagumo's choices were to recover the Midway strike group while he finished rearming his bombers or to immediately dispatch a strike carrying the wrong weapons and without fighter escort. Rear Admiral Tamon Yamaguchi, commander of the 2nd Carrier Division in the *Hiryu*, favored a quick attack with all aircraft without escort, but Rear Admiral Ryunosuke Kusaka, Nagumo's chief of staff, and Commander Minoru Genda, his air officer, counseled delay. Having just witnessed the defeat of the unescorted Midway strike, Nagumo was reluctant to send out a high-level dive-bombing attack without escorts, so he directed that the Midway strike group be recovered, that the bombers be armed with antiship weapons, and that a large strike of 36 Val dive-bombers and 36 Kate torpedo planes, escorted by a dozen Zeros, be readied for launch at 10:30. At 08:37, the Mobile Force turned into the wind to recover aircraft. By dithering, Nagumo ceded the initiative to the enemy and was on course to lose the battle as a result.

Admiral Fletcher learned that the Midway search planes had located the Mobile Force at 05:34. Fletcher's battle tactics comported with US Navy carrier doctrine, developed over years of annual prewar fleet exercises. He separated his task forces by 20 miles, enough distance so that the enemy could not easily locate both at the same time, but close enough so that the air groups could provide mutual support. Fletcher planned to launch a massive attack once the enemy was located. Admiral

Spruance planned to launch a strike from the *Enterprise* and *Hornet* of 70 Dauntlesses and 20 Devastators, escorted by 20 Wildcats. A handful of fighters would be held on CAP. Although the fighter-director officer in the *Enterprise* was responsible for all CAP and escort for all three carriers, no one was responsible for coordinating the bombing attacks, a costly shortcoming.

At 06:03 Fletcher received another message from a PBY-5 Catalina flying boat providing the exact location of the enemy carriers, about 175 miles from his position, and at 06:07 he ordered Spruance to turn to the southwest, close the distance with the enemy, and launch an attack. TF 16 separated into two task units and began putting up aircraft at 07:00. The TF 16 had 26 Wildcats, 67 Dauntlesses, and 29 Devastators, a total of 116 planes, either launched or launching when, at 07:45, Spruance, anxious over delays in launching, ordered the ill-coordinated flight to depart.

The crew of the *Yorktown* was given more time to ready its strike group because Fletcher, with the Coral Sea action in mind, withheld his bombers until he was certain that he had located all of the opposing carriers. Having determined that the enemy had deduced his location, he decided to launch a "limited strike" composed of 17 Dauntlesses and 12 Devastators escorted by six Wildcats, a total of 39 aircraft. Always cautious, Fletcher withheld 17 Dauntlesses and six Wildcat fighters in reserve.

The search for the Mobile Force proved that in an ocean as large as the Pacific, even the largest ships are small. Recovering the Midway strike planes at 09:18, Nagumo turned his ships northward to prepare for the attack, a movement that compounded an error in the initial report and made the formation even more difficult for the American flights to locate. The *Hornet* dive-bombers flying at high altitude missed the enemy altogether and continued flying to the southwest until they ran low on fuel. Twenty-one returned to the carrier, and the rest flew on to Midway. All of their escorting fighters ran out of fuel and ditched. However, at 09:20, the *Hornet* torpedo-bombers found the Mobile Force, but they were ambushed by Zeros, which splashed all 15 Devastators. Moments later, at about 09:25, the *Enterprise* torpedo-bombers, also unescorted, arrived. Dividing into two sections to attack from opposing sides, they were overwhelmed by the CAP, which downed 10 of 14 Devastators, none of which scored a hit.

Flying at high altitude like the *Hornet* dive-bombers, the *Enterprise* Dauntlesses also could not find the enemy at the expected position, so the flight leader, Lieutenant-Commander "Wade" McClusky, turned his planes to the north to search an enlarging square when he chanced upon a straggling Japanese destroyer, which he trailed back to the Mobile Force. Approaching from the south when he sighted the enemy at 10:00, McClusky's flight divided into two sections, which rolled over and descended on the *Akagi* and *Kaga*, then positioned at the south and west corners of a diamond-box formation. At 1,800 feet, the first pilot "reached for the handle on his left, pulled the bomb release, and cleared out as fast as he could. One after another 25 planes did the same, as the whole world seemed to erupt beneath them."[35] The *Akagi's* flight deck, littered with planes, fuel, and weapons, was hit by two bombs. Four bombs struck the *Kaga*. Her island was shredded and secondary explosions from bombs and fuel on the deck wreathed the ship in flame. Both sank that evening. By happenstance, the *Yorktown* strike group, approaching from the east, reached the Mobile Force at the same time. Lieutenant-Commander Maxwell Leslie led his flight toward the *Soryu*, the closest carrier on the east corner of the box. Five Avengers launched torpedoes, but none scored a hit and only two planes survived the enemy defenses to return to the carrier. Then, with the sun at their backs, the Dauntlesses nosed over into their dives. There was no fighter opposition and little antiaircraft gunfire, and the first 13 dive-bombers left the *Soryu* in flames. She was abandoned within a half-hour.

Returning to the task force, McClusky and Leslie left behind three burning Japanese carriers. The Americans caused immense damage, despite scoring relatively few direct hits, because they struck when the enemy decks were crowded with refueling aircraft and unloaded ordnance. When Nagumo transferred his flag from the crippled *Akagi* to the cruiser *Nagara*, only the undamaged *Hiryu*, now steaming northeastward, could still operate aircraft. Admiral Kondo was told to detach escorts from the Invasion Force to strengthen the screen of the Mobile Force.

The Japanese struck back with their remaining arm. While the Americans punished the other carriers, the *Hiryu* recovered the Midway strike and rearmed her planes. Admiral Yamaguchi launched an attack of 18 Vals, escorted by six Zeros, beginning at 10:45. A second strike of her reserve aircraft, nine Kates escorted by three fighters, followed an hour later. Shadowing American aircraft returning to the *Yorktown*, Lieutenant Michio Kobayahsi led his flight in low under the radar screen. The incomers were not found by the *Yorktown*'s radar until 11:32, when they were spotted closing fast from 32 miles to the southwest. Fletcher had the returning bombers waved off, all planes launched from the *Yorktown*'s deck, and a total of 28 Wildcat fighters from all three carriers were vectored out to intercept the Japanese.

The *Yorktown* CAP splashed 11 of Kobayashi's Val dive-bombers, but seven survived, nosed over, and scored three hits and several damaging near-misses. The first bomb holed the flight deck, the second went down to the fourth deck and detonated, and the third damaged the boiler room. However, repair parties quickly fixed the deck, the boilers were relit, and the ship was making 20 knots and refueling fighters soon afterward. Then, at 14:30, the *Yorktown*'s radar identified more incomers about 40 miles out. The refueling was ended and CAP was ordered to launch and fly out to engage the attackers, but planes were still launching when the Japanese appeared. Moreover, observed Captain Worthington, the CAP "was high up trying to break up the formation" but the "low-level torpedo attack was directly opposite from the earlier dive-bomber attack."[36] As a result, several of the second *Hiryu* flight of Kates survived the CAP and the screening antiaircraft fires, bore in on the sharply maneuvering carrier, and launched several torpedoes. Captain Buckmaster maneuvered to avoid one pair, but a second pair entered the port side amidships and exploded. The ship lost power, stopped, and listed 26 degrees to port. With the vessel in danger of capsizing, Fletcher transferred his flag to the cruiser *Astoria* – the second commander to abandon his flagship that day – and turned over tactical command to Spruance in the *Enterprise*. Buckmaster ordered the *Yorktown*'s crew to abandon ship.

Meanwhile, a scout plane launched earlier by the *Yorktown* reported that the *Hiryu* was steaming 100 miles to the northwest of TF 16. Spruance immediately readied another strike of 24 bombers from the *Enterprise* and 16 from the *Hornet*. Launched at 16:00 without fighter escort, which was withheld to provide CAP, the *Enterprise* planes found three burning carriers to the south and the unscathed *Hiryu* to the north. She was launching a desperate twilight strike of five Vals and five Kates escorted by 10 Zeros – her surviving aircraft – when the *Enterprise* attackers struck. The few remaining Zeros on CAP splashed three Dauntlesses, but the survivors placed four bombs in the *Hiryu*. When the *Hornet* bombers arrived a half-hour later, the fourth Japanese carrier was covered by flames.

Yamamoto, thinking that Midway aircraft had only disabled the *Kaga*, *Akagi*, and *Soryu*, and that the *Hiryu* would handle the one Pacific Fleet carrier on the scene, was ready to proceed according to plan. He ordered the transports to retire temporarily and Kondo to reinforce the Mobile Force. Then, at 17:30, he was told that the *Hiryu* was also burning and that none of the four carriers could be saved. Shaken by the disaster, Yamamoto resolved to recover by taking the offensive with an order to the Main Body to steam eastward in the hope of engaging the Pacific Fleet ships in a night gunnery duel.

Admiral Spruance, alert to this danger, also headed eastward and kept open the distance between the two forces. At 02:55, Yamamoto realized that the American ships were sailing away and that, shorn of his CAP, he had best cancel the MI operation and order a general retreat. Soon after, Spruance reversed course and pursued the enemy on the 5th and 6th while avoiding ambushes at night. On June 6, *Enterprise* patrols spotted heavy cruisers *Mikuma* and *Mogami* to the west. Spruance launched three attacks in succession, sinking the *Mikuma* and putting the *Mogami* out of action for a year. When he got low on fuel and turned TF 16 back to Hawaii, the crippled *Yorktown* was still afloat. Buckmaster boarded the carrier with a survey party on June 5. Admiral Nimitz had deployed the minesweeper *Vireo* to the scene to take the *Yorktown* under tow; the destroyer *Hammann* came alongside on the 6th and put a salvage party on board. Then, at 13:35, the submarine I-168 closed on the ships and fired four torpedoes. One sank the destroyer and two entered the carrier, which rolled over and went under on the morning of the 7th. One day earlier, the *Saratoga*, now repaired, stood into Pearl Harbor.

The tactical results of the battle of Midway were one-sided. The Pacific Fleet lost only two ships, the *Yorktown* and the *Hammann*, 132 carrier- and land-based aircraft, and 307 killed in action. Losses to the Combined Fleet were staggering. They numbered four carriers and one heavy cruiser, 275 aircraft, and 3,500 killed in action. American matériel advantages partly accounted for this outcome. Shipboard radar provided superior air early warning, which meant that the defending CAP met incomers further from the carriers. The Japanese torpedo was a far superior weapon, but the American aircraft, especially the SBD Dauntless dive-bomber and the F4F-4 Wildcat fighter, were more rugged and able to absorb more combat damage. Vastly better American intelligence was the product not only of longstanding naval policy, but also wretched Japanese communications, security, matériel and procedures. Superior American tactics also partly explained the outcome. Pacific Fleet searches were more numerous and more aggressive, whereas the Japanese relied too much on cruiser floatplanes.[37] At first, both sides believed the torpedo plane to be more lethal than the dive-bomber, but the Japanese allowed this wrongheaded conviction to dictate their CAP tactics, whereas the Americans were more conservative.

Command was another major factor. Nagumo's congenital indecision, evident at Pearl Harbor, burdened Japanese tactics at Midway. Fletcher, who commanded Pacific Fleet carriers in two of the six major battles of the Pacific War, made rational, timely decisions, but his luck, evident at Midway, ran out later that year in the South Pacific and he was effectively – and, perhaps, unfairly – sidelined by King for the rest of the war. Whereas Nimitz remained at Pearl Harbor to direct strategy, Yamamoto put to sea in his flagship to be on the scene, a foolish decision that prevented him from contributing to the decisive action. At the highest level of command, Japan's witless military leaders were at the mercy of one of history's most lethal strategists in Admiral King.

Finally, Japanese grand strategy leading up to the Coral Sea and Midway reflected a crabbed, regional view of geopolitical realities and the shifting balance of power in the Pacific occasioned by American belligerency. For the Japanese, the defeat at Midway signaled the end of the offensive campaign begun on the Kra Isthmus and at Pearl Harbor. For the Americans, Coral Sea and Midway meant that "the mostly defensive phase of the war [in the Pacific] was over."[38]

Despite the strategic victories in the Coral Sea and off Midway, King was never able to implement wholly his preferred grand strategy of assailing Japan on many fronts. The British resisted American pressure to move against Burma until 1944; the Chinese proved unwilling or unable to take the offensive until early 1945; and the Soviets, while profiting from their 1941 Neutrality Pact with Japan, extracted postwar territorial concessions from Washington in return for promises to enter a conflict with Japan that they intended to enter anyway, once Germany capitulated. This meant that the burden of defeating Japan fell largely on the American forces in the Pacific theaters. King's explanation of the meaning of the victory at Midway to Roosevelt in the White House on June 10 convinced the President to approve the admiral's planned counteroffensive in the South Pacific, which got underway on Guadalcanal in early August. After Midway, Japan was forced on the defensive for the remainder of the struggle, absorbing one gnawing blow after another until the final shocks of Hiroshima and Nagasaki compelled an unconditional surrender. Thus the actions in the Coral Sea and Midway in 1942 set in train the replacement of Japanese with American power in the Pacific, a major military feature of the Cold War and the New World Order.

## Chapter 6

# Learning from Defeat
## The Burma Campaign

*Dr Daniel Marston*

The Burma Campaign has often been called a sideshow in terms of its relevance to the war against Japan. This statement is partially true; strategically, Burma's location was not as significant as the Philippines or Iwo Jima or Okinawa. The engagement and eventual defeat of the Imperial Japanese Army in Burma was, nevertheless, significant in a number of ways. First, the British/Indian Army tied down and later destroyed a major component of the IJA – one that otherwise might have been sent to other theaters to defend Japanese interests. Second, the reforms that the British/Indian Army carried out during the Burma Campaign, particularly the expansion of the officer corps to include South Asians, ultimately had profound impact on the development of the independent states of the Indian subcontinent, particularly India and Pakistan. Finally, the Burma Campaign was significant because it changed perceptions of the IJA. From the fearsome, unbeatable fighting force of 1942, the IJA came to be viewed, as the British/Indian Army reformed, adapted, and grew stronger, as mere mortals who underestimated their opponents and made costly mistakes as a result.

## FIRST BURMA CAMPAIGN

The First Burma Campaign began on December 11, 1941, and ended in May 1942 as the longest retreat in British military history. Though soundly defeated, the British managed to escape into India, bringing with them a wealth of experience that would provide the framework for a reformed and eventually victorious British/Indian Army.

Field Marshal Sir William Slim, commander of Burma Corps (BURCORPS), described the retreat in his memoirs:

On the last day of that nine hundred-mile retreat I stood on a bank beside the road and watched the rearguard march into India. All of them, British, Indian and Gurkha, were gaunt and ragged as scarecrows. Yet as they trudged behind their surviving officers in groups pitifully small, they still carried their arms and kept their ranks, they were still recognizable fighting units. They might look like scarecrows, but they [looked] like soldiers too.[1]

The principal reason for the Japanese offensive into Burma was to safeguard Japan's advances into Malaya and the Dutch East Indies. They also wished to destroy the Burma Road, to prevent supplies from American forces getting to the Chinese Nationalist Armies. The Japanese plan for Burma was straightforward: the Fifteenth Army, veteran troops from China, under the command of Lieutenant-General S. Iida, launched an attack through the southern region of Tenasserim.

The British defense of Burma was, at first, rudimentary. The 1st Burma Division (BURDIV) was in the process of being formed when the campaign began. The campaigns in Europe, the Middle East, and Malaya had been given priority by the British Army, which meant that units in Burma (Burmese, British, and Indian), and indeed the whole of the Indian Army, were not equipped with the latest equipment and were short of ammunition.

In 1939, the Indian Army stood at some 200,000 men. By 1941, rapid expansion had brought the figure to more than 1.5 million men, and had, not surprisingly, diluted the quality of officers and men. The formation of new units meant that older units were often depleted (or "milked") of officers and NCOs. Ongoing equipment shortages meant that units often did not receive Bren guns or mortars until they arrived in Burma, and then were still short of ammunition, for both training exercises and battle engagements.

Training of the units stationed in Burma and in India created further complications. Most units had been trained for deployment to the Middle East, where the terrain indicated conventional, open-style warfare. Only a few officers recognized that the campaign in Burma might require different tactics to contend with the jungles in the southern and northern reaches of the country. Even those who did recognize it could do nothing, as there was no training regime for jungle fighting and no time to develop one. One junior officer recorded a conversation about training between his commander and a staff officer shortly after his arrival in Rangoon; when asked about training, the staff officer responded: "Training – you can't do any training because it is all bloody jungle."[2]

The British Commander-in-Chief, India,[3] General Sir Archibald Wavell, issued a plan for the defense of Burma involving major air force reinforcements, the erection of defenses in the Shan States, the creation of mobile guerrilla forces, two divisions transferred from India, and "staff conversations" with Chiang Kai-Shek to have Chinese forces move into Burma to help with defense. The air reinforcements never arrived, due to the requirements of other theaters, so the Japanese outnumbered the Royal Air Force (RAF) and Indian Air Force (IAF) nearly five to one. The 17th Indian Division – the equivalent of a division and a half of partially trained soldiers – was sent to Burma. A later reinforcement by the veteran 7th Armoured Brigade was important, but arrived too late in the campaign to shift the balance. The Chinese also provided a sizeable force, but they too were outfought by the Japanese, and forced to withdraw to their home nation.

As the 17th Indian Division took up positions in Moulmein and points south in early January 1942, the Japanese massed on the border. After seizing Victoria Point, the Japanese 55th Division headed north to Moulmein, and struck across the border. British intelligence about where the Japanese were heading was insufficient, a failing that confounded the British throughout the campaign. The Japanese advance was swift, reaching and seizing Moulmein by January 31. The 17th Indian Division withdrew towards the Bilin River. While it fought well, it was threatened with encirclement, and was forced to withdraw towards the Sittang River. The Japanese forces, by this time comprising two divisions, moved quickly to destroy the 17th Indian Division before it could withdraw across the Sittang River. On the night of February 23, the bridge was blown with two brigades of the 17th Division still on the eastern side of the river.[4]

This episode marked the beginning of the end of the campaign. The 17th Indian Division was below 40 percent strength, and 1BURDIV was moved south to provide reinforcements. The Japanese moved quickly to negotiate the Sittang River (which they crossed on March 3), surround the British, and force a decisive battle for Rangoon.[5] Units of the 17th Indian Division responded, attempting to force a breakthrough to the north. They succeeded on March 7, but Rangoon fell on the 9th, essentially cutting the Burma Army off from the outside world. The Burma Army headed north to attempt to hold a defensive line against the Japanese.

The Japanese had not been idle. With Rangoon in their hands, they were able to reinforce the Fifteenth Army.[6] By March 19, the British created a formal corps structure, BURCORPS, led by Lieutenant-General William Slim. The campaign entered its final phases, a continuous withdrawal. Chinese forces entered Burma and took up positions, covering the Sittang River Valley and the plains towards Mandalay. BURCORPS was given the responsibility of the western side of Burma, following the Irrawaddy River Valley to the north.

By the end of March, the RAF was forced to withdraw from Burma, leaving BURCORPS without air support or reconnaissance. The 17th Indian Division was forced to withdraw from Prome after heavy fighting, while BURCORPS withdrew towards Magwe. On April 10, the Japanese followed up the withdrawal, hoping to open a wedge between the 17th Division and 1BURDIV. This forced another major withdrawal for the British, sending units towards the oil field region of Yenangyaung. The Japanese launched a series of attacks against the Chinese forces in the Shan States to coincide with the drive on Yenangyaung.

The oil fields were prepared for demolition, and on April 15, orders were given for their destruction. 1BURDIV moved towards Yenangyaung, but the Japanese were able to get around the flanks of BURCORPS and enter Yenangyaung before 1BURDIV. This left 1BURDIV cut off from the north, and Chinese forces were drafted in to help the 1BURDIV to break out to the north. The breakout plan was scheduled for April 18–19. The Chinese attack faltered, and 1BURDIV's first attempt was not successful either. Even a series of attacks, from both the Chinese and the 1BURDIV sides, failed to engineer a breakthrough. Commanders decided to abandon the motor transport and heavy equipment, and have the men attempt to break out in small groups. This accomplished the breakout but meant that the 1BURDIV, already weakened, ceased to exist as a formation.

By the end of April, matters had deteriorated further. BURCORPS was below strength, and the Chinese forces in the Shan States and on the flank of BURCORPS were collapsing. BURCORPS was ordered to fall back towards Meiktila, with the Japanese close on their heels. On April 28, in the face of unrelenting Japanese pressure and a collapsing front, the high command decided to withdraw the remainder of BURCORPS to India.

BURCORPS made the long journey towards Imphal over difficult tracks, with the Japanese close behind, through the monsoon. By late May, the last men from BURCORPS entered Imphal.

## 1942/1943

The period between the First Burma Campaign and the Japanese offensives of 1944 was a testing time for the British and Indian forces stationed in India. Another defeat awaited the British in the Arakan, as well as a partially successful operation by the Chindits, a complete evaluation of training and doctrine, and the creation of a new command structure, South-East Asia Command (SEAC). The Japanese reached their highest level of success during this period.

### The First Arakan offensive

The backing of a limited offensive in the Arakan region rested with India Command and Eastern Army HQ.[7] By July 1942, only a few months after the defeat in Burma, a minor offensive was ordered to clear the Mayu Peninsula and seize Akyab Island and its strategic airstrip, a distance of 90 miles from the British front lines. The Mayu Peninsula comprised a range of jungle-covered mountains more than 2,000 feet high. Intelligence had stated that only four Japanese battalions were protecting the area. However, the British and Indian forces earmarked were not veteran troops and had minimal jungle warfare training.

After a series of proposals that had included amphibious operations, a stripped-down plan was put into operation in December 1942. The 14th Division was the main component, commanded by the Eastern Army, led by Lieutenant-General N. M. Irwin.

The advance began well. The 14th Division seized Maungdaw and Buthidaung, and by the end of December had reached the outskirts of the village of Donbaik, 10 miles short of the end of the peninsula. The Japanese, initially caught off guard, began to reinforce both sides of the range at Donbaik and Rathedaung, and repulsed attacks against both towns.

By the end of January, five brigades had reinforced the 14th Division, bringing the total of brigades deployed to nine. Despite the increase, the

14th was still commanded by a divisional commander. Slim, the XV Corps commander, called for a corps command, but no change was forthcoming. Through the whole of February and into early March, the units of the 14th Division threw themselves against the Japanese defenses, with little success. Many of the attacks were frontal and were easily repulsed by Japanese flanking fire. General Wavell commented on reviewing his troops' performance that "we still have a great deal to learn about jungle fighting."[8]

Irwin sent Slim to the Arakan to assess the situation. Slim called again for a corps command, but Irwin still disagreed. Slim also visited units in the field, and reported back that morale was low. By mid-March, the situation appeared to be a deadlock.

At this point, the Japanese 55th Division counterattacked the British and Indian troops on the eastern side of the Mayu Range. They had infiltrated behind and between the various units, using the terrain to their advantage once again. The British and Indians, still heavily dependent upon overland communications by road, had not secured the range. The troops opposite Rathedaung were forced to withdraw to the Mayu River. Irwin relieved General Lloyd of his command and took over command of the 14th Division and attached brigades himself. This seemed to help stabilize the situation, and Irwin handed over command to Major-General Lomax.

The Japanese, still on the move, next attacked the lines of communication supporting the units on the western side of the range, forcing them to retreat northwards. On April 5, Slim was finally called in to form a corps HQ to try and remedy the deteriorating situation. After a further month's fighting and continuous retreat, the remainder of the 14th Division and associated brigades had withdrawn to their starting positions. The operation had been a complete failure and further damaged the already fragile morale of the British and Indian units in India. As a result, Irwin was replaced as commander of Eastern Army by General Sir George Giffard.

## The First Chindit operation

The Chindits were in some ways the product of Wavell's efforts to form a guerrilla force in the First Burma Campaign. A Bush Warfare School was created at Maymyo, Burma. Brigadier Orde Wingate, a specialist in irregular warfare, was sent to centralize all the various schools and training. Along with the rest of BURCORPS, they had to withdraw to India, and remnants of the Bush Warfare School, along with other commandos from Europe, created a second establishment in India. Wingate was given command of the 77th Indian Brigade, and expressed his wish to deploy it in carrying out an unorthodox raid, in support of a Chinese offensive, into Northern Burma.

Wingate's brigade had been trained for jungle warfare and the units were not tied to the roads. Their columns consisted of mule transport, and their resupply was to be carried out by air. The brigade of 3,000 men was split into eight columns and three independent units. They planned to march overland from the Imphal region and strike into upper Burma, where they intended to raid and destroy the railway lines between Mandalay and the north.

On February 13, 1943, Wingate's units crossed into Burma, surprising the Japanese. They were quick to recover, however, and set out to destroy all of the columns. After a series of setbacks, Wingate ordered the columns to break up into smaller parties and make their separate ways back to Imphal. By May 26, the surviving Chindits had returned to Imphal, less two-thirds of the forces who had been killed or captured. This offensive has generated considerable controversy as to its value and outcome, but it unquestionably provided a morale boost for the British and Indian units, as well as some valuable lessons on the need for air superiority and effective air–ground communications.

## Buildup of the British and Indian Units

Between the end of the First Burma Campaign and the beginning of the Second Arakan offensive in late 1943, the British and Indian Army units underwent a major transformation. Some divisions, such as the 17th, 20th, and 23rd, attempted to devise new tactics and training for the war in Burma. They carried out exercises to learn the lessons from various battles. While these efforts were undoubtedly important, such grassroots innovation meant that the training and tactical doctrine being devised was not uniform or consistent. After the end of the First Arakan offensive, GHQ India set out to formalize training and doctrine for operations in Burma. The Infantry Committee, India, ordered that all units and reinforcements must be trained in jungle warfare, and ordered the creation of two training divisions and the development of a training pamphlet, known as the *Jungle Book*. By the end of 1943, many divisions and units were receiving training for jungle warfare. Their reinforcements were also receiving training as a matter of course, and divisional organizations were assessing and incorporating lessons learned in battle.

Throughout this period, senior commanders such as Slim set out to establish an adequate supply network for the Eastern Army (Fourteenth Army), which necessitated the construction of railway lines and better roads. Ultimately, however, the Fourteenth Army subsisted on much lower levels of supplies than the British armies in Europe. It is a tribute to Slim and his commanders that they were able to achieve so much with, relatively speaking, so little.

In the course of these preparations, the Army also undertook a medical offensive against malaria and other illnesses prevalent in a jungle climate. Medical camps were set up, and medical air evacuation was established to get men out of theater and into hospital. At this time, soldiers were often likely to spend months in hospital; this decreased to weeks with the introduction of forward medical units and air transport.

The command structure for the Burma campaign changed fundamentally after the Quebec Conference in July 1943. In August 1943, SEAC was organized under the command of Admiral Lord Louis Mountbatten, although it was not formally invested with operational command until November 15–16, 1943.[9] India Command, GHQ India, was to provide the logistical and training grounds for SEAC; it was headed from July 1943 until the end of the war by General Claude Auchinleck. General Slim, in discussing Auchinleck, said that "the 14th Army, from its birth to its final victory, owed much to his unselfish support and never-failing understanding. Without him and what he and the Army in India did for us we could not have existed, let alone conquered."[10]

Having absorbed the lessons of previous campaigns, all members of SEAC and Fourteenth Army recognized the need for proper air support. The RAF and USAAF received better aircraft, and larger numbers of fighter, bomber, and transport squadrons. The two air forces set out to dominate the skies of eastern India and Burma. Their units were structured into specific commands, such as the Third Tactical Air Force, Strategic Air Force, and Troop Carrier Command.

# 1944 CAMPAIGNS

The 1944 campaigns were both a turning point and proving ground for the Fourteenth Army. The First Chindit operation had heightened the fear within the Japanese high command that the British were close to taking the offensive. The Japanese planned offensives that were intended to disrupt any prospective British plans to invade Burma. In doing so, however, Japanese military intelligence failed to recognize that the Fourteenth Army and SEAC had reformed and reorganized their assets into a force considerably different than the one they had previously faced.

## Operation *Ha-Go*

By the end of 1943, the Fourteenth Army had prepared plans for a second limited offensive into the Arakan. This plan differed from the First Arakan offensive in many respects. For starters, both the 5th and 7th Indian divisions had been properly trained and organized for conflict in the hilly jungle environment of the Arakan. Both divisions were also planning to advance down the Mayu Range and to patrol the hilly range themselves, thus denying the Japanese access to the area.

The two divisions were assigned the task of seizing Maungdaw and Buthidaung, as well as the road network between the two. The 5th Division was to advance along the western side of the range, while the 7th Division moved along the eastern side. The 81st West African Division would operate further east, to offset any Japanese moves against the offensive, and would be resupplied by air. The 5th and 7th divisions built up the tracks into roads, understanding that they would have to stand and fight in defended boxes if the Japanese launched a counterattack.

By late November 1943, the offensive was on the move, and captured Maungdaw in January 1944. Reinforcements had been sent over the range to support the 7th Division's advance on Buthidaung. At about this time, Slim and the commanders in SEAC began to receive intelligence that the Japanese were going over to the offensive in the Arakan, and possibly in the Assam/Imphal region as well. The Japanese 55th Division made the first moves in the Arakan, hoping to attack the British advance, tie down many of the Fourteenth Army's reserves in the area, and then carry out a larger offensive against the major British supply depot of Imphal on the central front.

The 55th Division was divided into four major columns, one of which caused the most damage to the British advance. They were able to find gaps in the lines between the 81st and the 7th divisions, from which they headed straight for the 7th's main supply depot, known as the Admin Box. They succeeded in cutting off the 7th Division from the 5th Division. While the 7th Divisional HQ was attacked and almost wiped out, the various units of the division were able to fall back and create strong boxes to provide all-round defense against the Japanese attack. The clash for control of the area turned into a bloody battle of attrition. Most of the 55th Division moved in, in an attempt to destroy the 7th Indian Division. The British did not fall apart and retreat north, as the Japanese commanders had anticipated; rather, they stood and fought and resupplied by air. Over 2,300 tons of supplies were air-dropped to the 7th Division, while the 5th and 26th Indian divisions moved to destroy the Japanese forces caught between their units and the area around the Admin Box.

By February 24, the 7th Division linked up with reinforcements from the north. The 5th Division returned to the western side of the Mayu Range, while the 26th and 7th divisions set out to destroy the 55th Division, launching a counterattack in early March aimed towards Buthidaung and the road and tunnel networks. By June 1944, Japanese forces were withdrawing from the region, buckling under the constant pressure. Not only had the Japanese plan ended in conclusive defeat, it had also failed in its stated intention of drawing off the Fourteenth Army's reserves to the Arakan. While reserves were sent into the Arakan, Slim and SEAC were able to shift forces to Imphal quickly by air as the main offensive came in. Both the 5th and 7th Indian divisions were in the fighting in Imphal by the end of April.

## Operation *U-Go*

As stated previously, Slim and the Fourteenth Army became aware of plans for Japanese offensives in the Arakan and Imphal by late January 1944. The main force stationed in the Imphal Plain, 40 by 20 miles, surrounded by jungle-covered hills, was IV Corps, comprising the 17th, 20th, and 23rd divisions as well as the 254th Armoured Brigade and 50th Indian Parachute Brigade.

Imphal had a few airfields and was connected to the outside world by a road to the north through Kohima and Dimapur, which was the major railhead providing supplies to all of IV Corps. The Japanese plan of attack called for the Japanese Fifteenth Army, the 33rd, 31st, and 15th divisions, to attack all along the front and seize Kohima and Imphal. The 31st Division was given the task of seizing Kohima and pushing towards Dimapur, while the 15th Division was ordered to attack and cut off the Kohima and Imphal road, then strike from the north towards the Imphal Plain. The reinforced 33rd Division was to start its attack a week earlier, strike behind the 17th Indian Division and destroy it, and then strike towards Imphal from the south. At the same time, elements of the 33rd Division were to attack the 20th Indian Division and destroy it before it could reach Imphal. The 33rd Division began its move on March 9.

Slim and his staff did not want to withdraw the forward units until it was clear that the offensive had begun, because he feared that morale would be damaged. He did intend to withdraw both the 17th and 20th divisions to Imphal, and force the Japanese into a battle of attrition. Imphal would be held by all the units and resupplied by air as reinforcements attempted to break the surrounding Japanese forces. The plan did not go entirely as planned; the 17th Indian Division had a more difficult time withdrawing towards Imphal than anticipated. The 20th Division's withdrawal, although not easy, was not as difficult, and they were able to inflict heavy damage on the Japanese.[11] Both divisions were able to get back and form up strong positions within the plain.

The Japanese 15th and 31st divisions, meanwhile, were pushing hard to cut the Imphal and Kohima road. The 50th Indian Parachute Brigade put up a staunch defense at Sangshak; this held up the advance towards both Kohima and the Imphal from the northeast, but the threat to Kohima did not diminish. Slim ordered the 161st Brigade from the 5th Indian Division in the Arakan to be flown to the Kohima area at the end of March. The units moved into place and set up defensive positions just as the Japanese closed in. The two remaining brigades of the 5th Division were flown into Imphal to help defend the Urkhrul area to the northeast. By the end of March, the Japanese had succeeded in cutting the road between Kohima and Imphal. The British, however, had been able to extricate both the 17th and 20th divisions into Imphal by April

5 and had been reinforced by the 5th Indian Division. The Japanese offensive was not going to plan.

Between April and late June, a battle of attrition raged in Imphal. The British were able to hold their ground and be resupplied by air,[12] and thus continue the fight. The Japanese had failed to adapt their tactics to counter the newly developed jungle prowess of the British and Indian troops. The 17th Indian Division covered the southern entrances to the plain, while the 23rd moved into the Shenam region to the southeast and the 20th and 5th divisions were moved into the north and northeast regions.

The beginning of the end for the Japanese came from the north. While the 161st Brigade fought an attritional battle in Kohima, it was not alone. The XXXIII Corps was activated and the 2nd British Division sent from India via Dimapur to relieve pressure. On April 20, the garrison at Kohima was relieved and the 7th Indian Division sent in as the second major reinforcement in both the Kohima and Imphal areas. The 2nd British and 7th Indian divisions[13] pushed south to destroy the Japanese 31st and 15th divisions and link up with Imphal. A British officer described the heavy fighting: "first they came in ones and twos, and then larger parties… This was too good to miss. … [O]ur gunner got the artillery 3.7 inch guns on them… [W]e were carrying out real controlled fire at the Japanese… [W]e must have hit them fairly hard."[14] After much heavy fighting, units from the 5th Indian Division met up with the relieving forces from Kohima on June 22. The road had been reopened and the Japanese forces in the northern area of the plain were falling back.

Meanwhile, the fighting in the south continued unabated. After a series of headlong attacks against the 17th Indian Division in the south, the Japanese commanders finally realized that the offensive was over. On July 9, the Japanese Fifteenth Army ordered a withdrawal. The order came too late; Japanese units were losing cohesion and were in general disorder. Slim decided to keep the pressure up, and ordered the 5th Indian Division to head south along the Tiddim Road and destroy the 33rd Divisional Group. The 11th East African Division was ordered to follow along the flank to the east and destroy elements of the Fifteenth Army.

The Japanese offensives of 1944 had been soundly defeated. By the middle of the summer, the initiative clearly rested with the Fourteenth

Army and Slim and his commanders did not hesitate to take advantage. They moved to strike and destroy the Japanese Burma Army once and for all in the autumn of 1944.

## The Second Chindit operation

The Second Chindit operation differed from the first in 1943 in a few significant ways. Most important, the numbers of men involved were much greater. The first operation comprised a brigade of about 3,000 men. The second operation included six brigades, totaling more than 23,000 men. The structure of the second operation also highlighted the division of effort and perspective between the American and British forces. The British viewed the campaign as the recapture and occupation of Burma, and the destruction of the Japanese Burma Army. The Americans viewed the campaign as an opportunity to create a new Burma road, from Ledo in Assam to Yunnan, in order to provide the Chinese Nationalists with equipment and resources to wage war against the Japanese.

The three aims of Wingate's brigades in the Second Chindit operation were as follows: support Lieutenant-General Stillwell's advance on Myitkyina by attacking the 18th Japanese Division's lines of communications; induce the Chinese Expeditionary Force from Yunnan to cross into northern Burma; and raid and destroy communication and supply lines for the Japanese forces in northern Burma. Five of the brigades involved were to be flown into various landing areas, backed by Chindit-specific air support, the 1st Air Commando. Only one brigade was to march overland to the area. Three landing sites were set up, and elements of three brigades had landed by the evening of March 11 without alerting the Japanese defenders. The various units were to move out and create "strongholds," from which mobile columns would operate to destroy Japanese communications. On March 24, a second phase of troop deployment began; Wingate died in an air crash during this phase, and was succeeded by Brigadier Lentaigne.

The Japanese responded quickly to clear the threats to their northern forces, attacking each of the strongholds and setting up for battles of attrition. The Chindits were not intended for this sort of operation and, after a series of heavy battles, abandoned some of the strongholds and created new ones. The Japanese pressed the attack, attempting to clear the area of Chindits throughout May and June. Meanwhile, the Chinese advance proceeded slowly towards Myitkyina. On June 4, Chindit brigades attacked towards the area around the town of Mogaung, while remnants of the other brigades headed towards Myitkyina to support Stillwell's attack. The Chindits were being bled white in this operation, having stayed in the field longer than anyone intended. Brigadier Michael Calvert commented, after the fighting in Mogaung: "I was not going to ask any more of my men. I was haunted by the fact that we had been the willing horse, and that I had allowed them to be flogged until they could hardly stand... I was prepared to take on my own shoulders any blame for not fighting."[15]

By late June, the situation for the Chindits looked dire, and the decision was finally made to withdraw the Chindits as the Chinese and American forces made contact. When the remaining Chindits returned to India, the unit was disbanded. Those who survived and were fit to fight were, in many cases, sent as reinforcements to the Fourteenth Army.

## 1944/1945 CAMPAIGNS

While the Fourteenth Army pressed the advance against the retreating Japanese Fifteenth Army, the rest of the units and divisions carried out a much-needed rest and re-training. The Fourteenth Army did not rest on its laurels, but set out to assess and incorporate the lessons from the fighting in the Arakan and Assam. Slim and his commanders recognized that combat in Burma would ultimately encompass more open style fighting, so some units were re-equipped with motorized transport or trained to be air-landed units. Joint training was carried out with armored units, and units from XV Corps carried out intensive amphibious warfare training.

The campaigns of 1945 marked the reconquest of Burma, and included two major offensives. One was in the Arakan region and was carried out to support the larger offensive in central Burma. By May 1945, Rangoon would be recaptured and the Japanese would be in full retreat. Many would die in further fighting in July, as Japanese troops attempted to break out towards Thailand.

### Arakan

XV Corps began its offensive in the Arakan in December 1944, under orders to seize the Arakan region through a series of overland and amphibious attacks. They were also ordered to take the strategic islands of Akyab and Ramree, and to tie down the two Japanese divisions operating in the region. The offensive was under direct command of Allied Land Forces South East Asia,[16] while Slim and the Fourteenth Army focused on central Burma.

After a series of advances in the region British and Indian troops seized the Mayu Peninsula and Akyab Islands in January. This provided a boost to the advance in central Burma, as the airfields in the region were built up to provide air support. In late January, the 26th Indian Division was landed on Ramree Island, where they spent the month of February clearing Japanese positions. By the end of February, additional airfields were established on the island to support the advance.

The XV Corps carried out further attacks in the Arakan to tie down the Japanese. The 26th Indian Division was withdrawn for additional amphibious training and, in late April, ordered to land south of Rangoon. They advanced and seized the city on May 3.

## Operation *Extended Capital*

Elements of the Fourteenth Army had continued to pressure the retreating Japanese forces after Operation *U-Go*. By late November 1944, they had established two bridgeheads across the Chindwin River. The Japanese Burma Army, under the command of Lieutenant-General Hyotaro Kimura, had under its command ten divisions of infantry and two mixed brigades. Four of the divisions had been badly mauled, but the Burma Army received thousands of reinforcements for the final battle.

Slim sought a decisive battle. He knew his lines of communications were going to be stretched; the tracks from Imphal had been built up, but were still limited. Air resupply was going to be necessary.[17] Slim needed to destroy the Japanese Burma Army and advance quickly to Rangoon before the monsoon broke. His first plan, Operation *Capital*, envisioned that Kimura would remain on the Shwebo Plain, between the Chindwin and Irrawaddy Rivers, and fight. The offensive began early in December, when the 19th and 20th Indian divisions crossed the Chindwin and began to cross the Shwebo Plain. The divisions encountered some opposition, but it rapidly became clear to Slim and his commanders that Kimura was not going to seek a decisive battle on the plain. Kimura had withdrawn most of his forces to the opposite side of the Irrawaddy River, and Slim immediately revised his plan.

Slim's new plan, Operation *Extended Capital*, was a masterstroke. He had the divisions on the plain continue the advance towards the Irrawaddy River, while most of IV Corps was ordered to push through Kalewa and cross the river at Nyaungu. IV Corps was to operate in radio silence. Meanwhile, the units on the plain, XXXIII Corps, were to advance towards the Irrawaddy River, make their way across, and threaten Mandalay. This was intended to force the Japanese to send most of their troops to destroy the bridgeheads north and south of Mandalay. IV Corps would then surprise the Japanese southern defenses, launch an attack across the Irrawaddy River, and strike towards the communication center of the Japanese defensive lines along the river, at Meiktila. Slim explained it thus: "If we took Meiktila while Kimura was deeply engaged along the Irrawaddy about Mandalay, he would be compelled to detach large forces to clear his vital communications. This would give me not only the major battle I desired, but the chance to repeat the hammer and anvil tactics: XXXIII Corps the hammer from the north against the anvil of IV Corps at Meiktila and the Japanese between."[18]

The 19th Indian Division crossed the Irrawaddy River to the north of Mandalay on January 7 and 11. The Japanese sent forces to counter this apparent threat, in a series of counterattacks that were repulsed by the attacking British/Indian troops. The 19th built up its bridgeheads in preparation for the push south to Mandalay. On February 12, the 20th Indian Division crossed the Irrawaddy River south of Mandalay, forcing the Japanese to divide their focus, in order to contend with this new threat. On February 14, an even bigger surprise for the Japanese developed further south.

Kimura had received reports stating that British troops might be moving in the south. He had done nothing about these reports, however, and so on February 14, the 7th Indian Division (IV Corps) was able to cross and land at Nyaungu, against minimal opposition. To make matters worse for the Japanese, the 2nd British Division crossed the Irrawaddy River to the south of Mandalay on February 24. At this point, the 19th Indian Division began its drive to seize Mandalay. By mid-March, most of the Japanese forces in Mandalay were withdrawing after difficult fighting at Fort Dufferin and Mandalay Hill.

Japanese military intelligence had failed to identify the advance of the 7th Division. During the fighting it failed, once again, to recognize that the 7th Indian bridgehead had been reinforced by 255th Armoured Brigade and the 17th Indian Division. The divisions of XXXIII Corps, to the north, were busy trying to destroy the Japanese to the south of Mandalay. The 17th Indian Division and 255th Brigade made their attack towards Meiktila on February 21. After heavy fighting, Meiktila was seized on March 3. The 17th and 255th were cut off, but received reinforcements and supplies by air. The units in Meiktila were to be the anvil, and so they had to hold the area. The Japanese launched countless attacks to try to dislodge the British and disrupt their vital communications. Most attacks failed; the British had adopted an "active" defense of the area, and the Japanese were unable to counter their actions. As the isolated units fought an aggressive and attritional battle, units from the XXXIII and IV Corps advanced towards Meiktila, destroying the Japanese in between.

From March 22 to 24, a formal link with the units in Meiktila was established. The Japanese were being destroyed, and Slim's plan was working. Units of the Fourteenth Army were able to shift tactics for the open terrain of central Burma; some operated as motorized units and cooperated closely with tank units in the heavy fighting along the Irrawaddy River defenses.

The Race to Rangoon followed this offensive. The advance took place along two axes. The primary axis was along the Meiktila–Rangoon road, where the 5th and 17th Indian divisions leapfrogged one another and air resupply supported the advance. The second axis was carried out along the Irrawaddy River basin by the 20th and 7th Indian divisions. On May 6, units from the 17th and 26th Indian divisions met up, signaling a victorious end to the offensive. Intermittent heavy fighting continued over the course of the summer,[19] however, as Japanese forces attempted to break out towards Thailand.

Many Indian divisions were sent to reoccupy Malaya, French Indo-China, and the Dutch East Indies following the Japanese surrender. The divisions remained in the various areas for more than a year, fighting "Nationalist" guerrillas. Many units of the 5th Indian Division lost more men in the Dutch East Indies than during the Burma Campaign.

Chapter 7

# General MacArthur's War
## The South and Southwest Pacific campaigns 1942–45

*Professor David Horner*

The President of the United States ordered me to break through the Japanese lines and proceed from Corregidor to Australia for the purpose, as I understand it, of organizing the American offensive against Japan, a primary objective of which is the relief of the Philippines. I came through and I shall return.[1]

With these comments to reporters, who met his train north of Adelaide, Australia, on the afternoon of March 20, 1942, General Douglas MacArthur set the agenda for the Allied military campaign in the Southwest Pacific for the next two and half years. It was immaterial to him that Churchill and Roosevelt had agreed that the priority was to "beat Hitler first." The campaign to recover the Philippines would become his personal crusade and all else would be subordinate to it.

Two days earlier, having just arrived in northern Australia, he had learned that his new command, to be known as the Southwest Pacific Area, would include all Australian and American forces in and around Australia. As he journeyed south through the vastness of the Australian outback, first by aircraft and then by a small rickety train, he was stunned to learn that there were only about 25,000 American troops in Australia. American troops had started to arrive in December 1941, as a step on the way to the Philippines, but as the Philippines had become isolated the troops had remained in Australia, with additional forces arriving as the Americans belatedly built up for a later offensive. On the train from Adelaide to Melbourne, MacArthur heard more about the inadequacies of Australia's defenses. "God have mercy on us!" he exclaimed.[2]

Aged 62, MacArthur had already had a long and distinguished military career. In World War I he had been chief of staff of a division and had later commanded a brigade. By 1930 he was Chief of Staff of the US Army. He served in this capacity under President Roosevelt, with whom he had significant differences. Later he became military adviser to the government of the Philippines, during which time he retired from the American Army. He was recalled in July 1941 to command the United States Army Forces in the Far East. His command in the Philippines, once Japan entered the war, had not been successful. His air force had been destroyed on the ground by Japanese air attacks, and his troops, who withdrew to the Bataan peninsula, were shortly to face a disaster exceeded only by that of the British at Singapore. He should have been relieved of his command, but Roosevelt needed a well-known general to boost America's reputation in Australia.

MacArthur's defeat in the Philippines rankled deeply within him. Aloof, highly intelligent, widely hated and also admired throughout the American Army, he believed that it was his destiny to lead an Allied force to victory in the Pacific. Lieutenant-General George Brett, whom MacArthur succeeded as the senior US officer in Australia, described him as "a brilliant, temperamental egoist; a handsome man, who can be as charming as anyone who ever lived, or harshly indifferent to the needs and desires of those around him."[3]

MacArthur was a man of contradictions. As US Chief of Staff he had kept a Eurasian mistress, formerly a Shanghai chorus girl, while his mother, ignorant of this arrangement, helped him with official entertainment. He married for the second time while in the Philippines, and arrived in Australia with his wife, young son, and amah. In January 1942, in the midst of his defensive campaign in the Philippines, Filipino President Quezon secretly awarded him $500,000 as "recompense and reward" from the Filipino people.

Yet for all his faults, MacArthur gained the confidence of the Australian government, which hoped that his appointment would ensure American support. He harassed Washington for more troops and slowly put together his new command. Australia provided most of the ground troops and the US provided the majority of the ships and aircraft, although the numbers were still relatively small. Initially it was not possible to mount any offensive. The Japanese had the initiative; they had bombed northern Australia and had seized most of New Guinea.

The pressure on Australia was eased by the battle of the Coral Sea on May 7–8, in which MacArthur's command played only a minor role. Most of the American ships deployed, including two aircraft carriers, came from the nearby South Pacific Area under Vice-Admiral Robert Ghormley. The South Pacific Area was a largely US Navy command that was based on New Zealand and New Caledonia, and reported to Admiral Chester Nimitz in Hawaii.

The battle of the Coral Sea and, more importantly, the battle of Midway on June 4, changed the whole complexion of the war in the South and Southwest Pacific. The Japanese high command had originally planned to capture Port Moresby (in Australian-controlled New Guinea) and the southern Solomon Islands and "to isolate Australia" by seizing Fiji, Samoa, and New Caledonia. Circumstances forced a postponement of plans to take these latter islands; instead, the capture of Port Moresby became imperative, so that the Japanese could use it to dominate the Coral Sea. The loss of four large carriers at Midway meant that an amphibious operation was no longer possible, and on June 7 Lieutenant-General Harayoshi Hyakutake in Rabaul received orders to plan a land approach over the forbidding Owen Stanley Range to Port Moresby. The scaling down of the Japanese offensive plans indicated that, strategically, the tide of war was beginning to turn. Nevertheless, the Japanese remained capable of mounting a deadly offensive. The stage was set for major battles in New Guinea and the southern Solomons.

## GUADALCANAL AND PAPUA

Urged by MacArthur and encouraged by the victory at Midway, on July 2, 1942, the US Joint Chiefs of Staff in Washington ordered an offensive to recapture the Japanese base at Rabaul. The US Navy chief, Admiral Ernest King, was a ferocious advocate for the Pacific theater, but refused to contemplate placing his forces under MacArthur's control. Thus the offensive was to be shared. As the Japanese were already building an airstrip on Guadalcanal Island in the southern Solomon Islands, the Joint Chiefs ordered Ghormley's South Pacific Area to seize Guadalcanal, for which he was allocated the 1st US Marine Division under Major-General Alexander Vandegrift. Once the Marines had landed on Guadalcanal,

MacArthur was to occupy the Buna area on the north coast of Papua, where airstrips would be prepared to support his advance towards Rabaul.

Unfortunately for these optimistic plans, the Japanese struck first. On the night of July 21, advance troops landed at Buna, to be met by only light resistance. Major-General Tomitaro Horii, commander of the Japanese South Seas Detachment in Rabaul, was next ordered to attack Port Moresby over the range. Belatedly, MacArthur began to send reinforcements to New Guinea. Earlier, in May, his chief of intelligence had downplayed the importance of decrypted Japanese signals indicating their intentions to advance overland.

The landing of the US Marines at Guadalcanal on August 7 threw the Japanese off balance. Not pleased to be pushed off their new airstrip, the Japanese responded by attacking the Americans with aircraft based at Rabaul. In a controversial decision, Vice-Admiral Frank Jack Fletcher cautiously withdrew his three aircraft carriers, exposing the remaining amphibious forces to the Japanese. On the night of August 8, Japanese cruisers, under the aggressive and talented Vice-Admiral Gunichi Mikawa, struck, and in the battle of Savo Island the Australian cruiser *Canberra*, and three US cruisers were sunk – one of the worst losses ever suffered by the US Navy.

Following up this victory, the Japanese landed 1,000 men on Guadalcanal to drive off the Americans. On August 21, in the battle of the Tenaru, the Japanese lost heavily in an ill-prepared attack on the perimeter of Henderson airfield. While the Americans held the airstrip, where US Marine aircraft were based, they controlled the surrounding seas by day. At night, however, the Japanese dominated. Each night their warship and transports – the so-called Tokyo Express – sailed down the "Slot" between the islands to bring reinforcements for another effort to seize the vital airstrip.

In Papua, MacArthur's Australian forces faced a similar challenge. The Japanese offensive began on August 26 with simultaneous attacks – one on the Kokoda Trail that wound over the Owen Stanley Range, and the other a landing by Japanese marines at Milne Bay on the southeast tip of New Guinea. Fearful for his own position, MacArthur blamed the Australians for their allegedly poor fighting ability, and warned General Marshall in Washington that the situation might become critical unless he was provided with naval support.

In truth, MacArthur's strategy was at fault. He had based the defense of Port Moresby on the belief that a garrison at Milne Bay and a picket on the crest of the Owen Stanleys, in addition to air and naval forces, would be sufficient while he prepared for his offensive. But now his strategy was looking dangerously unrealistic. The Japanese had decimated the US Navy in the Solomons and were challenging the security of Milne Bay and the Owen Stanley Range.

By September 6, two Australian brigades at Milne Bay had defeated the Japanese, forcing them to evacuate. On the Kokoda Trail, however, Australian troops were undertaking a desperate withdrawal. Eventually the Japanese failed; the track was much more difficult than they had expected, and they had made insufficient provision for supplies. Their advance had been seriously delayed by the hard fighting of the Australians, which had bought time for reinforcements to arrive and forced the Japanese to exhaust their supplies. Importantly, the Guadalcanal campaign caused the Japanese high command in Rabaul to divert resources to that area, and eventually in late September to halt the Owen Stanley offensive.

Meanwhile, the fighting on and around Guadalcanal turned into a campaign of attrition. During September and October, the Japanese made repeated efforts to recover Henderson airfield. In the battle of Bloody Ridge, 2000 Japanese attacked in massed waves, approaching to within 900 meters of the airfield. If they had succeeded in taking it, they might well have won the campaign. Lieutenant-Colonel Merrit A. Edson, commander of the forces defending the ridge, was awarded the Congressional Medal of Honor. Marine Corps aircraft of the "Cactus Air Force" operating from the airfield supported the defenders, but in October Japanese ships began bombarding the airfield, putting it temporarily out of action.

Naval engagements continued, and in the battle of the Eastern Solomons in late August, one US aircraft carrier was sunk and another damaged. Slightly wounded, Fletcher accompanied the damaged carrier back to the United States. As one historian put it, he had "drifted from prudence into paralysis."[4] Still another carrier was lost on September 15, reducing the US Navy in the South Pacific to one undamaged carrier, USS *Hornet*. With the outcome of the campaign hanging in the balance, President Roosevelt was taking a personal interest. On October 15,

Nimitz reported that his forces were "unable to control the sea in the Guadalcanal area... The situation is not hopeless but it is certainly critical."[5] Guadalcanal became the focus of all American effort in the Pacific. Success would be a turning point for the Allies' fortunes, but failure would set the Allied cause back by months and perhaps even result in Admiral King's dismissal. King decided to move first, and on October 18, Vice-Admiral William "Bull" Halsey took over command from the defeatist Ghormley.

The naval battle of Guadalcanal began on November 12 and lasted for three days. In the first 24 minutes, the Americans lost six ships and the Japanese three, including a battleship. Eventually the odds began to tilt towards the Americans. By December the 1st US Marine Division had been withdrawn, but the 2d Marine Division and two US Army infantry divisions, under a US Army corps commander, Major-General Alexander Patch, were advancing slowly across the island.

In Papua, the 7th Australian Division began the counteroffensive back over the Kokoda Trail to the north coast, where they were joined by the 32d US Division. Exhausted, sick and with little support, the Australians and Americans were confronted by well-constructed Japanese defenses in jungle and swamp. Anxious to score a victory before the Navy did so at Guadalcanal, MacArthur demanded swift results, telling the US corps commander, Lieutenant-General Robert Eichelberger, "to take Buna, or not come back alive."[6] By the time the Japanese had been driven into the sea at Sanananda on January 22, 1943, they had suffered more than 13,000 killed. The Australians had lost more than 2,000 killed and the Americans more than 600. Almost 20,000 Australian and American troops were sick from malaria.

The Japanese faced a similar outcome on Guadalcanal, and in one of the crucial decisions of the Pacific War, their high command ordered evacuation. This took place in February. During the campaign the Japanese lost perhaps 24,000 killed, while American land force deaths numbered only some 1,600. US Navy casualties were high – 5,000 killed and nearly 3,000 wounded. Many of Japan's best-trained pilots were killed and its naval air force never recovered. Both the Japanese and US navies lost heavily, but the Americans could replace their ships quickly; the Japanese could not. After the war, Admiral Osami Nagano, the Japanese chief of naval staff, told his captors: "I look upon the

Guadalcanal and Tulagi operations as the turning point from offensive to defensive, and the cause of our setback there was our inability to increase our forces at the same speed as you did."

The campaigns in New Guinea and Guadalcanal had revealed considerable shortcomings in the performance of the American higher commanders. MacArthur had underestimated the Japanese, had been reluctant to reinforce his forces in New Guinea, had not understood the difficulties of the terrain or the determination of the Japanese defenders, and had been pushed into the campaign by Japanese initiatives. There is nothing in the campaign to support the popular image of MacArthur as a brilliant, far-sighted commander. Planning Guadalcanal, the Americans had not realized how difficult it would be to maintain a force on a hostile shore. If they had understood the logistic risks they were facing, they might not have initiated the campaign. It was the soldiers who bore the outcome of these decisions, fighting their battles in thick tropical jungles, on precarious mountain tracks, and in fetid swamps. Resupply was difficult, and in New Guinea the Allies were relying on native porters and airdrops. Tropical illnesses were as deadly as the enemy's bullets.

The Japanese made one last offensive thrust, towards Wau in New Guinea, but this was thwarted when an Australian brigade was flown into the area. Seeking to build up their defenses, the Japanese created the Eighteenth Army and planned to use it to reinforce New Guinea. Warned by signals intelligence and reconnaissance aircraft, the commander of the Allied air force in the Southwest Pacific Area, Lieutenant-General George Kenney, ordered the Japanese convoy to be intercepted in the Bismarck Sea.

Allied code-breakers also gave warning that Admiral Isoroku Yamamoto, Commander-in-Chief of the Japanese Combined Fleet, would be visiting Bougainville in the northern Solomons. American P-38 Lightnings from Henderson Field were waiting at his destination, and on April 18, 1943 they downed his aircraft in flames. This was a further blow to the Japanese who were already on the defensive in the Southwest Pacific.

# THE *CARTWHEEL* OPERATIONS

Having cleared Papua, MacArthur was anxious to continue the offensive, but the Joint Chiefs did not issue new orders to capture

Rabaul until March 28, 1943. Again the tasks were shared between the US Navy and Army. South Pacific Area forces, under Halsey, were to advance from Guadalcanal towards Rabaul, with the intermediate objective of Bougainville in the northern Solomons. Meanwhile, MacArthur's Southwest Pacific Area forces would seize the Huon Peninsula area of New Guinea and the western end of New Britain, thus opening the Vitiaz Strait. Halsey was to operate under MacArthur's general strategic direction, to ensure cooperation during the Allied operation known as Operation *Cartwheel*.

In preparation for this offensive, MacArthur was assigned a small naval amphibious force serving under Rear-Admiral Daniel Barbey. During 1942, two US infantry divisions had been deployed to his theater; these were to be joined by the 1st US Marine Division (in Australia, recuperating after Guadalcanal) and two more infantry divisions. This was much less than he had asked for, and it meant that, at least initially, he would need to rely on Australian troops.

Opposing the Allied forces was Lieutenant-General Hitoshi Imamura's Eighth Area Army with its headquarters at Rabaul. Lieutenant-General Hyakutake's Seventeenth Army defended the Solomons and New Britain with three divisions, while Lieutenant-General Hatazo Adachi's Eighteenth Army, also with three divisions, was in New Guinea. The Japanese strength was between 80,000 and 90,000, with reinforcements of about 60,000 available within three weeks. The Japanese had about 320 combat aircraft, with another 270 ready to be flown in within 48 hours.

Operation *Cartwheel* began on June 30, 1943, when Halsey's troops made their main landings on the islands of New Georgia and Rendova. The same day, American troops under MacArthur landed unopposed on Kiriwina and Woodlark Islands, as well as at Nassau Bay on the north coast of New Guinea. Both wings of the *Cartwheel* campaign were to continue for the remainder of 1943.

Responding to the New Georgia landing, the Japanese dispatched reinforcements from Rabaul, escorted by warships that clashed with the US Navy. Generally superior in night fighting, the Japanese Navy sank or damaged several American and Australian ships. For their part, Allied forces succeeded in sinking three Japanese transports in one engagement, with the loss of perhaps 1,500 men drowned. Avoiding the next strongly held island, American forces jumped to the island of Vella

Lavella, and by October, American and New Zealand troops had landed on several islands near to Bougainville.

On November 1 the 3d US Marine Division landed at Empress Augusta Bay on the west coast of Bougainville, bypassing a large concentration of Japanese forces occupying the southern end of the island. The following morning, a US Navy task force destroyed a cruiser and a destroyer from the Japanese Eighth Fleet. When a powerful Japanese task force under Vice-Admiral Takeo Kurita appeared at Rabaul, Halsey took a great risk and sent his two-carrier task force within range of Japanese air power. Supported by Kenney's land-based Fifth Air Force, US naval aircraft caused such damage that Kurita was forced to withdraw to Truk. Further Allied air attacks forced the Japanese to withdraw their air and naval units from Rabaul. After the Americans on Bougainville resisted a full-scale counteroffensive in March 1944, there was a virtual truce until the Australians took over the area towards the end of the year.

The fighting in the New Guinea area was characterized by fewer naval engagements but larger land operations than that in the Solomons. MacArthur's land forces were nominally under the Australian General Sir Thomas Blamey, but the commander of the US Sixth Army, the veteran professional soldier Lieutenant-General Walter Krueger, controlled most American operations. Blamey commanded New Guinea Force, which consisted of mainly Australian units. Between March and August 1943, the 3rd Australian Division, supported by the US troops that had landed at Nassau Bay, slogged through jungle-covered hills from Wau towards Salamaua. The Japanese Fourth Air Army rushed additional aircraft to New Guinea, but Kenney's Fifth Air Force, warned by Allied code-breakers, deployed aircraft to newly constructed forward airfields and caught the Japanese planes on the ground, with devastating losses.

Kenney was one of the outstanding air commanders of the war, but his greatest achievement was to win the support and confidence of MacArthur. Soon after his arrival in July 1942, he had concluded that the most effective way to conduct the war was not by confronting the main Japanese land forces, but by seizing airfields, preferably in areas where the Japanese were weakest. MacArthur accepted this strategy, but the relatively small size of his naval force meant that his main striking power was his air force, based on jungle airstrips rather than on aircraft carriers. The Army's role was to seize and hold the areas for the airstrips and for the naval anchorages and bases. In pursuing this strategy, MacArthur was assisted by signals intelligence in selecting areas that were held lightly by the enemy – although, perversely, he sometimes ignored his intelligence.

On September 4, 1943, Australian troops landed near Lae, the first step in New Guinea Force's campaign to clear the Huon Peninsula. After capturing Lae, the 7th Division advanced west into the upper Ramu Valley to secure airfields for Kenney's Fifth Air Force. The 9th Division landed at Finschhafen and, against strong opposition at Sattelberg, eventually cleared the western shore of the Vitiaz Strait.

Meanwhile, Krueger's Alamo Force had begun clearing the opposite shore of the strait, with American infantry landing on the southern coast of New Britain on December 15. On January 2, 1944, the 32d US Division landed at Saidor on the New Guinea coast; the Japanese 20th and 51st divisions escaped, but they had been roundly defeated.

Having opened the way through the Vitiaz Strait, MacArthur could advance westwards. As early as August 1943, the Joint Chiefs had declared that there was no need to capture Rabaul and had permitted MacArthur to go west to the Vogelkop Peninsula instead, with the implication that he could eventually proceed to the Philippines. For their part, on September 30 the Japanese high command ordered its main forces to withdraw behind the Absolute National Defense Zone in western New Guinea, leaving the garrisons at Rabaul, Bougainville, and in eastern New Guinea to fend for themselves. In December, the Japanese Second Area Army was formed to control operations to the west of Hollandia.

By 1944, the Americans and Australians had learned a considerable amount about jungle warfare. In Malaya, Burma, the Philippines, and New Guinea, the Japanese had caught their opponents off-guard. Lightly equipped and accustomed to hard living, the Japanese infantry moved quickly through deep jungle, bypassing static Allied positions. On the defensive, the Japanese constructed well-camouflaged strong points and fought with determination and skill. Their commanders perhaps lacked imagination in planning and did not seem to appreciate fully the effectiveness of massed firepower. As the Americans began to dominate the seas, the isolated Japanese defenders (for whom surrender was not an option) often had little alternative but to fight to the death.

The Americans had at first seemed bewildered by jungle warfare, but they learned quickly and fought the war in their own way. As an American divisional historian put it: "The Yank style of fighting was to wait for the artillery and let the big guns blast the enemy positions as barren of all life as possible. It saved many American lives and got better results although it took longer."[7] More broadly, the Americans brought to bear the full range of naval and air resources to support their land operations. All of this was backed by a massive logistic effort. The Allies had far better medical support than the Japanese, especially for coping with tropical diseases such as malaria.

The American historian, Ed Drea, has pointed out that between January 1943 and January 1944, the Allies conducted a grinding war of attrition in which "Australian infantrymen carried out the bulk of ground combat while the Americans reconstituted, reinforced, and readied themselves for the maneuver phase of the campaign." The series of breathtaking landings of the following year "were the fruits of the Australians' gallant effort in eastern New Guinea."[8]

# THE ADVANCE TO THE PHILIPPINES

MacArthur's campaign from late 1943 onwards was only the southern arm of a two-pronged American offensive in the Pacific. Having secured eastern New Guinea and neutralized the Japanese at Rabaul, the Americans could well have concentrated all their efforts in the Central Pacific. Admiral King had always advocated using US naval power there, but MacArthur had argued strongly for resources to advance through New Guinea towards the Philippines. Whatever the political and strategic merits of liberating the Philippines might have been, MacArthur had made it a personal crusade, and he had the necessary prestige and influence to win the argument. In any case, if both the Central and Southwest Pacific thrusts could be sustained, they would throw the Japanese comprehensively off balance.

Fortunately, the United States had the resources necessary to sustain this two-pronged attack. By mid-April 1944, MacArthur had 450,000 American army and air personnel under his command, including seven infantry divisions, three separate regimental combat teams, and three engineer special brigades. The Australian divisions that had fought in New Guinea returned to Australia for rest, while other Australian divisions occupied fairly static positions in New Guinea. With his extra American divisions, MacArthur could continue the advance without the Australian infantry.

As the US Navy's Central Pacific campaign gathered pace in the latter months of 1943, however, MacArthur became fearful of being left behind. On February 29, 1944, in a daring and risky "raid," his forces seized Los Negros in the Admiralty Islands, completing the ring around Rabaul. Any ideas of attacking Rabaul were henceforth abandoned, and the huge Japanese garrison was to play little further part in the war. Instead, MacArthur directed a series of landings by American troops along the northern New Guinea coast that isolated 40,000 Japanese forces operating in the Wewak area. His forces landed at Aitape and Hollandia on April 23, Sarmi and Wakde on May 17, Biak on May 27, Noemfoor on July 2 and Sansapor on July 30. In three months, MacArthur's forces advanced 1,400 kilometers.

With no aircraft carriers of his own, and receiving limited aircraft carrier support from the Central Pacific, MacArthur's forces constructed airfields at each landing to provide land-based air support for the next assault. On some occasions these positions were captured relatively easily; on others, there was grim fighting. One such was the 41st US Division landing at Biak on May 27, where troops were confronted by more than 12,000 Japanese defenders. MacArthur immediately issued a communiqué which read, "For strategic purposes this marks the practical end of the New Guinea campaign."[9] Despite this assurance, however, American aircraft did not begin operating from the captured airstrips until June 22.

MacArthur's advance showed him at his best as a commander. He was not interested in liberating New Guinea for its own sake, but viewed it merely as a provider of sufficient positions to enable him to continue his advance. He gave considerable freedom to his subordinate commanders, so long as they understood the need for speed. Each operation involved the coordination of land, air, and naval forces, and often several operations took place at the same time. The advance was also a huge logistic undertaking. New Guinea lacked any modern infrastructure, and all the force's requirements had to be brought into the theater by ship. Intermediate ports and logistic facilities had to be constructed in jungle and swamp. The hot and humid climate affected men and machines, while tropical disease posed a constant threat. At Biak, for example, American battle casualties were 400 killed and 2,000 wounded. Non-battle casualties – mostly from scrub typhus or an undiagnosed fever – exceeded 7,000.

MacArthur had at least two motives for pursuing his rapid and, at times, risky offensive. First, it kept the enemy off balance. With the advantage of excellent intelligence, he generally knew where the enemy was weakest, and with superior naval and air resources, he had greater capacity for maneuver than his opponents, whose large static garrisons could be left to wither on the vine. Second, MacArthur was fighting a ruthless campaign to win the battle for public opinion and to persuade the Joint Chiefs to continue to support his ambition of recovering the Philippines. Thus the Los Negros operation was driven as much by the need to influence the Joint Chiefs as it was to complete the encirclement of Rabaul. A relentless barrage of optimistic and extravagantly worded communiqués accompanied all operations. At the end of July, MacArthur visited Hawaii for a meeting with Roosevelt and Nimitz. Roosevelt seemed to accept MacArthur's argument in favor of capturing the Philippines, but MacArthur had not yet received a directive from the Joint Chiefs.

On September 15, MacArthur's forces seized a forward base at Morotai, between New Guinea and the Philippines. Following this capture, MacArthur reorganized his command. He had been given control of the American forces in Bougainville, and thus had a total of eighteen divisions under his command. Once he had handed responsibility for Bougainville and New Guinea to the Australians, he could use most of the Americans for an attack on the Philippines. In addition to Krueger's Sixth Army, he formed a new army, the Eighth, under Lieutenant-General Robert Eichelberger.

Decisions about the future shape of the Pacific War were made at important meetings in Quebec and Washington in mid-September and early October 1944. At Quebec, Churchill, Roosevelt, and their Chiefs of Staff agreed that the Americans should land at Mindanao in the southern Philippines. In the midst of the conference came further news from the Pacific. Between September 7 and 14, Halsey's carrier force struck vigorously at Yap, the Palaus, Mindanao, and the central Philippines. He reported excitedly that he had found little opposition in the Philippines; he believed that Yap, Talaud, and Sarangani could be bypassed and the forces scheduled for those islands used against Leyte in the central Philippines. On September 15, the US Joint Chiefs approved a landing by MacArthur's forces on Leyte, beginning on October 20. The landing on Mindanao was abandoned.

Finally, in Washington on October 3, the Joint Chiefs resolved the issue that had been simmering for six months, namely whether the United States should invade Luzon (the main island of the Philippines group) or Formosa (now Taiwan). It was agreed that MacArthur's forces would invade Luzon on December 20, 1944. Nimitz's Central Pacific command would seize Iwo Jima in late January 1945, and move on to Okinawa on March 1.

# THE LIBERATION OF THE PHILIPPINES

The Leyte landing on October 20, 1944, was one of the larger military operations of the war. The invasion force consisted of the US Seventh Fleet, under Vice-Admiral Thomas Kinkaid, and four infantry divisions of Krueger's US Sixth Army. Admiral Halsey's powerful US Third Fleet, with 16 carriers, provided support. Assembled at short notice, the total force numbered 700 ships and some 160,000 men, and was mounted from bases more than 1,000 kilometers distant.

MacArthur waded ashore at Leyte on the afternoon of October 20, the occasion well captured by waiting photographers. President Sergio Osmena of the Philippines accompanied him, and both of them delivered radio broadcasts. "People of the Philippines, I have returned!" said MacArthur. "By the grace of Almighty God, our forces stand again on Philippine soil... Rally to me!"[10] A few days later, MacArthur established his headquarters ashore.

Meanwhile, the Japanese Navy, under the tactical command of Vice-Admiral Jizaburo Ozawa, converged on the US fleet. Ozawa lured Halsey north, away from the landing area, while he sent two striking forces into the Leyte Gulf. MacArthur was dismayed at the loss of his air cover, and ordered Kenney to get his Fifth Air Force to Leyte as fast as possible. "I'm never going to pull another show without land-based air," he told Kenney, "and if I even suggest such a thing I want you to kick me where it will do some good."[11]

The battle of the Leyte Gulf, which began on October 24, was the largest and one of the most decisive naval battles in history. With the battle in the balance, the commander of one of the Japanese striking forces, Vice-Admiral Kurita, called off the engagement and retired. By October 26, the Japanese had lost four carriers, three battleships, nine cruisers, and ten destroyers. Before the landing, the US Navy had destroyed over 500 Japanese carrier- and land-based aircraft. The Japanese Navy never recovered from this defeat.

Defeated at sea, but aware of the danger if the Americans gained a foothold in the Philippines, the Japanese high command mounted a desperate counteroffensive. They were aided by the Americans' failure to maintain air superiority; many American carriers had withdrawn for other tasks, and the captured airfields on Leyte were in such poor condition that only a few aircraft could use them. The Japanese were therefore relatively free to send convoys of reinforcements to Leyte, while their aircraft attacked American transports resupplying the Leyte beachhead. Advancing cautiously from its beachhead, the US Sixth Army met strong resistance from skilful and determined Japanese troops. In an audacious but uncoordinated attack, Japanese paratroops dropped onto the American airfields, but were destroyed in a four-day battle. The Sixth Army deployed seven divisions, lost almost 3,000 killed and 10,000 wounded, and accounted for 56,000 Japanese casualties before MacArthur announced the successful conclusion of the campaign on December 25. A week earlier, he had been promoted to the new five-star rank of General of the Army. Of course the campaign was not over. Eichelberger, commander of the relieving US Eighth Army, claimed that in the mopping-up period between December 26, 1944 and May 8, 1945, his forces killed more than 27,000 Japanese.

On January 9, 1945, the Sixth Army landed at Lingayen Gulf, on the main Philippines island of Luzon. Attacked by Japanese *kamikaze* (suicide) planes, the Americans had 25 ships sunk or damaged, but 175,000 men were put ashore. The subsequent land campaign, against a Japanese army of 260,000 serving under the highly capable General Tomoyuki Yamashita, was the second largest conducted by the American Army in the entire war, after that in northwest Europe in 1944–45. The Sixth Army deployed ten divisions, and the campaign involved tank battles, amphibious landings, parachute drops, and guerrilla warfare. By the end of June, the Luzon campaign was over. The Sixth Army had lost 8,000 killed and 30,000 wounded. The Japanese had suffered 190,000 casualties.

# UNNECESSARY CAMPAIGNS?

Following the end of the Luzon campaign, the Sixth Army began to prepare for the invasion of Japan. Meanwhile, the Eighth Army undertook a series of amphibious operations throughout the southern Philippines to eliminate large pockets of Japanese. These operations helped liberate extensive areas, but did not contribute directly to the defeat of Japan.

The same criticism can be leveled at the Australian Army's campaigns in Bougainville and New Guinea in 1945. MacArthur was, at best, lukewarm about the justification for these offensives, but he enthusiastically ordered the 1st Australian Corps to conduct operations in Borneo. There was even less justification for these later operations, as once Central Pacific forces landed at Okinawa on April 1, 1945, all campaigns to the south were strategically irrelevant.

Some historians have made the same point about all of the Southwest Pacific Area's operations during this period. Stanley L. Falk argued that "Japan's surrender would have come no later had Southwest Pacific ground forces simply remained in place in the final year and a half of the war and allowed the Japanese in that area to wither away under the mounting pressures of American air and seapower."[12] The liberation of the Philippines would have been delayed slightly, but would not have been accompanied by the deaths of more than 100,000 Filipino civilians. Nearly 16,000 Americans were killed in western New Guinea, in the islands taken to support the Philippines landings, and in the Philippines itself.

Other historians have argued that the main American effort should have been made in the Southwest Pacific. In the Central Pacific, the Americans need only have deployed sufficient forces to persuade the Japanese to retain their garrisons on the islands. This would have saved the lives of the American soldiers lost in the island–hopping campaign. With the full weight of the US Navy, MacArthur's thrust from the south would have been even more powerful. Of course, the US Navy would never have countenanced placing the main campaign in US Army hands.

MacArthur won the argument to be permitted to invade the Philippines by his personality and political influence, and bolstered his case with brilliant victories during 1943 and 1944. He did not know that America had developed the atomic bomb, and did not expect the Japanese to surrender quickly. He needed to secure the Philippines to provide a firm base for the invasion of Japan for which he had been nominated to plan and command. Yet even without the atomic bomb, air and sea power might have starved and battered the Japanese into submission. Leaving aside these questions, there can be no denying the military achievement of the Southwest Pacific Area's forces in conducting a successful three-year campaign over thousands of kilometers, in extremely difficult conditions of terrain and climate and against a brave and determined foe. Nor can there be any doubt that this was, unequivocally, Douglas MacArthur's campaign.

Chapter 8

# The ANZAC Contribution
## Australia and New Zealand in the Pacific War

*Professor David Horner*

Australia and New Zealand's contributions to World War II were out of proportion to their size. As small English-speaking democracies that looked to Britain for security, it was not surprising that in 1939 both countries joined with Britain in the war against Germany, and that both made remarkably large commitments, especially considering their remoteness from the main theaters of war. But their attitudes to the war changed dramatically in December 1941, when they were thrust directly into the Pacific War. Suddenly and frighteningly, the long-promised assistance from Britain evaporated. Until help arrived from the United States, Australia and New Zealand were on their own.

Australia carried a much heavier burden in the Pacific War than New Zealand, mainly because, unlike New Zealand, it received direct attacks on its territory. Japanese bombers struck at the northern port of Darwin, and Japanese troops invaded Australian Papua as well as its League of Nations-mandated territory of New Guinea. Such a threat demanded a full-scale response. In addition, Australia's population of 7 million was vastly larger than New Zealand's 1.6 million, and it had a stronger industrial base; its capacity for raising and sustaining forces was much greater. Finally, the New Zealand government decided that, despite the outbreak of the Pacific War, it would continue its main military effort in Europe; the prospect of an actual Japanese invasion presumably seemed more remote than it did to the Australians.

The nature of Australia and New Zealand's military contributions were determined partly by the size and capability of their prewar forces. Before the war, both countries had miniscule regular armies, and their land forces consisted of part-time militias. In 1939, they both raised voluntary expeditionary forces to serve in Europe and the Middle East. The Second Australian Imperial Force (2nd AIF) – "second" because the first had served in World War I – consisted of four infantry divisions, of which three (the 6th, 7th, and 9th) served in the Middle East in 1940–41. Australia retained the 8th Division nearer to home; most of it went to Malaya in 1941, while single battalions were deployed to New Britain, Ambon, and Timor respectively. The 2nd New Zealand Expeditionary Force (2nd NZEF) consisted primarily of the New Zealand Division; it too served in the Middle East in 1940–41.

Both countries had small regular navies that served in distant theaters under British command during 1940–41. Both lacked proper shipbuilding industries, making it difficult to expand their navies with major warships. As the war progressed, Australia was able to construct corvettes and smaller craft, and built up its Navy with these vessels. Both Australia and New Zealand also had great difficulty in purchasing modern aircraft from Britain and the United States to enable them to expand their small air forces for home defense. However, both countries provided large numbers of personnel to be trained as aircrew as part of the Empire Air Training Scheme for service in Britain – a commitment that continued throughout the war.

The outbreak of the Pacific War found both countries exposed to Japanese attack. The impact of this threat on each country and the manner in which it contributed to the Pacific War was different; so their stories are best told separately. Australia's contribution – much larger and more diverse – will be described first.

## AUSTRALIA AND THE JAPANESE THREAT

Australians were closely involved in the Pacific War from the outset. By mid-January 1942, the 8th Division was in action in Malaya, where it incurred heavy casualties. The division lost 1,700 killed and 1,300 wounded before the remaining 15,000 were captured at the fall of Singapore on February 15. Meanwhile, Australian battalions were in action in New Britain, Ambon, Timor, and Java. Most of these troops also were captured, and about one-third of those captured later died in captivity.

These were huge losses for the Australian Army, and for a short while Australia seemed vulnerable to a Japanese invasion. The experienced 6th and 7th divisions were, however, heading home to Australia, although the 9th Australian and New Zealand divisions remained in the Middle East, continuing to take part in major operations during 1942.

When General Douglas MacArthur took command of the Southwest Pacific Area in April 1942, the Australian forces were struggling to come to a war footing. The 7th Division and elements of the 6th had returned to Australia, while the militia divisions (mostly conscripts) had gone onto full-time service. Five militia infantry divisions, two militia cavalry divisions, and the AIF armored division (still being formed) were deployed for the defense of Australia; but they were inadequately trained, and lacked modern weapons and equipment. Some of the ships of the Royal Australian Navy (RAN) had returned to Australian waters; but the RAN's major ships, its cruisers, had been reduced to four in number: HMAS *Sydney* had been sunk in November 1941, as had the *Perth* in the Sunda Strait in March 1942. The Royal Australian Air Force (RAAF), although expanding rapidly, lacked modern aircraft.

Threatened by invasion, Australia's Labor government, headed by the Prime Minister, John Curtin, instituted strict wartime measures, including ordering men and women to work in industries that directly supported the war. Australia's fledgling industries began producing ships, aircraft, guns, and electrical equipment.

In response to the emergency, the government placed all its forces under MacArthur, and strongly supported his efforts to persuade the Joint Chiefs to send additional forces to Australia. MacArthur became Curtin's principal military adviser, and exercised unprecedented influence over the government.

MacArthur was supposed to head an Allied command, but he jealously excluded Australian officers, and for that matter US Navy officers, from his headquarters. His land force commander was an Australian, General Sir Thomas Blamey, a tough, experienced officer who had commanded the Australians in the Middle East, but MacArthur was already scheming to ensure that Blamey would not be permitted to command American troops in action. MacArthur's naval and air force commanders were Americans, each commanding Allied forces that included Americans and Australians and, in the case of the air force, some Dutch units.

MacArthur later claimed that he had decided to take the fight to the Japanese in New Guinea as soon as he arrived in Australia. In truth, however, he could not do so initially. He had insufficient naval and air resources to support the deployment of large land forces to New Guinea, which remained garrisoned by a small number of militia troops and RAAF units. After the battle of the Coral Sea MacArthur slowly began to reinforce New Guinea, but he kept back his best troops, the 7th Australian Division, for his planned offensive. Meanwhile, in preparation for the offensive, he moved his headquarters forward, from Melbourne to Brisbane.

## THE PAPUAN CAMPAIGN

When the Japanese landed at Buna on the north coast of Papua on the night of July 21, MacArthur did not take the threat seriously. This left the incompletely trained and inadequately equipped 39th (militia) Battalion fighting desperately around the small town of Kokoda. The Japanese intended to advance over the towering Owen Stanley mountain range along a small footpath, later known as the Kokoda Trail, to the main Allied base at Port Moresby. In March 1942 the Japanese high command had decided to put aside its plans to invade Australia and to focus instead on isolating Australia by occupying Port Moresby, the Solomons, Fiji, Samoa, and New Caledonia. If the Japanese could take Port Moresby, their aircraft could dominate the Coral Sea and strike at mainland Australia. But who knows? If the Japanese had secured Port Moresby, they might have changed their plans, and mounted amphibious raids on the Australian coast. Either way, it was vital for the Allies to hold Port Moresby.

When he eventually realized the gravity of this threat, MacArthur ordered the 7th Division to New Guinea. Before it could be fully deployed, however, the Japanese began their main offensive on August 26, landing at Milne Bay and attacking along the Kokoda Trail at Isurava. At Milne Bay, in swamp and jungle, a brigade from the 7th Division and a militia brigade drove back the Japanese marines and forced them to evacuate.

Meanwhile, at Isurava the depleted 39th Battalion was engaged in an unequal struggle, although Australian reinforcements were arriving. The 21st (AIF) Brigade started to reach the battle area on the evening of

August 26 to relieve the 39th. Major-General Horii, commander of the Japanese South Seas Force, had some 13,500 troops in a well-balanced fighting group of five infantry battalions, mountain and antiaircraft artillery, engineers, and pioneers. Of course not all these troops could be deployed, so realistically, at Isurava about 5,000 Japanese attacked a force of about 1,800 Australians.

It is hard to imagine a worse location in which to conduct military operations. The track wound its way through thick jungle and across raging mountain streams. All supplies had to be brought forward by native porters, and casualties had to be carried back in the same manner. During the day it was hot and humid; at night the troops were lashed by chilling rain. Soon they were sick with tropical diseases. Supplies were inadequate. There were attempts to drop supplies by parachute, but many of these disappeared into jungle-covered crevasses.

In these conditions the 21st Brigade, under Brigadier Arnold Potts, fought one of the crucial battles in Australian history. Bravery was commonplace. On August 29, Private Bruce Kingsbury of the 2/14th Battalion won the Victoria Cross posthumously when he attacked the Japanese with his Bren gun. At the height of the battle, 30 walking wounded of the 39th who had been evacuated heard of their comrades' plight. All but three immediately, and at their own initiative, returned to the forward area; of the three who did not, one had lost a foot, one a forearm, and the third had been shot in the throat.

The Australians delayed the enemy for four days and inflicted heavy casualties in the process. For the next two weeks the brigade conducted a fighting withdrawal, always keeping itself between the Japanese and Port Moresby. For the wounded, this was a harrowing ordeal. Corporal John Metson, shot in the ankle at Isurava, refused to be borne on a stretcher. "It will take eight of you chaps to carry that thing," he said. "I'll get along somehow."[1] He wrapped torn blankets around his hands and knees and began crawling through mud and rain toward Port Moresby, 130 kilometers across the mountains. Two days later, the war correspondent Osmar White found him, still crawling, and offered to find some stretcher-bearers. "If you can get bearers," Metson snarled, "then get them for some other poor bastard! There are plenty worse off than me."[2] A party of wounded soldiers, cut off by the Japanese, set out on an unmapped alternative route, living off sweet potato plants that they found along the way. The Japanese overtook and killed the helpless men, including Metson, who had been crawling for nearly three weeks.

The fighting withdrawal delayed the Japanese long enough for the 21st Brigade to be relieved by the 25th Brigade, which had just arrived in New Guinea. MacArthur, who had not been to New Guinea and had no idea of the terrain or relative strengths in the forward area, was highly critical of the Australians, claiming that they were unable to match the Japanese in jungle fighting and that aggressive leadership was lacking. Convinced that the Australian commanders had failed, MacArthur advised Curtin to order Blamey to New Guinea. In fact, the Australian commanders had not failed, and the tide of battle had already turned. The Guadalcanal campaign was demanding the Japanese main effort, and on September 18 General Hyakutake, in Rabaul, ordered the Japanese South Seas Force in the Owen Stanleys to withdraw to the north coast of Papua. Reinforced by a brigade of the 6th Division, the Australians began their counteroffensive back over the mountains.

From mid-November onwards, the 7th Australian and 32d US divisions fought grim battles of attrition at Buna, Gona, and Sanananda on the north coast of Papua, where the Japanese were holding well-defended positions in jungle and swamp. By this stage, the Allied force in New Guinea had been built up to include three Australian divisions and one American division. MacArthur moved to Port Moresby, where Blamey was Commander New Guinea Force. Lieutenant-General Edmund Herring commanded the 1st Australian Corps on the north coast.

It came as a great shock to MacArthur to find that his American infantry had performed poorly at Buna. When the fighting ground to a halt, with heavy casualties, MacArthur offered to bring the 41st US Division up from Australia. Blamey told him frankly that he would prefer to send in more Australians, "as he knew they would fight." As American General George Kenney, who was present, recalled, "it was a bitter pill for General MacArthur to swallow."[3]

By January 22, 1943, the Australians and Americans had driven the Japanese into the sea, bringing the Papuan campaign to its conclusion. Most of the burden had been borne by the Australian Army, as demonstrated by the casualties; the Australians lost more than 2,000 killed, the Americans 600.

# THE NEW GUINEA CAMPAIGN

Having gained firsthand experience of jungle warfare, the Australians spent the first half of 1943 training vigorously in northern Queensland, preparing for further operations. Lacking the weight of firepower and lavish supplies available to their American counterparts, they concentrated on patrolling skills and infantry tactics. Meanwhile, the 3rd Australian Division advanced through jungle and mountains, from Wau to Salamaua. For MacArthur's main offensive during 1943, the Australian Army again provided the majority of his land forces. Blamey was again Commander New Guinea Force, while Herring commanded the 1st Australian Corps. After the experience in Papua, MacArthur was determined not to place his main American formations under the Australians, and he appointed Lieutenant-General Walter Krueger to command Alamo Force, which would come directly under his command. But Alamo Force would not see action until December.

The New Guinea Force operations involved the orchestration of land, sea, and air forces in several amphibious and air-land operations. On September 4, the 9th Australian Division (which had returned from the Middle East earlier in the year) conducted an amphibious landing to the east of Lae. Next day, an American parachute regiment landed at Nadzab, inland from Lae. The first troops of the 7th Australian Division flew into Nadzab airstrip, and advanced on Lae from the west. Lae was captured on September 16. Salamaua had already fallen on September 11.

The Australians, demonstrating great flexibility, maintained the offensive. The 7th Division reversed its axis, and, moving troops forward by air, advanced into the Ramu Valley to secure sites for airfields. On October 2, the 9th Division conducted an amphibious landing at Finschhafen. The enemy counterattacked in strength and the 9th Division did not clear the area, including the key Sattelberg feature, until November 25.

Australian tanks and artillery supported the final assault on Sattelberg, but success was ultimately achieved by the bravery and expertise of the forward infantry. Sergeant Tom Derrick was commanding the leading platoon when the battalion commander ordered a withdrawal. Derrick appealed to his company commander: "Bugger the CO. Just give me twenty minutes and we'll have this place."[4] It was a one-man front up an almost vertical incline covered in jungle. In peacetime the climb is barely possible using both hands and feet. Covered by his platoon members, Derrick alone clambered up the cliff, holding on with one hand, throwing grenades with the other, pausing to fire his rifle. He cleared ten machine-gun posts before, at dusk, he reached an open patch, just short of the crest. Fifteen Japanese dead remained on the spur. Derrick's platoon occupied the area. That night the remaining Japanese withdrew. Awarded the Victoria Cross, Derrick said that the achievement was due mainly to his mates.

Meanwhile, the 7th Division was moving into the Finisterre mountain range, dominated by Japanese positions on the razorback Shaggy Ridge. The high point was taken on January 31. The 11th Australian Division relieved the 7th and on April 24, 1944 its troops entered Madang on the New Guinea coast, meeting up with the leading elements of the 5th Division, which had relieved the 9th and advanced along the New Guinea coast. By this time American troops had taken over the main offensive and most of the Australian divisions had returned to Australia for rest and retraining.

The New Guinea campaigns of 1943 were the largest and most complicated carried out by the Australians during the war. Between March 1943 and April 1944, under Blamey, Australia deployed five infantry divisions, losing about 1,200 killed. Japanese losses in the same period numbered about 35,000. The campaign included the first opposed amphibious operations in MacArthur's command, and relied heavily on the transport of troops by air. The Australians showed that they had mastered the tactics and techniques of jungle warfare and were superior to the Japanese in this regard.

## THE SCALE OF AUSTRALIA'S CONTRIBUTION

Australia's major contribution to MacArthur's operations represented only part of its war effort. Substantial forces remained committed to the defense of Australia, while others were deployed further afield, under British command. Thus, although the Army deployed three divisions to Papua in 1942, and five to New Guinea in 1943, the remainder defended the coast of Australia. For example, a division defended Darwin in case the Japanese followed up their air attacks with an actual landing. In April

1943 the Army consisted of the equivalent of twelve divisions. At its largest (in August 1943) it numbered 540,000, and throughout the war 735,000 personnel served – about one-tenth of the population.

After December 1941, most ships of the RAN returned to Australia, although some destroyers continued to serve with British forces in the Indian Ocean. By June 1943, the RAN's combat force included three cruisers (HMAS *Canberra* had been lost at Guadalcanal), ten destroyers, three sloops, 48 corvettes, 16 launches, and three landing ships. From mid-1942 a British officer, Rear Admiral Victor Crutchley, commanded the Australian naval squadron and he was given command of a task force of Australian and American cruisers and destroyers that supported MacArthur's operations. In mid-1944 an Australian officer, Commodore John Collins, succeeded Crutchley. Six destroyers and 13 corvettes were serving with the British Eastern Fleet and thus were also involved in the war against Japan. Meanwhile, most of the corvettes and some sloops conducted defensive operations, including convoy escort, around Australia – an important task because of Japanese submarine attacks. At its largest, in March 1945, the RAN numbered 40,000 personnel.

By August 1943, the RAAF numbered 48 squadrons and had a strength of 156,000 (it would later reach 181,000). But 17 squadrons were operating in Europe, while other RAAF personnel were serving in British squadrons there. A total of 20,000 RAAF personnel were in Europe, and those serving in Bomber Command in raids over Germany and other occupied countries were to suffer the highest RAAF casualties of the war. Back in Australia, RAAF squadrons were deployed on home defense tasks, while bomber squadrons in northern Australia conducted a bombing offensive against Japanese bases in the Netherlands East Indies. The RAAF received aircraft as part of the Allied allocation to the Southwest Pacific Area, and thus was equipped with Kittyhawks, Spitfires, Hudsons, Liberators, Catalinas, Dakotas, Beaufighters, and Australian-made Beauforts. The RAAF also had obsolete aircraft and aircraft types that had been released by the Americans because they were not popular with their air forces.

During the campaigns in New Guinea during 1942 and 1943, the RAAF deployed an operational group as part of the US Fifth Air Force. In 1942, Australian Kittyhawks defended Port Moresby and provided ground support at Milne Bay. Australian Beaufighters played a key role in the battle of the Bismarck Sea in March 1943, and Australian aircraft supported Australian and American operations in 1943 and 1944. In October 1944, the Australian operational group was retitled the First Tactical Air Force, under the command of an air commodore. It included eight flying squadrons and four airfield construction squadrons – an important contribution to MacArthur's strategy of seizing and developing airfields.

## THE FINAL CAMPAIGNS

Clearly, MacArthur could never have conducted his operations during 1942 and 1943 without the Australians. The Australian Army provided most of his land forces, and the Australian Navy and Air Force supplemented his forces substantially. Furthermore, Australia provided MacArthur with crucial logistic support and an indispensable mounting base.

Yet as increasing numbers of American troops, aircraft, and ships arrived in the theater, MacArthur became determined to exclude Australian land and air forces from his offensive operations. In March 1944 he told the Australian Prime Minister, Curtin, that the spearhead of his advance would be three Australian divisions and an American paratroop division; but in fact his plans did not include the Australians. As he began concentrating his forces for operations in the Philippines, he ordered Blamey to relieve the six American divisions engaged in garrison or holding operations in the Solomons and New Guinea. Blamey produced plans to use seven Australian brigades. MacArthur insisted that Blamey use twelve brigades – or four Australian divisions – thus leaving fewer Australian divisions available for operations in the Philippines. Furthermore, MacArthur destroyed the myth that Blamey had any role as Commander Allied Land Forces when he dissolved Alamo Force and gave orders directly to Krueger's Sixth Army. The truth was that MacArthur had no intention of using the Australians in what he wanted to be a purely American operation in the Philippines. In effect, he was holding the Australians in reserve.

Some Australian units were, however, involved in the Philippines campaign. The Australian naval squadron supported the landings at Leyte in October 1944 and at Lingayen in January 1945, coming under heavy *kamikaze* attacks.

Other Australians involved in the Philippines campaign came from signal intelligence units. In 1942, MacArthur had formed the Central Bureau to provide signals intelligence for his command. It consisted primarily of Australian Army and Air Force and American Army personnel. Central Bureau and the US Navy Fleet Radio Unit in Melbourne (FRUMEL) gave MacArthur access to priceless intelligence about Japanese strengths and intentions. The most important break came in January 1944, when Australian infantry at Sio on the New Guinea coast captured the entire cipher library of the Japanese 20th Division. MacArthur was able to plan his operations during 1944 with full confidence in his understanding of his adversary's capabilities. By May 1945, when the Central Bureau began moving from Brisbane to Manila, it had a strength of 4,000 scattered across the theater; about half of these were Australians.

From October 1944, troops of the First Australian Army under Lieutenant-General Vernon Sturdee began relieving American divisions in Bougainville, New Britain, and New Guinea. In New Britain, the 5th Division conducted a containment operation, and at the end of the war the Japanese garrison at Rabaul was found to number almost 70,000 personnel. In Bougainville the 2nd Australian Corps (3rd Division and two brigades of the 11th) began a slow and careful offensive, which was still proceeding at the end of the war. In New Guinea, the 6th Division captured Wewak, driving the Japanese into the mountains. Theoretically the Australians were still under MacArthur's command, but Blamey ordered the offensives with little reference to MacArthur. In the absence of American air and naval support, the Australians provided their own.

Many commentators (and participants) have argued that these unnecessary campaigns did not affect the outcome of the war, but Blamey believed that Australia had a duty to liberate its own territory. He could not know that the war would end in August, and he considered that the best way to withdraw his troops from these "back" areas was to eliminate the Japanese forces there, thus meeting the demands for demobilization, and also making troops available for the invasion of the main island of Japan in March 1946.

In March 1945, Blamey established his forward headquarters at Morotai, from where he could command the First Army in New Guinea, and the 1st Australian Corps (under Lieutenant-General Sir Leslie

Morshead) once it began operations in Borneo. Also located at Morotai was the headquarters of RAAF Command, under Air Vice-Marshal William Bostock, who was given responsibility for all Allied – primarily Australian and New Zealand – air operations south of the Philippines.

The 1st Corps' operations in Borneo began on May 1, 1945, when the 26th Brigade, supported by the 1st Tactical Air Force and an Allied fleet, including Australian ships, landed on the island of Tarakan, off the northeast coast of Borneo. The purpose of the operation was to seize an airfield to support further operations in Borneo, and to gain control of the oil installations. The airfield could not be repaired in time for the coming operations and the oilfields took a year to bring back to production. The next landing took place on June 10 when two brigades of the 9th Division landed on Labuan Island and the Brunei mainland. Again the 1st Tactical Air Force, under Air Commodore Frederick Scherger, provided support.

Blamey had generally supported the first two operations in Borneo, even though it was soon obvious that they had no effect on the outcome of the war. But he was now more wary and opposed the landing of the 7th Division at Balikpapan on the east coast of Borneo. MacArthur warned the Australian government that to cancel the operation would disorganize Allied strategic plans; unable to dispute MacArthur's assertion, the government approved the landing, which took place on July 1. Actually, MacArthur's motivation was probably to demonstrate to the Dutch government that he had attempted to recover part of its territory.

In July 1945 Australia had more infantry divisions (six of its seven) in action at one time than in any other month of the war. Australia was the only Allied country that had proportionally more divisions in action after the defeat of Germany than before. With the advantage of hindsight, it is easy now to question the value of Australia's 1945 campaigns. But several matters must be considered in doing so. First, the Australian forces were still under MacArthur's strategic direction, although perhaps that command arrangement should have been reviewed during the previous year. Second, the Australian government had not developed an effective process for determining strategic policy, and the ineffective process that was in existence was hampered by the sickness of the Prime Minister after October 1944.

Third, once the Americans deployed their powerful naval and air forces against Japan in 1945, there was never going to be much scope for an Australian involvement. After carrying much of the burden in the Southwest Pacific in the earlier stages of the war, the Australian government was determined that Australia would have some say in the peace process. Australia was no longer fighting for its survival. It could no longer even make a major contribution to the defeat of Japan; but the government had a responsibility to look to the nation's future security. This meant that Australia needed to continue playing a role in the war and also to nurture its alliance with the United States. Australia's campaigns in 1944–45 were conducted for these reasons.

## NEW ZEALAND'S ROLE

By comparison with the Australia, New Zealand made only a modest contribution to the Pacific War, even though proportionately it made a greater contribution to the entire war than any part of the British Empire. After the outbreak of war with Japan, New Zealand considered whether to withdraw its infantry division from the Middle East. President Roosevelt offered to send the 1st US Marine Division to New Zealand and the New Zealand government, under the Prime Minister Peter Fraser, decided to leave its division in the Middle East. New Zealand was therefore unable to contribute land forces to the 1942 offensives. Initially, the headquarters of the South Pacific Area, under American Vice-Admiral Robert Ghormley, was established in New Zealand, but it moved to New Caledonia in July 1942. The two cruisers of the Royal New Zealand Navy served as part of the South Pacific command's naval forces in the Guadalcanal campaign.

In May 1942, the 14th New Zealand Brigade was deployed to Fiji to join the 8th Brigade, which had been defending the island since late 1940. These brigades came under the newly formed 3rd New Zealand Division. The New Zealand division in the Middle East was designated as the 2nd Division. After it fought in the battle of El Alamein in October–November 1942 the question was again raised as to whether it should return home, in the same manner as the 9th Australian Division was returning. The government decided again to keep its division in the Middle East. This decision strained relations between the New Zealand and Australian governments, as Australia considered that it was carrying an unequal share of the fighting in the Pacific. The question was raised again after the Tunisian campaign in 1943, and in 1944 during the Italian campaign. On both occasions New Zealand re-confirmed its earlier decisions, and the 2nd Division continued in the Italian campaign through to the capture of Trieste in April–May 1945.

The 3rd New Zealand Division returned to New Zealand from Fiji, and under Major-General Harold Barrowclough, moved forward to Guadalcanal. In September 1943, the 14th Brigade landed on the island of Vella Lavella, in the central Solomon Islands, to take over mopping-up operations from American troops. In October, the 8th Brigade captured Treasury Island. The following February, the 14th Brigade landed on Green Island, north of the Solomons, thus completing the encirclement of the Japanese garrison on Bougainville. By this time, New Zealand's severe manpower shortages were making it extremely difficult to maintain the 2nd Division in Italy. As a result, the 3rd Division was disbanded to enable reinforcements to be sent to Italy, and also to return some men to essential industries in New Zealand.

The Royal New Zealand Air Force (RNZAF) made a considerable contribution to the Solomons campaigns, beginning with the arrival of a squadron of Hudsons at Guadalcanal in November 1942. A squadron of Warhawk fighters joined the campaign in June 1943. By mid-1944, eight RNZAF squadrons (four fighter, two bomber-reconnaissance, one dive-bomber and one flying boat) were operating in the northern Solomons. When the Australians took over from the Americans in Bougainville in October 1944, they were supported by RNZAF Corsairs operating under the control of the commander of RAAF Command, Air Vice-Marshal Bostock. About one-third of the 45,000 New Zealanders in the wartime RNZAF served in the Pacific. Nearly 600 New Zealanders lost their lives in the Solomon Islands campaigns, including 345 RNZAF personnel.

On September 2, 1945, General MacArthur accepted the Japanese surrender on the battleship *Missouri* in Tokyo Bay. General Sir Thomas Blamey signed on behalf of Australia, and the New Zealand Chief of Air Staff, Air Vice-Marshal Leonard Isitt, signed on behalf of New Zealand. At Morotai on September 9, Blamey accepted the surrender of 126,500 Japanese troops in the East Indies from Lieutenant-General Futsataro Teshima, commander of the Japanese Second Area Army.

Chapter 9

# The Shortest Road to Tokyo
## Nimitz and the Central Pacific War

*Professor Theodore Gatchel*

During World War II, US forces under the Command of Admiral Chester W. Nimitz planned and conducted a series of naval campaigns in the Central Pacific that still stand as a model for conducting joint operations in a large theater against a powerful and determined enemy.

Because of the tenacious resistance offered by the Japanese and the gallantry of American servicemen required to overcome it, island battles such as Tarawa, Iwo Jima, and Okinawa have become legends in US military history. The spectacular nature of those battles has tended to focus attention on the tactical aspects of warfare and limit discussion of the many important challenges faced by Nimitz and his subordinates during campaign planning and joint operations.

In the fight against the Japanese, Nimitz was simultaneously forced to resolve a seemingly never-ending series of disputes between his planners and the Joint Chiefs of Staff (JCS); between himself and the commander of the Southwest Pacific Area (SWPA), General Douglas MacArthur; among the US services; and even among the different warfare communities within the US Navy. Nimitz was, however, largely spared one problem that faced both Eisenhower in Europe and MacArthur in the SWPA: dealing with allies. Until the arrival of British carriers at the very end of the Central Pacific War, Nimitz's forces were entirely from the United States.

## BACKGROUND TO THE CENTRAL PACIFIC CAMPAIGNS

Prewar planning by the US services had focused on the Central Pacific and the need for the Navy to fight its way from Hawaii through the Marshall, Caroline, and Mariana Islands at the start of war. These actions would be necessary to relieve beleaguered American forces in Guam and the Philippines or to recapture those islands if they had already fallen. No plans were made for operations in the region between the Philippines and Australia.[1]

Not surprisingly, Imperial Japanese Navy planners anticipated US moves and developed a strategy to counter them. In one sense, the two navies were remarkably similar. The leaders of both largely adhered to the concepts delineated by the nineteenth-century American naval strategist Alfred Thayer Mahan. Mahan believed strongly in the importance of destroying an enemy's fleet in a decisive sea battle, and both sides actively sought such a battle during the war.

The Japanese, however, faced one serious obstacle to winning a decisive fleet engagement: the size of their fleet. Given their defensive posture and what they considered to be superior tactics, training, and *esprit*, Japanese planners estimated that they had a 50/50 chance of success with a fleet that was 70 percent the size of their opponent's. In 1922 and 1930, however, the Japanese had accepted treaties that limited their fleet to 60 percent of the US fleet.[2]

To overcome that disparity, the IJN developed a strategy of "gradual attrition." Under this plan, it would employ submarines, land-based bombers, and light surface forces to whittle down the approaching US fleet to a size that the Japanese could defeat in a fleet-versus-fleet battle. To implement the strategy, the Japanese would use bases in the Marshall, Caroline, and Mariana Islands that they had taken over under a League of Nations Mandate after World War I.

When war started, however, the attack on Pearl Harbor eliminated any possibility of the US fleet coming to the immediate relief of Guam and the Philippines. Additionally, the speed with which Japanese forces overran the Bismarck Archipelago, the Solomons, and most of New Guinea placed the Japanese in position to threaten not only the sea lines of communication (SLOCs) between the United States and Australia, but also the Australian continent itself.

That immediate threat was the one that faced JCS planners in March 1942, when President Roosevelt approved a plan that divided the Pacific into two separate theaters.[3] In principle, the services agreed on the need for unity of command in the Pacific, but could not agree on who should be invested with the resulting power and responsibility. The Army wanted General Douglas MacArthur, but the Navy was unwilling to entrust command of the fleet to an Army officer, and no naval officer was senior enough to warrant making MacArthur a subordinate.

Unable to break the deadlock, the JCS created two independent theaters of war in the Pacific: the SWPA, under MacArthur, included the Philippines, the Netherlands East Indies, and Australia and the Pacific Ocean Areas (POA) that covered the remainder of the Pacific. Command of the POA fell to Nimitz, who had become Commander-in-Chief of the US Pacific Fleet on December 31, 1941. His command was divided into three subordinate areas, encompassing the south, central, and north Pacific respectively. An admiral who reported to Nimitz, but coordinated his operations closely with MacArthur's, commanded the South Pacific. Nimitz personally commanded operations in the other two regions.

Although Great Britain and the United States had agreed on the principle of defeating Germany first before the US entered the war, the specifics of implementing that principle remained vague. The growing Japanese threat to Australia, combined with the inability of the Allies to launch a cross-channel invasion of France in either 1942 or 1943, caused the Americans to propose a limited offensive in the South Pacific and SWPA. Its objective was to capture the main Japanese air and naval base at Rabaul, on New Britain.

The US/British Combined Chiefs of Staff (CCS) eventually approved this limited offensive, but could not agree on what should follow it. The British generally preferred a defensive posture in the Pacific until Germany was defeated. American leaders, particularly Admiral Ernest J. King, Commander-in-Chief of the US Fleet and Chief of Naval Operations, pushed for continued offensive operations from both the SWPA and the Central Pacific to maintain an unrelenting pressure on the Japanese.

The argument over whether to have one or two axes of advance against the Japanese was directly related to the issue of unity of command that had resulted in two theaters of war. When MacArthur left the Philippines in March 1942, he made his famous pledge, "I shall return." In his view, that pledge required a return to the Philippines through the SWPA. Nimitz and most other naval officers regarded the narrow seas of MacArthur's theater, in which ships were always under the threat of land-based aircraft, as the worst possible place to conduct naval operations. In the view of most naval strategists, an advance on the Philippines through the Central Pacific was clearly the proper choice.

In theory, the interior geostrategic position occupied by the Japanese in the Pacific gave them an advantage over the Americans. Operating from its base at Truk in the Carolines, the Japanese Combined Fleet, which included the two most powerful battleships ever built, could respond quickly to a threat from either US axis of advance, defeating it before forces from the other US theater could intervene. Although perhaps true initially, this Japanese positional advantage was ultimately to be negated by the growth of US naval forces.

The JCS resolved the issue of how to proceed strategically in favor of a two-axis advance, using a process that set the pattern for planning in the Central Pacific. By agreement with the CCS, the US JCS retained overall strategic control of the war in the Pacific.[4] The JCS, in turn, coordinated the efforts of the two theaters, the SWPA and POA, by selecting strategic – and sometimes operational – objectives, allocating resources, and generally overseeing the plans and operations of the two theater commanders. During the course of the war, for example, Nimitz had 18 face-to-face meetings with Admiral King, the Navy's representative on the JCS.

During his 36-year naval career, Nimitz had commanded both surface ships and submarines. Like most American officers of the time, however, little in his background had prepared him to command large forces from the other services.[5] To overcome that potential weakness, Nimitz created joint organizations to plan and command multi-service operations.

Forgoing the traditional commander's prerogative of a flagship, Nimitz established his headquarters ashore, overlooking Pearl Harbor. He added officers from each of the services to his staff and combined his intelligence units into the Joint Intelligence Center Pacific Ocean Area (JICPOA), an all-service, all-source, intelligence organization.

In his role as fleet commander, Nimitz instituted organizational changes needed to prepare his naval forces for operations in the Central Pacific. He created a fleet structure under which the fleet stayed forward fighting the Japanese, while two fleet commanders, Admirals Raymond Spruance and William "Bull" Halsey, rotated with their staffs back to Hawaii to plan future operations. When Halsey commanded, it was designated Third Fleet. When Spruance took command, it became Fifth Fleet.[6]

Nimitz also created an amphibious force, subordinate to Fifth Fleet, to plan and conduct the landings that would become the salient characteristic of the naval war in the Central Pacific. Rear Admiral Richmond Kelly Turner, who had commanded amphibious forces at Guadalcanal, took command of this new organization. It controlled the Navy's amphibious forces as well as landing forces from the Army and the Marine Corps, headed by Marine Corps Major-General Holland M. "Howlin' Mad" Smith.[7]

An experienced submariner, Nimitz realized that only submarines could initially carry the war deep into enemy-controlled areas of the Pacific. Accordingly, he directed them to attack the Japanese merchant marine in order to sever the sea lanes that Japanese industry and military forces relied upon for vital raw materials, such as oil and rubber from Southeast Asia. He also organized his submarines as a separate command designed to implement that strategy.

The final piece of Nimitz's naval organizational puzzle involved the role of naval aviation. The demise of the battleships at Pearl Harbor made the aircraft carrier the fleet's capital ship by default. Although carriers demonstrated at Coral Sea and Midway that air attacks represented the future of naval warfare, American naval aviators were unhappy. Admiral Frank Jack Fletcher, who had commanded at Coral Sea, and Admiral Spruance, who had served with Fletcher at Midway, were both surface officers. Aviators believed strongly that only fliers were capable of realizing the full potential of carriers. To placate the aviators and to gain a personal source of aviation expertise, Nimitz selected Vice-Admiral John H. Towers, the Navy's longest serving aviator, to be his deputy.

Having made those organizational changes by mid-1943, Nimitz was ready to begin an offensive in the Central Pacific. The big question was where to start.

# THE GILBERTS (OPERATION *GALVANIC*)

Most planning for the Central Pacific, from the prewar "Orange" series to the "Strategic Plan for the Defeat of Japan" (approved by the CCS on May 19, 1943), envisioned beginning the drive to victory with objectives in the Marshalls. As Nimitz's planners began to prepare for such an operation, a debate arose concerning the feasibility of the Marshalls as a first step. The issue involved whether or not such an operation could be supported by carrier-based naval aviation alone. At the time, the nearest US air bases to the Marshalls were beyond the range of land-based planes. Naval aviators such as Admiral Towers were convinced that naval aviation was up to the task, but US amphibious doctrine of the period expressed reservations about the ability of carrier planes to overcome land-based opposition.[8] Preferring to err on the side of caution, Nimitz chose to seize bases in the Gilbert Islands as a prelude to moving against the Marshalls.

Nimitz eventually settled on a plan using the 2d Marine Division to capture Tarawa Atoll, and a regiment from the Army's 27th Infantry Division to seize Makin Atoll. Makin was lightly defended, but Tarawa was another story. As the US Army's official history of the Gilberts operation noted, "With the possible exception of Iwo Jima, its beaches were better protected against a landing force than any encountered in any theater of war."[9]

Planning for *Galvanic* revealed a number of issues for the attacking forces. The Marines were concerned that the Navy might abandon them, as happened at Guadalcanal, if the American carriers were threatened. The Navy, on the other hand, was worried that the Japanese might attack while the US fleet was forced to remain tied to the landing sites to protect the invasion forces.

The Navy's concern was justified. The Pacific was a naval theater and the Japanese relied primarily on the Combined Fleet to defend it. Although the Japanese had redrawn their defensive lines in September to place the Gilberts and Marshalls outside of the area critical to Japanese security, Spruance was concerned about an attack by the Combined Fleet and wanted to be fully prepared to deal with one. In his general instructions to his flag officers, he wrote, "If, however, a major portion of the Japanese Fleet were to attempt to interfere with GALVANIC, it is obvious that the defeat of the enemy fleet would at once become paramount."[10]

Even if the Japanese had planned to commit the Combined Fleet to a fight for the Gilberts, events in the SWPA conspired to make such an action unlikely. On November 1, 1943, US Marines landed on Bougainville in the Northern Solomons. In response, the Combined Fleet left Truk for the site of the landing. While refueling at Rabaul, part of the fleet was caught in a devastating air raid by American forces. As a result, the Combined Fleet was unable to react when US forces landed in the Gilberts on November 20.

Even without interference from the Combined Fleet, the Marines had their hands full. Tarawa represented the first attempt to seize a highly defended beachhead in daylight, and, although doctrine proved generally sound, many details needed refinement. Overcoming an unusual tide that prevented landing craft other than amphibian tractors from reaching the beach, inadequate air and naval gunfire preparation, and defenders who killed themselves before allowing themselves to be captured, the Marines secured the atoll's main island, Betio, in 76 hours. The cost was enormous: 1,115 Marines and sailors killed or missing and another 2,292 wounded.[11]

Makin proved to be a much easier target. Despite the lesser resistance, the Army attackers moved much more slowly than the Marines on Tarawa, which precipitated a dispute between the Army division commander, Major-General Ralph Smith, and the overall landing force commander, Marine Major-General H. M. Smith. The Army's position was that their more deliberate tactics saved soldiers' lives. The Navy countered that the longer combat lasted ashore, the longer the fleet was tied to the beachhead, thereby exposing its sailors to greater risk of a Japanese naval attack. Because of this concern, Nimitz told Spruance, "Get the hell in, then get the hell out!"[12] The Navy's view was reinforced when a Japanese submarine sank a US escort carrier off Makin, a day after the plan called for securing the island. When the Navy's casualties are added to those ashore, Makin's toll approached that of the much fiercer battle at Tarawa.

# THE MARSHALLS (OPERATIONS *FLINTLOCK* AND *CATCHPOLE*)

By capturing the Gilberts, Nimitz seized the initiative from the Japanese, tested his amphibious doctrine, and positioned his forces for the next move. On January 15, 1944, he released Campaign Plan Granite that delineated the general course of a Central Pacific advance in compliance with the strategic guidance from the CCS. The planners agreed that the next step would be into the Marshalls, a course that the Japanese correctly anticipated. Given the immense size of the island group, however, there was much less agreement about exactly which atolls to attack.

The Marshall Islands comprise 29 atolls in two chains covering 750,000 square miles of ocean.[13] Because the Japanese could not predict exactly where the Americans would attack, they were forced to disperse their forces throughout the Marshalls.[14] Spruance and his two

Troops of the 1st US Marine Division board landing ships at Cape Sudest (Papua) in preparation for the main New Britain landing at Cape Gloucester on December 26, 1943. After hard fighting they established a perimeter but did not press the advance on Rabaul. (Australian War Memorial; Neg. No. 128393)

General Douglas MacArthur wading ashore at Leyte on October 20, 1944. (NARA)

Troops of the 39th Australian Infantry Battalion on the Kokoda Trail in August 1942. Troops arrived in the forward area exhausted after marching for days up and down lung-busting mountains. The track was awash with mud and soldiers pulled themselves up the slopes by holding onto protruding roots. (Australian War Memorial; Neg. No. 013288)

Troops of the 7th Australian Division land at Balikpapan, Borneo on July 1, 1945, in the last large-scale amphibious operation of the war. In the campaigns of late 1944 and 1945, the Australians lost more than 1,500 killed. (Australian War Memorial; Neg. No. 128283)

US marines take cover on Red Beach No.3 during the Tarawa landing. It took two years for the US to gain the experience and tactical mobility needed to assault such a heavily fortified position, and Tarawa was the first test of US amphibious doctrine. (NARA; 532385)

"Quiet Lagoon," Tarawa Atoll, 1943. The three-day victory at Tarawa came at a high cost. (USMC)

Five Essex Class carriers at Ulithi Atoll, December 8, 1944. (NARA; 80-G-294131)

B-29s of the Twentieth Air Force, based in Guam, bombing targets in Japan. (USAAF)

Lieutenant Kentaro Mitsuhashi prepares to lead the first suicide attack on Okinawa using the rocket-propelled *Ohka* bomb. Although powerful, the *Ohka* was difficult to control and sank only one US ship. Overall kamikaze attacks at Okinawa sank 34 Allied ships and damaged 368. (United States Naval Institute Photo Archive)

Leading the waves of troop-carrying LVTs ashore at Okinawa were these armored amphibians with their snub-nosed 75-mm howitzers and .50cal machine guns. The US Tenth Army landed 16,000 troops the first hour and a total of 60,000 by sunset. (USMC)

Assault waves approach the landing beaches of Iwo Jima at H-Hour on February 19, 1945. Extensive underground defenses, including those on Mount Suribachi, forced an intense battle that cost the Marines and supporting naval personnel more than 25,000 casualties, of which more than 6,000 were killed in action or later died of wounds. (NARA; 80-G-415308)

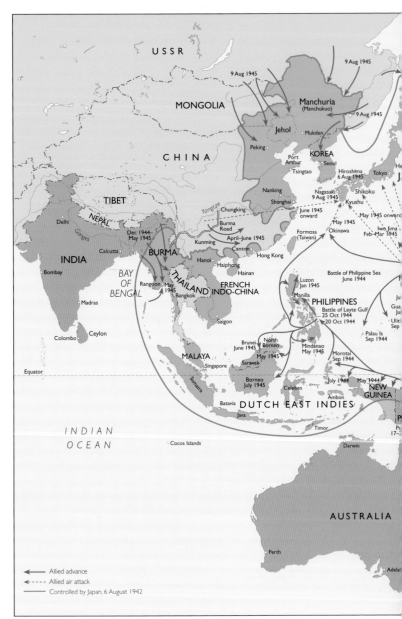

The Allied Counteroffensive

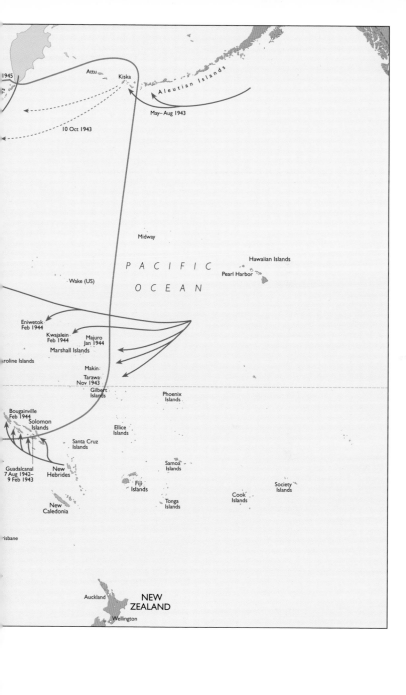

1945

Attu    Kiska

*A l e u t i a n   I s l a n d s*

May–Aug 1943

10 Oct 1943

Midway

P A C I F I C

Hawaiian Islands

Pearl Harbor

Wake (US)

O C E A N

Eniwetok
Feb 1944

Kwajalein
Feb 1944    Majuro
Jan 1944
Marshall Islands

roline Islands

Makin
Tarawa
Nov 1943
Gilbert
Islands

Phoenix
Islands

Bougainville
Feb 1944
Solomon
Islands

Ellice
Islands

Santa Cruz
Islands

Guadalcanal
7 Aug 1942–
9 Feb 1943

New
Hebrides

Samoa
Islands

Fiji
Islands

Tonga
Islands

Cook
Islands

Society
Islands

New
Caledonia

risbane

Auckland    **NEW
ZEALAND**

Wellington

The uranium bomb nicknamed "Little Boy" levelled Hiroshima on August 6, 1945. (NARA)

The formal surrender of the Japanese government was signed on USS *Missouri* on September 2, 1945. (Army Signal Corps Collection, NARA)

amphibious commanders, Turner and H. M. Smith, recommended seizing Maloelap and Wotje, in the eastern chain, before proceeding to the principal objective, Kwajalein. Bolstered by the successes in the Gilberts and confident that the problems discovered there could be corrected, Nimitz overruled his advisers and directed them to bypass the eastern islands and directly attack Kwajalein.[15]

The assault on the Marshalls was planned in two phases: first, the capture of Kwajalein (Operation *Flintlock*), followed in several months by the capture of Eniwetok (Operation *Catchpole*). To reduce the ability of the Japanese Combined Fleet to interfere with these operations, Nimitz preceded them with a major carrier strike on the Japanese air and naval base at Truk in the Carolines.

US intelligence was unaware at the time that aircraft and ship losses in both Pacific theaters had forced the Japanese to rethink their plans and redraw their defensive lines. Under the new scheme, the Marshalls were outside the area in which the IJN would commit the Combined Fleet to oppose a US landing. Freed, therefore, from major naval opposition, Spruance's Fifth Fleet conducted a textbook operation at Kwajalein from January 31 to February 2, 1944, in which the 4th Marine Division captured the connected islands of Roi and Namur and the Army's 7th Division took Kwajalein Island. Both objectives were achieved with moderate casualties, and with a speed that allowed Spruance to attack Eniwetok only 15 days after the fall of Kwajalein, using forces that had been designated as the reserve for Kwajalein. Operations in the Marshalls demonstrated that Nimitz's forces had largely mastered the technique of seizing coral atolls. Shortly, however, those forces were to face a new challenge.

## THE MARIANAS (OPERATION *FORAGER*)

Although the Granite plan envisioned moving from the Marshalls into the Carolines, Nimitz's planners began to consider a different approach. Under the new concept, Japanese bases in the Carolines, especially Truk, would be bypassed and periodically bombed to keep them from presenting a serious threat to US forces. The Central Pacific drive would then head directly to the Marianas. Doing so would recapture Guam, an American territory seized by Japan at the start of the war, continue the advance towards the Japanese home islands, and secure air bases from which Army Air Forces (AAF) B-29 bombers could reach the Japanese home islands. Although the AAF had initially used bases in China, the Marianas were easier to defend and support logistically.

Nimitz's planners faced two major changes from the Gilberts and Marshalls. First, the islands were fundamentally different. Instead of small, low-lying coral atolls, the Marianas were large, volcanic islands with rugged, heavily vegetated terrain. Where Betio was smaller than New York City's Central Park, Saipan covered 85 square miles. The enemy had also changed. For the first time in the Central Pacific, the Japanese Army brought divisions from China to defend the Marianas. Consequently, the Japanese defense shifted from holding at the water's edge to a more flexible concept that included tank attacks and falling back to prepared inland positions in order to prolong the defense.

Two issues that had surfaced initially in the Gilberts arose again in the Marianas, with serious consequences. The first was the Army–Marine Corps dispute over infantry tactics. The second was the tension between the Navy's competing missions of protecting the forces fighting ashore, and fighting a major sea battle to destroy the Japanese fleet.

Both of these issues were brought to a head by the way in which the Japanese chose to defend the Marianas. The Japanese fully understood the strategic consequences of the loss of the islands and had therefore designated them an "absolute strategic area."[16] Because of their importance, the IJN planned to commit the Combined Fleet to their defense in order to precipitate the much-sought-after decisive fleet battle. In anticipation of the battle, the Japanese had formed, under Vice-Admiral Jizaburo Ozawa, a mobile fleet closely resembling an American carrier striking force. To employ this new fleet, the Japanese created one of their typically elaborate plans that required a high degree of synchronization.

The Japanese plan envisioned attacking the American ships, both with land-based aircraft from the Marianas and carrier aircraft. The carrier aircraft would land in the Marianas after attacking the Americans, rearm, refuel, and then attack again on their return to their carriers. In theory, the longer range of the Japanese aircraft would allow them to strike the US fleet, while remaining out of range of American retaliation.

Unfortunately for the Japanese, Spruance had a copy of a Japanese plan captured in the Philippines that gave him a general idea of his enemy's concept of operations.[17] Aware of the concept and alerted to the pending attack through highly classified radio intercepts, Spruance attacked the Japanese airfields in the Marianas. Those attacks largely eliminated Japan's capability to execute the land–based portion of their plan, but, exhibiting a pattern that plagued Japanese commanders during the war, the air commander in the Marianas failed to inform Ozawa of the problem. Unaware of this change, Ozawa proceeded as planned.

Spruance, on the other hand, made several important changes to his plan. Instead of keeping the Army's 27th Division afloat as a reserve, he ordered Turner to land it starting on June 16, the day after D-Day, and then take the amphibious ships east of Saipan, where they would be protected from Japanese air strikes. Spruance and the fast carriers of Task Force (TF) 58 then sailed west to intercept Ozawa.

Ozawa struck first on June 19, but his large airborne raid against Spruance's carriers was intercepted by American fighters. The poorly trained Japanese aviators were no match for their US counterparts, and during the course of the resulting battle, the Japanese lost about 400 aircraft. Officially designated the battle of the Philippine Sea, the action became better known in the US fleet as the "Marianas Turkey Shoot."

During the battle, a dispute arose over what actions Spruance should take. He was concerned primarily with protecting the beachhead, and the possibility that parts of Ozawa's force might evade him and attack the amphibious ships. The aviators urged Spruance to focus his efforts on the Japanese carriers, and he belatedly agreed. Search planes were unable to locate Ozawa's force until late the next day. Spruance ordered a strike at maximum range that sank one carrier. Because of the range, however, many US planes ran out of fuel before they could return, and had to ditch in the ocean.

American submarines sank two more Japanese carriers, but Ozawa escaped with six of his original nine. In a reprise of the debate that had occurred in the Gilberts, US naval aviators again expressed their disgust with what they considered excess caution by Spruance. In their view, if an aviator had commanded the Fifth Fleet, Ozawa would not have escaped.

Ashore on Saipan, a second dispute from the Gilberts was being replayed. The corps commander, Lieutenant-General H. M. Smith, had placed the 27th Division between two Marine divisions, and he believed that its slow progress was unnecessarily endangering the Marine units by exposing their flanks. After repeated admonitions to its commander,

Major-General Ralph Smith, the Marine relieved the Army commander of his command, after receiving authorization from Spruance. During the course of the war, Army generals had relieved numerous subordinate generals for a variety of faults without causing any serious repercussions. The relief of an Army general by a Marine, on the other hand, ignited a firestorm of controversy. Nimitz and Spruance both supported Smith's action, but the incident created bad blood between the Army and the Marine Corps that lasted throughout the war and, some would argue, into the Vietnam conflict.[18]

Although Ralph Smith's relief produced no immediate change in the tactical situation, US forces eventually drove the defending Japanese into the northern end of the island, where they ended their defense with the largest *banzai* attack of the war.

Following the end of combat on Saipan, the 4th Marine Division attacked nearby Tinian on July 24. Correctly assessing that the Japanese would expect a landing on the island's wide beaches in the south, the Marines conducted an amphibious demonstration off those beaches, while actually landing across two tiny breaks in Tinian's coral-lined northern coast. Three days before the landing at Tinian, Marines from Admiral Turner's Northern Attack Force had landed on Guam. When capture of the Marianas was completed on August 10, the Japanese knew they were in serious trouble. Emperor Hirohito had earlier told the Saipan garrison, "If Saipan is lost, air raids on Tokyo will take place often."[19] The Emperor was right on the mark. The AAF was already preparing bases in the Marianas from which to carry out the strategic bombing of the Japanese homeland.

## THE PALAUS (OPERATION *STALEMATE*)

While these actions were taking place, the JCS and Nimitz's staff were wrestling with the divisive issue of prospective objectives for the Pacific War. MacArthur remained focused on liberating the Philippines. Nimitz's revised Granite plan, on the other hand, envisioned moving to the southern Philippines and then Formosa, as a precursor to gaining a foothold on the China coast.[20] Admiral King supported the Formosa plan, and led a discussion of the CCS during the London meetings in June 1944, during which the idea of completely bypassing the Philippines was discussed.[21]

MacArthur prevailed, however, and the JCS settled on Leyte for the start of a Philippines campaign. With Leyte agreed upon, the debate moved to the next step, with the choice being either Luzon or Formosa. Once again, the JCS accepted MacArthur's proposal, and agreed on Luzon.[22]

Nimitz proposed using Central Pacific forces to attack Peleliu in the Palaus as a precursor to Leyte. A move into the Palaus had always been part of the Granite plans, but Nimitz was also concerned that the Japanese might use bases in the Palaus to conduct a flank attack on the Leyte invasion forces. As a result, Nimitz tasked Halsey to seize the Palaus before the Leyte operation. Halsey accomplished this in a bloody fight that lasted from September 12 to November 27 and caused nearly 10,500 US casualties.[23]

As the Japanese pulled back into a smaller defensive perimeter, their lines of communication to their homeland became shorter and, at least theoretically, easier to manage. Conversely, the American lines of communication became longer, which should have worked to their disadvantage. Unfortunately for the Japanese, two factors prevented them from being able to convert that theoretical advantage into a practical one.

First, Japan's geographic position presented the IJN with an unsolvable problem. Japan's fleet was built in shipyards in the homeland, and ships returned there for major repairs. As Japan's position deteriorated, the IJN also relied increasingly on the relative safety of home waters to train new naval aviators in the difficult art of carrier operations. At the same time, the IJN required immense amounts of fuel that could only be obtained from the East Indies. This forced the Navy to split the fleet between the two regions. The split eased the fuel situation, but caused operational problems that were never entirely solved.

The second factor was the innovative methods that Nimitz employed to support his forces. Engineers from all services became adept at repairing Japanese airfields and building new ones on captured islands in remarkably short times. In many cases, American aircraft began operating from such fields before the islands had been completely secured. Similarly, atolls, such as Ulithi in the Carolines, were turned into advanced naval bases where tenders and floating dry-docks allowed all but the most serious battle damage to be repaired in the combat zone. The US Navy also developed an impressive ability to resupply its forces at sea. Service squadrons accompanying the combat forces contained not only oilers and cargo ships to provide fuel, food, and ammunition, but escort carriers that could quickly replace losses on the fast carriers with new aircraft and pilots.[24]

The Navy's expeditionary support capability allowed Nimitz to establish an advanced base for submarines at Saipan that greatly reduced the distance the subs had to travel to rearm between missions. Although interdiction of Japanese SLOCs remained the submarines' primary mission, it was not their only one. The sinking of two Japanese carriers during the battle of the Philippine Sea illustrated just one of the varied roles that submarines played in the Central Pacific. They also laid mines, delivered reconnaissance teams to enemy beaches, conducted periscope photography of future landing sites, and rescued downed aviators.

# IWO JIMA (OPERATION *DETACHMENT*)

In his Campaign Plan Granite, Nimitz had identified his immediate strategic objective as obtaining "positions from which the ultimate surrender of JAPAN can be forced by intensive air bombardment, by sea and air blockade, and by invasion if necessary."[25] The services viewed the likelihood of each of those three methods succeeding differently, but all viewed Okinawa as a useful location from which to implement them. Given the long distance between the Marianas and Okinawa, however, a search began for possible intermediate objectives.

The AAF pressed hard for Iwo Jima, halfway between the B-29 bases in the Marianas and their targets in Japan. Strictly speaking, the B-29s were not Nimitz's problem, because they belonged to a recently-created organization under direct JCS control. AAF Major-General Curtis LeMay personally appealed to Spruance to take Iwo Jima as a base for fighter escorts, as well as an emergency field for bombers too badly damaged to return to the Marianas.[26] Although they remained concerned about predictions of excessively high casualties, Spruance and Nimitz, who had moved to a forward headquarters in Guam in January 1945, eventually accepted the AAF rationale for Iwo Jima.

On February 19, 1945, V Amphibious Corps assaulted the island with two Marine divisions in the assault and a third in reserve. The Marines needed more than a month to secure the small island, in what became the bloodiest battle in Marine Corps history and the only landing in which the Japanese inflicted more casualties on their enemy than they suffered themselves.

## OKINAWA (OPERATION *ICEBERG*)

The seizure of Iwo Jima had hardly been completed when Spruance's amphibians moved on Okinawa, only 320 miles southwest of Japan itself. The Army's 77th Division first landed in the Kerama Retto, a group of small islands 15 miles west of Okinawa, to provide a safe haven for damaged US ships and a base for seaplanes.

On April 1, 1945, two Army and two Marine divisions landed unopposed over beaches in the center of Okinawa. As US forces began to move south, however, General Simon Bolivar Buckner, commander of the US Tenth Army, who had replaced H. M. Smith as the senior landing force officer under Turner, found that lack of opposition at the beaches did not presage an easy time. Using techniques tested at Biak, Peleliu, and Iwo Jima, 100,000 Japanese soldiers on Okinawa had created an extensive, in-depth defense throughout the southern part of Okinawa.

The purpose was not to defeat the Americans, but to delay them. The Japanese knew that as long as they held out, the US fleet would remain close offshore. That, in turn, made the fleet an ideal target for a series of massive *kamikaze* attacks made possible by the proximity of Okinawa to the southern home island of Kyushu. US casualties from those attacks, when added to those ashore, totaled 49,151, making Okinawa the costliest operation of the Pacific War.[27] Regarding the attacks, the United States Strategic Bombing Survey noted that, if the Japanese had been able to sustain them, "they might have been able to cause us to withdraw or revise our strategic plans."[28]

## THE END OF THE WAR

The impact of those casualties did not go unnoticed by American planners working on Operation *Olympic*, a landing on Kyushu. Okinawa was widely regarded as a harbinger of what to expect from any invasion of Japan proper. Kyushu would have been the largest amphibious assault in history, and would also have seen a merger of the two Pacific axes. MacArthur would have commanded the ground forces and Nimitz the naval ones. Invasion was made unnecessary by the surrender of Japan on

August 15, 1945 following the dropping of atomic bombs on Hiroshima and Nagasaki, and the Soviet Union's entry into the war.

President Truman's decision to use the atomic bombs has been the subject of much heated debate. Similar, albeit less extensive, debate continues regarding other aspects of the Central Pacific War, particularly regarding Spruance's actions during the Marianas operation and whether or not the landings at Tarawa, Peleliu, and Iwo Jima were worth the cost of seizing them. The lack of unity of command is another frequently debated topic.

Those postwar debates reflect ones that occurred during the war that Nimitz, as theater commander, was forced to adjudicate. Because the services generally differed on how to deal with the problems, Nimitz frequently had to referee among the services over strongly held views. Some of Nimitz's decisions can be criticized individually. His insistence on taking Peleliu and his support for landings on Formosa and the China coast, for example, are difficult to defend in light of what we know today. Given the information available at the time and the competing pressures he faced, however, Nimitz's overall performance is hard to fault. His selection to sign the formal Japanese surrender documents for the US forces was a fitting tribute to the admiral who led US forces to victory in the greatest naval war in history.

# Chapter 10
# After Midway
## Japanese naval strategy 1942–45

*Professor H. P. Willmott*

More than a century before the event, the defeat of Japan was explained in a single sentence written by a relatively obscure Prussian army officer. In *On War*, Carl von Clausewitz wrote:

> The first, the grandest, the most decisive act of judgement which the Statesman and General exercises is rightly to understand [the nature of] the War in which he engages, and not to take it for something, or wish to make of it something, which [it is not and which] it is impossible for it to be.

In a sense, this is a comment that can be applied to virtually any war, because all states at some time or another have fought the "wrong" war or have been out-thought, out-fought, and defeated with virtually no redeeming feature. The defeat of Japan in the World War II, however, deserves special attention under the terms of reference provided by Clausewitz, and for obvious reasons. The alliance that she conjured into existence against herself, the nature of the defeat across an ocean, and the final manner of that defeat most certainly were awesome, if thoroughly unintended.

The relevance of this Clausewitzian observation lies in the simple fact that Japan's failing, in terms of understanding the nature of the war that she initiated, was multi-layered. The obvious and fundamental misunderstanding related directly to two matters: the failure to understand that this war's terms of reference were not Japan's to determine, and the failure to understand the American foe. The two were of course linked; Japan saw the war that she initiated in the western Pacific and Southeast Asia in December 1941 as a limited war. To the extent that Japan ever considered defeat as an alternative to victory, she considered it in the context of a limited war. In reality, the alternative to Japan's victory in a limited war was her defeat in a total war. There was in this thought process the failure to understand that both sides would determine the nature of the war, as well as Japan's fundamental error in underestimating the enemy.

Japan did recognize the industrial superiority of the United States, although the full enormity of national disparity could never have been anticipated in 1941. She failed to acknowledge, however, the capacity for American durability in a struggle lasting a number of years, and for obvious reason: a nation with no experience of defeat and, more importantly, a nation created by and watched over by the gods, and ruled by a god could not envisage defeat. This religious dimension provided the basis for the belief in the superiority of the Japanese martial commitment – *Yamato damashii* – that was the guarantee against national defeat.

The basis of the national plan for the conduct of the Pacific War was a naval concept of operations that had been two decades in the making, though certain of its ideas could be traced to Tsushima (1905) and the Russo-Japanese War. In essence, Japan sought to conduct a defensive war by overrunning Southeast Asia and then casting around her conquests a perimeter defense on which the Americans would fight to exhaustion. They would then accept a negotiated peace that would confirm Japan's possession of Southeast Asia. This concept had taken shape in the interwar period. Its success was predicated on the concept of a "decisive battle" that was to be fought in the general area of the Carolines and Marianas, against an American fleet moving into the western Pacific from its base at Pearl Harbor in the Central Pacific. This battle would commence off the Hawaiian Islands, using submarines that would initiate the battle of attrition. To this end, the Imperial Japanese Navy, the *Nippon Teikoku Kaigun*, developed three separate types of ocean-going units: the scout submarine, that came complete with seaplanes that would find the enemy; and command-submarines, designed to direct cruiser-submarines to the battle. Cruiser-submarines could reach a surface speed of 24 knots; the IJN calculated that such speed would enable these units to outpace American formations obliged to advance into the western Pacific at economical cruising speed. From there, they could mount successive attacks, up to the limit of their torpedo capacity, during this initial "approach-to-contact" phase.

Shore-based aircraft, operating from bases in the Marshalls, Carolines, and Marianas, would complement these operations as American formations came into the western Pacific. It was as part of this effort that the Japanese developed the Betty medium bomber that, in its day, was superior in range and speed to any other medium bomber in service anywhere in the world. According to IJN calculations, each of these forms of attack, by submarines and land-based aircraft, were anticipated to inflict one-tenth losses upon the enemy. They would also prepare the way for battle to be joined, initially by fast battleship and heavy cruiser squadrons, which would sweep aside enemy screening formations, allowing light cruiser and destroyer formations to conduct successive, massed night attacks on enemy lines. With midget submarines also laid across the American path, the IJN anticipated an additional 10 percent losses. With Japanese carriers operating ahead of the battle line, intending to neutralize their opposite numbers by dive-bombing attacks, the IJN expected that, with an American fleet blinded, weakened by losses, and its cohesion compromised, battle could then be joined by the battle force.

This was to be the decisive phase of "the decisive battle," and its main action would involve the most modern battleships, i.e. the Yamato class. This class was to have numbered four units and was planned as an interim measure: with the intention of building battleships armed with 19.7-in. guns, the IJN sought to provide itself with warships individually so superior to anything that the Americans possessed that overwhelming victory was assured. These ships would be the first to join battle, and their advantage of range and weight of shell were expected to provide an immediate advantage. When the older battleships joined the action, their combined efforts would result in the annihilation of the American fleet.

This account of IJN intent, prewar intent, is provided in some detail here, in a chapter concerned with IJN strategy in the aftermath of the battles of the Coral Sea and Midway, for one reason: it was a strategy that trapped the IJN, from which it could not escape, and which in very large measure left it with no means to confront the reality of defeat. Why this was so is complicated, but its recounting is essential to any genuine understanding of Japanese overall defeat in the war at sea and specifically of the situation in which the Imperial Navy found itself between May 1942 and May 1944.

Any understanding of Japan, the IJN, and the defeat in the Pacific War necessarily has to start with a naval doctrine that can certainly trace its origins to Saneyuki Akiyama, "the seven-stage plan of attrition," and Tsushima. Despite this, in its final state Japanese naval doctrine was flawed on any number of counts, few of which related directly to the experience of the Russo-Japanese War (1904–05). The most obvious of these weaknesses related to the perimeter defense which, by definition, consisted mostly of gaps held apart by the occasional island, garrison, and air base. To compound the problem, very few of these garrisons and bases had any chance of resisting attack; most were small, and lacked sufficient numbers of aircraft and dispersal facilities to enable them to survive attack. In reality, none of these bases was ever likely to be attacked, except by formations that were overwhelmingly superior. In the event, the Americans, after the start of the drive across the Central Pacific in November 1943, were able to bring massively superior force to bear, ensuring that any objective could be isolated and overwhelmed before any Japanese naval force could intervene. This imbalance pointed up the two major weaknesses of Japanese naval intent. First, the Japanese did not have the means to establish and then maintain forces that, by virtue of their defensive deployment, were neither concentrated nor able to concentrate quickly and effectively. Second, the IJN had no assurance that it could deploy fleet formations in a timely and effective manner to the support of forward bases under attack. In essence, the inferiority of Japanese forces in bases along a perimeter defense, combined with the inferiority of the Japanese fleet relative to its American counterpart, meant that Japan's only possibility of being able to mount a successful defensive campaign rested in land-based air power and the fleet complementing one another and producing a balance of forces or perhaps even a Japanese superiority of numbers. But such intent and hope was no more than illusion, and on several counts.

The basic reality counterbalancing this illusion was that the fleet could not be guaranteed to be "permanently ready." In fact, in December 1941 Japan went to war at a time when, of all her fleet units, just one destroyer was not in service. This situation highlighted one inescapable fact: not too far down the road, the demands of routine overhaul and refits, not to mention repair, were certain to begin to inflict major reductions upon available force. Attempting to maintain forward bases, given Japan's lack of available shipping, only compounded problems. Realistically, with the exception of Truk and Rabaul, none of the bases in the central and Southwest Pacific could be equipped on the scale required to meet an enemy which (and a point easily missed by virtue of the IJN's defensive intent) would be vested with the initiative and full range of choice in terms of when, where, and in what strength it was to mount its own, successive, offensive operations.

Such weaknesses on the part of Japan as a nation, and the IJN as a service, nonetheless represent nothing more than the start-line. There were at work various other weaknesses that, in association with each other and those stated here, rendered the Japanese position flawed beyond recall. The requirements of a single chapter preclude comprehensive analysis of these weaknesses, and it is sufficient to note three to indicate the scope of the problem.

The first flaw was the wholly unrealistic expectations of submarine success during the enemy advance to contact. The IJN confronted this reality in a series of exercises in 1939 that showed that the submarines could not mount successive attacks on enemy formations. Their advantage of speed over an enemy operating at economical cruising speed was not sufficient to allow their being able to sweep wide around an enemy force and thence be able to mount a second or third attack. Submarines had but a single chance, but even after the 1940 exercises, when the rules had been rewritten and the submarines still proved unable to overhaul the surface force, the IJN remained committed to this concept. In one sense it had no real option. Having built its submarines on the basis of this tactical plan, it had no choice but to live with its previous decision; but the fact was that the IJN went to war with a defensive doctrine that it knew was at very best dubious, and at worst flawed.

The second significant flaw was that IJN doctrine was concerned with battle, and that (as described elsewhere), by some mysterious process which must have been something like transubstantiation, what began as a service battle plan became an inter-service plan of campaign and, finally, a national war plan. Leaving aside this matter, fundamental though it is to Japanese defeat, it is important to note that the "proper" concern for the IJN was battle; but that the basic requirement of Japan was to wage war. The Japanese were not alone in failing to distinguish between the perspective of nations, which wage war, and services, which fight battles. Even so, the IJN obsession with battle came at the expense of trade defense, though the Japanese weakness in this matter did extend beyond lack of IJN interest, commitment, and resources. Japan's weakness lay in the fact that national shipping needs, given a level of imports that stood at about 48 million tons in 1940, were some 10 million tons. In 1940, foreign bottoms accounted for four million of these tons. From the time that she was subject to embargo, most of this shipping was lost to Japan, and there was no way in which Japanese shipyards could make good the loss of two-fifths of the nation's carrying requirement. This weakness was compounded by the division of the remaining shipping among the two services and the civilian economy. Once the services had taken roughly half of what remained, the state's shipping requirements amounted to just three million tons to meet the demands for food, goods, and raw materials, less those ships which, for one reason or another, were not in service. In December 1941, Japan had available only about one-quarter of the shipping that she needed to meet the demands of society, the economy, and war production. There was no way that her shipyards could simultaneously build warships, build service shipping and merchantmen, repair and overhaul warships, and repair and overhaul shipping. At the very best, Japanese yards had the capacity to build warships and also to modestly increase the size of the shipping pool, but they could not build and service simultaneously. And even these logistical considerations were only the beginning of the problem. Japan went to war with just four purpose-built escorts in service, and none of these had sonar. None of the 14 members of the Type A class were within two months of being laid down, and the 32 escorts and 26 chasers of all descriptions and origins that were in service in December 1941 were totally inadequate to meet Japan's needs, even with another 30 escorts and 16 chasers under construction or planned.

It was not until summer 1941 that the IJN undertook a staff examination of the losses that might be incurred at the hands of American submarines in an unrestricted *guerre de course* – a campaign against shipping. This examination concluded that Japan could expect losses of 75,000 tons of shipping a month, or 900,000 tons in a year. This total is particularly significant because the IJN had determined elsewhere that Japanese yards could be expected to produce some

900,000 tons of shipping in a year, notwithstanding the fact that yearly shipping production over the previous decade had been about half this amount.

Third, the basic IJN plan was wholly unrealistic. Not just the submarine component, but the whole concept, constructed around the decisive battle that was to be fought, belonged to another age. The Japanese plan was perfection at the point of obsolescence, the naval equivalent of a de Dondi timepiece – a majestic clockwork of wheels-within-wheels, representing the medieval European view of the universe: ingenious and imaginative, lovingly and beautifully crafted, hopelessly unrealistic. The concept of the battle line was one that the Japanese themselves had largely discarded, while the latter part of the 1930s saw the carrier really emerge as the warship that would determine the nature and size of tactical formations. This latter process was, of course, far from complete in December 1941 and arguably was not finished until 1943. Nevertheless, for much of the 1930s, naval orthodoxy pointed in the direction of task groups with single carriers, perhaps two carriers but certainly no more, and for the very simple reason that it was generally assumed that a carrier found by the enemy was a carrier sunk. The evidence of the first year of the Pacific War suggests that this calculation had some validity, but the use of radar, and voice radio in high-performance fighters, gave carrier task groups the means to conduct defensive battles with realistic hopes of success – as long as the task group was American.

The point of relevance relating all these matters to the situation in which nation and navy found themselves, after the defeat off Midway Islands in June 1942, is obvious: in the interwar period, the IJN had equipped itself with a doctrine, and then built warships in order to win the battle that it intended to fight. The problem was that as events unfolded, the only battle it could fight was the battle it intended to win, and the battle that it was called upon to fight differed significantly from the one that had been envisaged.

The IJN was, qualitatively, the best navy in the world in the second half of 1941. The evidence for a seemingly extraordinary statement is readily apparent upon examination: consider the attack on the Italian fleet at Taranto in November 1940, which was conducted by one carrier plus aircraft. Compare this to the Japanese attack on the US Pacific Fleet at Pearl Harbor in December 1941, which was conducted by six carriers and 355 aircraft in a two-wave attack. Add to this the fact that the opening Japanese moves came at a distance of some 4,500 miles from the home islands, across nine time zones and the International Date Line. However, by 1944, the United States had attained a true global reach that overshadowed the capability of any other nation, Japan and December 1941 notwithstanding. These facts illustrate the impossible situation in which the IJN found itself after the defeat off Midway Islands in June 1942. facing battles that were not those for which it had prepared. In a way that is very elusive, in terms of quality, the IJN was perhaps the best navy in the world in the second half of 1941, but it was a one-shot navy that lacked the strength in depth and the capacity to change and reconstitute itself.

The defeat at Midway left the IJN with no option but to abandon its plans to move against the islands of Hawaii and the Southwest Pacific, the latter specifically intended to sever American lines of communication with Australia. Since such a plan was clearly no longer possible, it points up the observation that if war with the United States in the second half of 1941 really was either desirable or inevitable, then Japan's only sensible course of action should have been the *koryaku* – the conquest of Oahu – as opposed to the *kogeki* – the strike against the US Pacific Fleet. Regardless of this, the reality was that, after Midway, Japan had to try to bring as many units, particularly carriers, into service as quickly as possible, while fighting a defensive battle on the perimeter that had been cast around conquests throughout Southeast Asia and the Southwest, Central, and northern Pacific.

The results of Japan's strategy were somewhat perverse. Over the next 18 months, very few islands changed hands. The Japanese suffered a series of defeats, none of any real significance, in eastern New Guinea and in the Solomons. In May 1943, their garrison on Attu in the Aleutians was overwhelmed, which compelled the Japanese high command, recognizing the inevitable, to cut its losses. The Japanese evacuated the Japanese garrison on Kiska in July 1943 without alerting the Allies, who subjected the island to an assault landing in August. By the end of October 1943, Japanese losses amounted to very little, and the Allied forces, with the exception of submarines, remained thousands of miles, and seemingly years away, from the home islands. Two months later, the

Japanese defensive perimeter in the Central Pacific had all but collapsed, and the Japanese defensive position at Rabaul rendered irrelevant.

The element of perversity lies in the fact that this period, between June and October 1942, is dominated by one campaign – the battle fought on, over, and off Guadalcanal in the lower Solomon Islands. It was in this campaign that the Japanese suffered all but comprehensive defeat at the hands of an American enemy that actually fought and won the defensive battle that had been the cornerstone of IJN doctrine. Of course, what the Americans had done was the mirror image of Japanese intent: in August 1942 they landed on Guadalcanal, seized the Japanese base and airfield that were under construction, and then moved aircraft into the suitably named Henderson Field.[1] Thereafter the US Pacific Fleet fought four major actions – the battles of the Eastern Solomons (August 22–25), of Santa Cruz (October 26–27), and the first and second naval battles of Guadalcanal (November 12–13 and 14–15) – that resulted in the defeat of a Combined Fleet laboring under the same handicaps that it had assigned the Americans in its prewar plans. Some 50 actions were fought off and over Guadalcanal from August 1942 to February 1943 between naval and air forces of the two sides, but two crucial points decided the outcome. The American ability to get air units into Henderson Field condemned the Japanese to fight the air battle from Rabaul, with very little chance of damaged aircraft ever making it home. Over the next three months, this meant American domination of the waters that washed Guadalcanal, at least during daylight. To compound this disadvantage, the Combined Fleet performed very poorly in the Guadalcanal campaign. It was very slow to recognize the seriousness of the situation that was developing in the lower Solomons, and its reaction was a piecemeal commitment of forces that was insufficient to secure a decisive victory. It was perhaps unfortunate that the first clash off Guadalcanal, the battle off Savo Island on the night of August 8–9, resulted in a Japanese victory, which may have created misperceptions about the realities of the situation. The irony was that in this particular battle, the Japanese comprehensively outfought an Allied formation, sinking four and damaging one of the five Allied heavy cruisers (and one destroyer) committed to the action. Having done so, however, the Japanese force did not dwell upon its victory; fearing American air attack with the dawn, the Japanese broke off the battle and headed for Rabaul, making no effort against the transport and support shipping off Guadalcanal. In reality, only a balanced Japanese force could have dealt with the latter, but another two weeks were to pass before the Japanese committed carrier forces to battle. The result was a draw: the Japanese lost a light carrier, and the Americans suffered one carrier damaged.

In the aftermath of the Eastern Solomons battle (August 24), the American had one carrier – the *Saratoga* – torpedoed (August 31) and another – the *Wasp* – sunk (September 15) by submarine attack. At Santa Cruz (October 26–27), the Japanese, despite the sinking of the *Hornet*, won only a pyrrhic victory: the losses incurred by their carrier air groups precluded their being able to exploit what amounted to a very real potential advantage.

In these actions the Japanese reduced American carrier strength in the Southwest Pacific to just the *Enterprise*, which was quite extensively damaged in the Santa Cruz battle. In fact, such was the weakness of the Americans that a British carrier had to be sent to the Southwest Pacific during the first half of 1943. With the carrier formations of both sides neutralized, the Americans and Japanese each committed battle and cruiser units to the battle. The piecemeal commitment of Japanese forces, without proper close support, left their units exposed to defeat in detail in the naval battles of Guadalcanal in mid-November 1942. The loss of two battleships in two actions was a massive shock to a Japanese Navy convinced of its advantages in night action, but in truth the setbacks and losses in these actions were but one aspect of defeat. The Japanese high command was forced to admit that the formations put ashore on Guadalcanal were not capable of overrunning the American defensive positions on the island and that with losses approaching four figures, their land-based aircraft likewise could not prevail. Perhaps more seriously, the Guadalcanal campaign represented a logistical commitment at the most distant part of the front, and one that by this stage involved something like 700,000 tons of shipping, which neither Japan as a nation nor the two services could afford. Accordingly, in December 1942 the Japanese high command took the decision to abandon the Guadalcanal commitment. The Japanese evacuated the island successfully, and without interference, in the first week of February 1943.

Immediately after this event, however, the Americans moved into the Russells. The defeat in the Bismarck Sea action in the first week of March led, in effect, to the Japanese high command writing off the eastern New Guinea commitment. Thereafter very little happened in the Southwest Pacific, the main American concern being to gather forces in readiness for the offensive effort that began in November. For the Japanese, this period of relative calm seemed to vindicate their strategic intent, though the comfort that they drew from the relative stability of the front was belied by two matters. In the surface actions in 1943 the Americans, by virtue of superior radar, radio, and numbers, worsted the Japanese. In terms of qualitative dimension, the Japanese advantage at the war's start had already disappeared: the Americans had secured the upper hand as a result of their victories and defeats, and the battle experience thus gained, and technological superiority.

The second matter was something that was to worsen as the war lengthened, and this was the Japanese inability to realistically assess losses and the course of battle. Vastly inflated claims of enemy losses proved to be a feature of battle on the part of the IJN. Thus, the loss of the battleship *Hiei* in the first Guadalcanal battle in November 1942 cost the Americans five heavy and two light cruisers and eight destroyers, with another two cruisers and six destroyers damaged to some degree – which was more than the Americans had in the battle. In April 1943, in the course of a four-day offensive, Japanese naval land-based aircraft conducted an offensive over the Solomons and eastern New Guinea that reversed all the defeats of the previous nine months. In October 1944, in the prelude to the naval battle for the Philippines commonly known as Leyte Gulf, on the basis of the claims presented to him by IJN representatives, claims that included the sinking of 16 carriers and overall more than half a million tons of American warships in six days, the Emperor issued a victory decree and there were celebrations throughout Japan. There were also victory celebrations in *Rikugun* headquarters throughout the Philippines. All armed forces of all nations overstate their own effectiveness, but with the Japanese services this approached an art form that was increasingly divorced from reality.

For most of 1943, with the Americans registering only minor gains in the northern and Southwest Pacific, the main IJN attention was directed to training replacement air groups for the carrier formations, in readiness for the coming "decisive battle." Attention also focused on the creation, in November 1943, of a convoy system, an undertaking that encountered horrendous problems. Escort numbers were insufficient; radar, radio, and weaponry – in terms of the numbers and the size and rate of depth-charges – were all inadequate for the escorts that were available. Many of these deficiencies were covered with the prefabricated Types C and D escorts – these had two radar systems, three sonar sets, throwers, and as many as 120 depth-charges – these did not enter service until spring 1944 and their commitment thereafter was to a losing cause. Moreover, coordination of effort between escorts and land-based aircraft was woeful and in any event Japanese land-based aircraft were armed only with bombs and lacked the depth-charges, rockets and radars so crucial to Allied victory in the North Atlantic, and in any event these assorted matériel weaknesses went alongside a fundamental lack of proper planning. The shipping of the services and civil economy were separated, with the result that it was not unknown for civil merchantmen and service ships to sail outward together, the former empty and the latter full, and return together, with roles reversed. Perhaps even more serious was the fact that naval shipping was very largely unprotected or very poorly provided, as indeed was much of the IJA's shipping. This fact was crucial in 1944, for a reason that is seldom properly appreciated in most histories of the Pacific War. Japan's worsening shipping situation over the course of 1943–44 is generally acknowledged, but not the fact that the greater part of losses were incurred not by merchant shipping but by service shipping. Nor is sufficient attention given to the fact that the greater part of losses were incurred after November 1943, as carrier aircraft took the tide of war through the Japanese perimeter defenses. With naval shipping obliged to operate in waters increasingly dominated by American carrier aircraft and increasingly infested by American submarines deployed in support of landing operations, Japanese shipping was subjected to well-nigh crippling losses, even before their landings in the Philippines placed the Americans astride Japanese lines of communication between the home islands and the southern resources area. In the period between November 1, 1943 and June 30, 1944, in which time the Americans broke through the Japanese defensive positions in the Gilbert and Ellice Islands and the Marshalls, side-stepped Rabaul and then moved along the coast of northern New Guinea and into the Marianas, Japanese service and merchant shipping losses were the equivalent of Japanese losses prior to October 31, 1943, and this merely heralded a worsening disaster. In this eight-month period, when the equivalent of the losses of a 23-month period were concentrated into one-third of the time, the Japanese suffered such disasters as the American carrier raid on Truk which, with almost 200,000 tons of service and merchant shipping destroyed, must represent the most destructive single day in mercantile history, and this toll was primarily exacted by carrier aircraft that failed to account for a single merchantman and just six service transports prior to February 1944. In this October 1943–June 1944 phase of the war the monthly rate of Japanese losses was the equivalent of 24.63 warships of 42,031 tons and 69.25 service and merchant ships of 287,596 tons, in the next phase of the war between July 1944 and March 1945, in which time the Americans moved into the Philippines, the monthly rate of Japanese losses was the equivalent of 47.33 warships of 100,004 tons and 84.33 service and merchant ships of 308,556 tons, and the latter losses represented a very considerable part of the sizeable and ocean-going ships that were available to Japan in summer 1944. The last ships to make their way to the home islands from the south did so in March 1945, and thereafter the Japanese were finished. The various convoy routes in the south had been largely abandoned in summer 1944, and the shipping that remained in the north, on the routes to Manchuria and Korea, were beset after March 1945 by an American mining of Japanese home waters – Operation *Starvation* – to which the Japanese simply had no response.

These and other matters came together in the Philippines, with the American landings on Leyte in October 1944. The IJN realized that the loss of the Philippines – which would sever trade with the southern resources area on which Japan depended – would be tantamount to enemy landings on the home islands. By this time, however, Japanese intention had unravelled on two previous occasions. In November 1943, the IJN had attempted to put its reconstituted carrier air groups ashore at Rabaul, in an effort to counter American moves into the upper Solomons and Bismarck archipelago. These formations were simply ripped to pieces by American carriers. The Japanese, as a result, decided to abandon the fight for most of the northern coast of New Guinea and to make a stand on the line of the Marianas, Palaus, and the Vogelkop. Despite losing Aitape and Hollandia to overwhelming attack in April 1944, the American landings on Biak in May provoked an attempt to give battle that was immediately countered by the American landings on Saipan. With the Americans having overwhelmed the various air bases in the Marianas and Bonins before the Japanese carrier groups (reconstituted for a second time) could join the battle, the latter, hopelessly outnumbered, were shattered – and this time beyond recall – in the battle of the Philippine Sea. Defeat in the battle that the IJN had designated "the decisive battle" left two options available: another "decisive battle" to defend the Philippines; and the introduction of a new type of offensive operation, the *kamikaze* attack.

The Imperial Navy favored another decisive battle, seeking "a fitting place to die," "the chance to bloom as flowers of death." The Imperial Army initially sought to thwart this plan, pointing out that the fleet belonged to the nation, not the Navy, not that so minor a matter had any significance for the IJN. The IJN's position on *kamikaze* attacks was more complicated. The high command was aware that its basic strategic policy was falling apart, but failed to grasp the significance of events in battle. Between November 24, 1943, when the escort carrier *Liscome Bay* was torpedoed off the Gilberts by the submarine I-175, and October 24, 1944, when the *Princeton* was lost off the northern Philippines as a result of attack by a land-based aircraft, Japanese shells, torpedoes, and bombs failed to account for a single US Navy fleet unit, other than the Fletcher class destroyer *Brownson*, which was lost to air attack on December 26, 1943 off Cape Gloucester, New Britain. In other words, the American effort that encompassed the breaking of the outer perimeter defense in the Central Pacific; the carrier forays into the western Pacific that resulted in the shipping massacres at Truk (February 17–18) and Koror (March 30–31); the landings at Hollandia and Aitape which took the tide of war from one end of New Guinea to the other in two months, and which finally led to overwhelming victory in the Philippine Sea (June 19–20); and the subsequent rampage throughout the Philippines cost the United States just one destroyer, plus the destroyer escort *Shelton*, which was sunk off Morotai on October 3 by the submarine Ro. 41. The Japanese recourse to *kamikaze* attack was not a case, as so often stated, of suicide attack representing the most effective means of resistance. It was in fact the only means of resistance available – and it was wholly inadequate to Japan's needs.

There are several reasons for this. First, by October 1944 the Americans had acquired such superiority of numbers – in the air, in warship numbers, and in assault and support shipping – that no amount of Japanese success was ever going to turn the tide. Second, American recasting of tactical formations, both in warships and air groups, combined with massively increased firepower of warships, increased American ability to out-fight the *kamikaze*. The reconstitution of air groups with very few strike aircraft (and in the case of one fleet carrier, a group with only fighters) was extremely important in this process. There was no overall reduction of offensive capability, because of the unprecedented number of carriers arriving on station. The cost in terms of ships lost, written off, or forced back to the yards was high, but ultimately the United States, and her allies, had the means to make good their losses. Third, and perhaps most intangible but crucial: Allied sailors who fought in order to live were more than a match for Japanese airmen who died in order to fight. Such were the realities of the naval war in the Pacific.

# Chapter 11

# Across the Reef

## Amphibious warfare in the Pacific

*Colonel Joseph H. Alexander, USMC (ret.)*

The Allied invasion of the southern Solomons on August 7, 1942, was a major turning point in the Pacific War. Rear Admiral Kelly Turner executed a primary amphibious landing on Guadalcanal and secondary landings 20 miles north across Sealark Channel (soon nicknamed "Ironbottom Sound") at Tulagi and the twin islands of Gavutu–Tanambogo. The small task force surprised the Japanese troops, allowing unopposed landings on Guadalcanal and Tulagi, but Turner lacked sufficient boats to carry out all three operations simultaneously. Turner had planned to retrieve the boats used in the initial assaults to strike Gavutu, then Tanambogo. Unfortunately, the Gavutu landing force had to wait seven hours until the boats returned. Given this reprieve, the Japanese defenders on the twin islands took to their caves, aimed their machine guns at the gap in the barrier reef, and waited.

Every aspect of the Gavutu landing was ineffective. The preliminary bombardment consisted of four minutes of naval shelling and ten minutes of dive-bombing strikes, both fruitless against the cave-sheltered Japanese. The landing boats, battling a punishing headwind, took an hour to reach the island. The reef channeled the boats into the preregistered fire of Japanese machine guns. The US Marine battalion commander fell in the opening fusillade. Other Marines struggled ashore and attempted to kill the machine gunners with rifles and grenades. More suitable weapons for cave fighting, such as demolitions and flamethrowers, were not available. Urgent requests for close air support by carrier-based aircraft resulted in the Marines twice being strafed by "friendly" planes.

Seeking to flank Japanese strong points on Gavutu, the senior US commander ordered a night attack on nearby Tanambogo by a rifle company embarked in seven landing boats. Three boats became lost in the darkness. The others were fatally illuminated in their final approach when a US destroyer's shells ignited a fuel dump. Japanese gunners on both islands opened a disciplined crossfire. The surviving Marines straggled back to Gavutu throughout the night. The next day, reinforced and more generously supported by naval gunfire and aircraft, the Marines swept across both islands, but it was an unexpectedly costly victory.

These initial landings in the southern Solomons illustrate both the promise and the hazard of amphibious warfare. Strategic surprise and high mobility rewarded the Allies with unopposed possession of Guadalcanal and its invaluable airstrip, yet the assault on Gavutu-Tanambogo revealed how much the Americans still had to learn about conducting an opposed amphibious landing.

The experiences of Gavutu-Tanambogo dismayed Major-General Alexander A. Vandegrift, commanding the 1st Marine Division, who concluded that "landings should not be attempted in the face of organized resistance if, by any combination of march or maneuver, it is possible to land unopposed and undetected."[1]

Vandegrift's warning remained relevant in subsequent amphibious campaigns in the Solomons, but the time came when neither march nor maneuver could avoid an opposed amphibious assault against Japan's island outposts in the Central and Western Pacific. These fortified bastions – in essence, the "stepping stones" leading from Pearl Harbor to Japan – required the United States to gather the means and the will to attack the strong points directly. Subtlety yielded to raw power. Colonel Saburo Hayashi, Imperial Japanese Army, described how the United States changed its operational mode. "The tactics of the Americans called for hurling enormous firepower against the enemy and then making forced landings frontally," he said after the war. "So-called 'storm landings' were common American practice."[2]

The struggle for victory in the Pacific required an amphibious war of unprecedented proportions. The harsh lessons of Gavutu-Tanambogo would eventually lead to the complex but well-coordinated assaults on Luzon, Iwo Jima, and Okinawa. In the end, the Allies would be poised at the doorstep of Japan, prepared to execute the most enormous forcible landing in history.

# THE ESSENCE OF AMPHIBIOUS OPERATIONS

An amphibious operation is an attack launched from the sea by naval and landing forces embarked in ships or craft involving a landing on a hostile or potentially hostile shore.[3]

Amphibious operations are not an end in themselves. Despite their scale and drama, neither the Normandy nor Okinawa landings ended the war in their respective theaters. Instead, such operations serve as a springboard for further combat operations, open a new front, or fix enemy forces in place, often by the forward presence of an amphibious fleet-in-being.

Amphibious assaults are widely regarded as the most difficult military operations to execute. The crucial requirement is for a rapid, uninterrupted buildup of combat power ashore, from an initial zero capability to full striking power. In the opposed landings of the Pacific War, the first man to splash ashore faced nearly impossible odds of survival. The second man fared slightly better, as did the tenth and the thousandth, incrementally. Speed of execution was critical. The surviving troops in the assault waves needed immediate reinforcement by infantry, tank, and field artillery units. Otherwise, the momentum of the assault became lost, the attack bogged down, and the congested beachheads invited disastrous counterattacks.

Chaos characterized even the best-planned beachheads in the Pacific War. Even in peacetime maneuvers, amphibious commanders found it extremely difficult to move large numbers of heavily laden troops from their transport ships, down the scramble nets into the landing craft bobbing alongside, and direct them through several miles of sea swells and plunging surf to the right beach, at the right time, and in the right order.

The ship-to-shore movement is inherently hazardous. Men drown in the surf, are squashed by shifting cargo, or get run over by combat vehicles. Enemy fire complicates an already difficult process. Landing craft are blown up or capsize in the surf. Troops struggle ashore without leaders, weapons, or ammunition. Units are scrambled. Instead of an orderly tactical displacement, the beachhead often resembles a shipwreck.

The inherent chaos and initial vulnerability of the amphibious assault demand exceptional teamwork and unity of command. The commanders of the amphibious task force and the landing force –

typically an admiral and a general, both with strong-willed personalities and competing priorities – must adhere to a strict sequence of responsibilities. Only one can exercise overall command at a time. Historically, the admiral retains command until the landing force is fully established ashore, at which time, as mutually agreed, the Marine or Army general assumes command of the battle beyond the beachhead.

The keys to success in the increasingly complex amphibious assaults of the Pacific War were joint teamwork, detailed planning, creative adaptability to chaotic conditions – and violent execution.

## ROOTS OF AMPHIBIOUS WARFARE

Ancient warriors often used amphibious operations. The Greek general Demosthenes landed a force of Athenians on the Spartan island of Pylos during the Peloponnesian Wars. In a striking application of a strategic offensive combined with a tactical defensive, the Athenians withstood waves of Spartan counter-landing efforts and came as close to winning the long war as they ever would. In 55 BC, Julius Caesar fought his way ashore near present-day Kent at the head of his Tenth Roman Legion, against well-armed British cavalry and spearmen. Naval and field commanders of the 18th and 19th centuries regarded opposed landings from the sea as dangerous but achievable missions.

The advent of machine guns, airplanes, mines, and submarines during the Industrial Revolution seemed to render amphibious landings too costly. The slaughter of the British, Australian, and New Zealand landing forces in the Gallipoli campaign of 1915 confirmed these suspicions. "A landing on a foreign coast in face of hostile troops has always been one of the most difficult operations of war," wrote the British military analyst Captain B. H. Liddell Hart. "It has now become much more difficult, indeed almost impossible, because of the vulnerable target which a convoy of transports offers to the defenders' air force. Even more vulnerable is the process of disembarkation in open boats."[4]

In the 1930s, the US Marines began to challenge the widespread belief that modern weaponry had rendered amphibious operations obsolete. The Marines, seeking a more distinctive mission within the Department of the Navy, analyzed the Gallipoli landings and concluded that the Allies may well have succeeded had they followed certain principles of amphibious warfare, among them unity of command;

seizing control of the sea and air around the objective; coordination of naval gunfire, aviation, counter-mine and antisubmarine operations; development of seaworthy, self-retracting landing craft; systematic delivery of high-priority cargo as requested by the landing force; and the concentration of combat power at the point of attack.

The Marines converted the principles derived from Gallipoli into a radical new doctrine of offensive amphibious warfare, first published in 1935 under the title *Tentative Manual for Landing Operations*. Although doubtful at first, the US Navy and Army soon adopted the doctrine as their standard operating procedure. As unprepared as America's armed forces were for global war in 1941, they at least entered World War II with an operational manual that would guide them, with remarkably few changes, throughout the greatest amphibious campaigns ever fought.

The new doctrine still lacked a full-scale trial by fire, which did not occur until the battle of Tarawa in late 1943. Only by then had the United States established operational and industrial supremacy in the Pacific, producing sufficient carriers, gunfire support ships, transports, specialized amphibious ships, and ramped landing craft to warrant such a risky undertaking.

# JAPANESE AMPHIBIOUS DEVELOPMENTS

Japanese strategic planners anticipated an amphibious war in the Pacific as early as the 1920s. Building on their experience in landing against German and Russian outposts in the Pacific during World War I, the Japanese developed armored landing barges and produced a joint Army-Navy manual, *Outline of Amphibious Operations*, well ahead of the United States or Great Britain. When Japan invaded China in the 1930s, American military observers reported the use of troop transports and ramped, shallow-draft landing craft by Japanese amphibious forces.

The Japanese followed their attack on Pearl Harbor on December 7, 1941 with a series of amphibious campaigns throughout the Pacific. With few setbacks, the Imperial Japanese Army and Navy used amphibious operations to accelerate the conquest of Guam, Hong Kong, Wake, the Gilberts, Thailand, Malaya, Singapore, the Philippines, the Dutch East Indies, northern New Guinea, and the Solomons. Their sea, air, and landing forces seemed invincible.

Yet the Japanese lacked the shipping to sustain a truly large amphibious force. They conducted most of their landings at night, typically along an undefended coast and limited in scale to a single battalion or regiment. Their landings were rarely opposed. The initial Japanese assault on Wake Island, in December 1942, met stout opposition and utterly failed. A second assault – larger and more powerfully supported by naval gunfire and aircraft – succeeded. Similarly, US and Filipino forces defending southern Luzon in early 1942 rebuffed a four-pronged Japanese amphibious assault, driving the invaders back into the sea. Imperial General Headquarters learned from these mistakes. Three months later, a Japanese battalion executed a masterful night landing on Corregidor Island that prompted the surrender of the besieged Allied garrison.

The Imperial Japanese Navy employed special naval landing forces, designated *rikusentai*, to spearhead amphibious assaults and establish base defenses ashore in the South Pacific. *Rikusentai* were sailors trained in infantry tactics and weapons by the Army, and they numbered 50,000 at the height of Japan's rapid conquests of 1941–42. When Japan yielded the strategic initiative to the Allies following Midway and Guadalcanal, the *rikusentai* became defensive specialists, notably at Tarawa and the Dragon's Peninsula of New Georgia.

## US AMPHIBIOUS DEVELOPMENTS

The United States essentially fought two wars in the Pacific. One occurred between December 1941 and November 1943; the second began with the battle of Tarawa in late November 1943 and continued through the end of the war in August 1945. Neither bore much resemblance to the other.

The first phase was a desperate, largely defensive war fought with inadequate resources against frequently superior Japanese forces and technology. Conservative holding actions, raids, and spoiling attacks were common. Such offensive campaigns as could be launched were risky affairs at best. This was the case at Guadalcanal and Bougainville, where Marines and Army soldiers executed surprise landings to capture beachheads and then dug in to defend against swarming counterattacks by Japanese land, sea, and air forces.

The first phase also coincided with the Allied strategic decision to accord the European theater top priority in troops, ships, aircraft, and tanks. It took America nearly two years to convert its industry to a full wartime basis. The nation's shipyards and ordnance plants could not produce sufficient matériel to equip simultaneous amphibious campaigns in both theaters until late 1943.

The second phase of the US war in the Pacific began with Operation *Galvanic*, the campaign to recapture Tarawa and the other British Gilbert Islands, in late November 1943. In contrast with the typically "bare-bones" Bougainville landing just three weeks earlier, the Tarawa task force featured new Essex class fleet carriers, high-speed battleships, tracked amphibian assault vehicles, and improved naval shore bombardment firepower. Each enhancement proved essential. As it was, the 2d Marine Division paid an exorbitant price to seize Tarawa. Such an undertaking would have been impossible earlier in the war.

The Allies used amphibious operations with increasing confidence and effectiveness in both major theaters in World War II. In Europe, the Allied landings at Casablanca, Sicily, Salerno, and Anzio set the stage for the massive "D-Day" assault on the Normandy coast of France on June 6, 1944, the largest amphibious operation of the war.

Commanders in Europe waged amphibious warfare differently than their counterparts in the Pacific. The long coastlines of North Africa, Italy, and France offered more opportunities for surprise landings, placing a premium on deception operations and speed of execution. Night landings were common in the European theater, and preliminary naval gunfire was limited in order to maximize the element of surprise. The fact that European coastal objectives typically included towns and cities also ruled out extensive naval bombardment. Open terrain inland from the beaches and a relatively short range from shore-based air bases enabled European theater commanders to employ night drops of paratroop and glider units to augment the amphibious landings.[5] The absence of offshore coral reefs meant Higgins boats could deliver assault troops directly on to European beaches with little need for tracked amphibian vehicles.

By contrast, the great expanses and small atolls of the Pacific required different amphibious assault tactics. While the element of surprise was critical in the first phase of the Pacific War, it gradually became secondary to the need for a methodical preliminary bombardment by ships and carrier-based aircraft against the fortified islands of the Central

Pacific. Similarly, Pacific commanders rarely conducted night landings, needing daylight to observe and adjust their preliminary shelling and conduct thorough minesweeping operations. The prevalence of coral reefs made it vital to use tracked amphibian vehicles in the assault waves. Dense jungles and steep terrain among the small Pacific islands provided few opportunities to use airborne troops in the assault.

Another significant difference between the amphibious battles of the European and Pacific theaters involved the nature of the enemies. While the Germans fought ferociously and employed greater firepower, they would eventually retreat or surrender to the Allied assaults. Not so the Japanese. In the amphibious battles for the Central Pacific, Japanese soldiers and sailors, bound by fealty to their emperor and imbued with the code of *Bushido* (essentially, "The Way of the Warrior"), either fought to the last man or committed ritualistic suicide. In fact, deliberate suicide tactics – *kamikaze* aircraft, "human bullet" antitank troops, "human torpedo" anti-ship sailors – appeared more frequently the closer the Allies advanced to the Japanese homeland. Each amphibious assault became a battle of extermination. In this close-quarter, point-blank fighting, the most effective infantry weapons of the US Marines became portable flamethrowers, submachine guns, and Ka-Bar fighting knives. The 1st Marine Division, for example, hurled 16,000 hand grenades (typical range: 20 yards) in its six-week effort to wrest Peleliu from diehard Japanese defenders.

## AMPHIBIOUS CHALLENGES

Allied amphibious commanders had to solve six daunting operational and logistical problems in the Pacific, each exacerbated by the theater's distinctive hydrography and Japan's tenacious defenders.

1. How to collect accurate intelligence on the target island's hydrography and defenses.
2. How best to quarantine the island against Japanese counterattacks.
3. Whether to seek surprise or conduct advance force operations, such as beach reconnaissance, underwater demolition, minesweeping, and extended preliminary naval bombardment.
4. How to land assault troops across a coral reef.
5. How to land tanks early on D-Day.

6. How best to provide logistic support to the landing force and avoid beach congestion.

Collecting amphibious intelligence remained challenging throughout the war. Available navigation charts for the Gilberts, for example, dated from the Wilkes expedition a century earlier. Human intelligence sources – especially the network of Allied "coast watchers" operating in places like Guadalcanal and New Georgia – were invaluable assets once ashore, but often difficult to contact in advance. Expatriate traders and loyal natives were helpful in the Gilberts and Guam, but the Japanese complicated matters by evicting the entire native populations from Betio, Peleliu, and Iwo Jima in advance.

Beach photographs taken from the periscopes of submarines rarely helped. Stealthy swimmers represented a critical breakthrough. Navy Underwater Demolition Teams (UDT) and Marine amphibious reconnaissance units appeared in 1944 and provided superb intelligence at Tinian, Iwo Jima, and Okinawa. Aerial photographs were extremely helpful at barren Tarawa, but virtually useless at jungle-shrouded Peleliu.

Protecting the amphibious task force and the beachhead from Japanese counterattacks was of paramount concern to the Allies. There is no more inviting target in naval warfare than a cluster of thin-skinned auxiliary ships loaded with troops and volatile fuel and ammo, all anchored around a new beachhead. While Allied amphibious forces were never at greater risk than during the battle of Savo Island on the second night of the Guadalcanal landing, the counterattack threat did not subside until the Japanese surrender. Even after the Allied defeat of enemy naval counter-thrusts at the battles of the Philippine Sea and Leyte Gulf, the Japanese still managed to severely threaten the US Fifth Fleet at Okinawa with massed suicide *kamikaze* attacks and a sacrificial sortie by the *Yamato*, the world's largest battleship.

The threat of Japanese fleet and aerial counterattacks shaped the nature of every Allied landing in the first half of the war. By Tarawa, however, Admiral Chester Nimitz had received a sufficient number of new warships to create a fast carrier task force, a striking fleet strong enough to attack enemy airfields and naval anchorages in the heart of Japanese territory. This operational initiative enabled Nimitz to assign the old, slower, Pearl Harbor-vintage battleships and small escort carriers in direct support of the amphibious task force. The dual concept worked handsomely at the Philippine Sea, Iwo Jima, and Okinawa, but less well at Leyte Gulf when Japanese deception tactics lured Admiral William "Bull" Halsey's Third Fleet far away from the vulnerable beachhead.

Advance Force operations were an unaffordable luxury where surprise was the overriding concern. Operational surprise was critical to the success of the early amphibious assaults in the Solomons and valuable for the landings at Tarawa, Kwajalein, Eniwetok, Hollandia, and Saipan. As Admiral Kichisaburo Nomura acknowledged to his interrogators after the war, "Everywhere you attacked before the defense was ready. You came more quickly than we expected."[6] Yet after seizing the Marianas, the United States forfeited tactical surprise in the Western Pacific in favor of prolonged Advance Force operations against the more heavily defended bastions of Peleliu, Iwo Jima, and Okinawa.

The most controversial element of Advance Force operations remained the extent of preliminary naval bombardment. Three hours of concentrated bombardment before H-Hour at Tarawa, which Navy commanders promised would "obliterate" the small island and its defenses, proved totally inadequate. The duration and effectiveness of preliminary shelling improved in subsequent operations, but the Marines always wanted more – except at Guam, when they benefited from 13 days of naval pounding by Rear Admiral Richard L. "Close-In" Conolly. Guam remained a rare exception. When Major-General Roy S. Geiger, commanding the III Amphibious Corps, left Guam for the staging base for the upcoming Peleliu assault, he was warned by his new Navy counterpart not to expect another Guam, declaring, "I don't have the ships and we don't have the ammo."[7] The assault on Peleliu suffered accordingly.

The most dramatic example of pre-H-Hour bombardment occurred at Iwo Jima, where the ships delivered a "rolling box" barrage just ahead of the assault waves, quite similar to the assault fires developed in the trench fighting of World War I.

The coral reefs of the Central Pacific mandated the use of tracked amphibian vehicles in lieu of Higgins boats as the primary ship-to-shore mobility for assault troops. The amphibian tractors had several names – "Alligators," "amtracs," or, officially, Landing Vehicles, Tracked (LVTs). Marine-owned and operated, the LVTs were capable of launching from amphibious ships at sea, traversing reefs and plunging surf, and negotiating marginal terrain inland. Initially assigned a logistic support role, LVTs were upgraded to lead the amphibious assault over Tarawa's fringing reef in 1943. Before the campaign, the 2d Marine Division hastily doubled the vehicle's machine guns, bolted armor plate to the driver's compartment, and installed grappling hooks to clear barbed wire obstacles. The gamble worked at Tarawa, where 90 percent of the modified vehicles survived the long run to the beach under fire to deliver 1,500 assault troops ashore. The Marines lacked sufficient LVTs to land the balance of the assault force, however, and the campaign nearly foundered on this shortfall.

Learning from Tarawa, Army and Marine units in the Pacific quickly acquired substantial numbers of LVTs, including improved troop-carrying versions equipped with stern ramps and new "armored" versions mounting a gyro-stabilized 75mm howitzer mounted in a center-line turret, designed to lead the first assault wave ashore by fire from the sea. The assault landings on Iwo Jima and Okinawa featured more than a thousand such amphibian vehicles.

The Alligators solved the problem of traversing reefs and beach obstacles to land infantry, but the imperative for rapid build-up of combat power ashore demanded the early landing of tanks to break out of the beachhead. Alligators, requiring positive buoyancy, lacked sufficient armor to serve as tanks; nor were they large enough to carry a tank.

Tanks provided the landing force with mobility, firepower, and shock action. US forces in the Pacific War favored the Sherman M4 medium tank with its 75mm gun and tough durability. Yet the Sherman's 34-ton weight complicated its embarkation, offloading, and landing. As late as Bougainville, the amphibious task force lacked the means for timely delivery of the 3d Marine Division's new Shermans, requiring the landing force to substitute Stuart M2 light tanks (whose small 37mm gun caused the infantry to nickname them "Tinker Toy Tanks").

The early method of delivering tanks was tedious and dangerous. Transports carried the tanks to the objective area chained to their open decks. Once anchored at the objective, the transports lifted each tank by swinging boom over the side and into a medium landing craft (LCM), an extremely tight fit and a decidedly hazardous operation for the boat crew. Each transfer took at least 15 minutes, a cycle easily doubled under conditions of enemy fire, rough seas, or pre-dawn darkness. With speed of attack so critical for success on D-Day, the inordinately slow process of unloading tanks from transports remained unsatisfactory. Until Tarawa, the only alternative was to leave the Shermans behind.

The technological breakthrough came at Tarawa. On D-Day, the US Navy unveiled its first dock landing ship, the LSD, an amphibious ship of British design with a stern gate and a floodable well deck. The revolutionary ship could ballast down at sea, lower its gate, and flood its well deck to float 14 LCMs, each preloaded with a Sherman tank. In this fashion, USS *Ashland* (LSD 1) launched its tanks in a matter of minutes at Tarawa, a quantum improvement. When the reef blocked the LCMs, the coxswains simply lowered their ramps onto the exposed coral, allowing each Sherman to trundle safely into the shallow waters of the lagoon.

Yet Tarawa's hellish lagoon revealed an unexpected hazard of its own. The tanks had arrived in the Pacific without their auxiliary fording kits, limiting their operating depth to three feet. Earlier Allied air raids had left the lagoon pocked with underwater shell holes, many ten feet deep and hidden by the turbid waters. When the tankers put men afoot in the lagoon to guide the vehicles clear of the craters, the Japanese shot them down. As a result, five of the 14 Shermans foundered in the unseen holes, drowning the crews and disabling the vehicles.

The Marines learned from this painful lesson. At Peleliu, the 1st Marine Division landed its Sherman tanks 19 minutes after H-Hour, a record for the war, by leading each column ashore behind an armored LVT. As long as the LVT clanked shoreward on its tracks in shallow water the tanks followed closely; if the lead amphibian suddenly floated, the tank crews knew to detour instantly to avoid the unseen crater.

For the 1945 Okinawa campaign, Pacific commanders borrowed a page from their European Theater counterparts at Normandy by welding flotation devices onto their Shermans. The assault force launched these modified tanks from landing ships well out to sea, dispatching them shoreward on their own power. Several tanks sank; others, launched too far from the beach, took five hours to arrive.

Sustainable logistic support was the most difficult of all ship-to-shore assault problems to solve. Everything required for rapid build-up of combat power and mobility had to be phased ashore with excruciating forethought. If combat support vehicles and matériel came ashore too soon, they clogged the beachhead, creating greater chaos. If the support waves arrived too late, the battle could be lost.

The Marines learned from their study of Gallipoli the value of "combat loading" amphibious ships. Combat loading ignores efficient use of cargo space in order to more fully support the landing plan and the scheme of maneuver ashore. What is likely to be needed first is loaded last, thus becoming the initial items accessible for debarkation at the objective.

Much of the chaos experienced during the early amphibious landings of the Pacific War resulted from hasty, indiscriminate offloading of the ships. Under the very real threat of Japanese fleet and aerial counterattacks, Navy commanders ordered their ships emptied in a matter of hours to expedite their departure from the vulnerable anchorage. The slap-dash offload left towering stacks of disparate supplies scattered along the beaches for days after the landing. Japanese aviators at Guadalcanal, Rendova, and Hollandia destroyed enormous stockpiles of Allied matériel left too long in the open.

Even at Tarawa, Admiral Nimitz's concern for a Japanese counterattack caused him to order his fleet commander to "get the hell in and get the hell out."[8] The close-quarters violence that characterized the 76-hour battle for Tarawa prevented boats from landing anywhere but the head of a pier. Congestion reigned. At one point, the senior Marine ashore had no way of telling which of the 300 boats milling about offshore contained the supplies he most critically needed. Nor could he use the boats to deploy one of his battalions to assault an enemy-held island nearby.

This debacle produced yet another valuable lesson learned from Tarawa. Thereafter the Navy agreed to offload only those supplies requested by the Marines ashore. The tactical situation on the beach would set the pace of offloading, not the perceived urgency to empty all ships as soon as possible. The Marines also agreed to make greater use of "floating dumps," large landing craft preloaded with such combat essentials as blood plasma, sand bags, flamethrower refills, fresh water, or radio batteries, that would circle "on call" near the line of departure, to shorten the delivery time.

Meanwhile, the Navy attacked the age-old problem of beachfront congestion by developing special Beach Master teams that would land with the assault waves and immediately take charge of the beachhead, directing boat traffic, managing unloading sites, establishing supply dumps, and evacuating the wounded. Said Lieutenant Edward J. Hagan, assistant surgeon for the 7th Marines at Peleliu, "The bravest men were the Navy Beach Masters, out there without cover, trying to create order out of chaos."[9]

Solving these special problems enabled the Allies to enhance the effectiveness of their seaborne assaults. By 1945, the 30th anniversary of Gallipoli, Allied task forces had developed the forces and firepower to land 68,000 troops on the first day at Lingayen Bay, 30,000 the first day of Iwo Jima, and 60,000 at Okinawa, all within a matter of 10 weeks.

Tarawa provided the operational and doctrinal watershed. Two months after that bloody battle, the US Fifth Fleet steamrollered its way through the Marshall Islands equipped with improved LVTs, underwater demolition teams and Marine amphibious reconnaissance units, command-configured amphibious force flagships, waterproof tactical radios, and greatly improved naval gunfire and carrier air support. Tarawa also validated the basic doctrine of assaulting a fortified beach. If it worked at Tarawa, despite the adverse tactical and hydrographic conditions, it would work at Normandy, or Iwo Jima.

## COLLISION COURSE

By contrast, no innovative defensive tactics seemed to work for long for the Japanese. In the Solomons and New Guinea, General Douglas MacArthur, commanding the Southwest Pacific Theater, bypassed the Japanese strongholds of Rabaul, Kavieng, and Kolombangara, always landing where defenses were thinnest or non-existent. MacArthur's masterful use of deception tactics in the Philippines consistently misled the enemy.

In the Central Pacific, the Japanese learned to expect Allied assaults on those islands possessing superior airfields or anchorages. Alerted by the early raid on Makin in the Gilberts, the Japanese knew that Tarawa Atoll, with its bomber strip on Betio Island, would be a logical target. They fortified the small island for 15 months, creating a network of coast defense guns, underwater obstacles, and some 500 pillboxes that, yard for yard, represented the most heavily defended shoreline in the Pacific. Betio fell in 76 bloody hours.

In the Gilberts, Marshalls, and Marianas, the Japanese followed the same doctrine of defending at the water's edge. But the increasing violence of the Allied shelling and the velocity provided by infantry-mounted LVTs crossing the reef regardless of tidal conditions led to convincing victories at Tarawa, Kwajalein, Eniwetok, Saipan, Tinian, and Guam. The loss of the Marianas motivated Imperial General Headquarters to publish an urgently revised doctrine for island defense. First manifested at Peleliu, the new defensive doctrine ordered island commanders to withdraw from the water's edge (leaving small forces to disrupt the landing) and, instead, concentrate the main defensive positions in underground positions inland, seeking to delay and bleed the attacking Allies. The objective was to make each assault so costly in time and blood that the Allies would seek an armistice short of invading the Japanese home islands.

The new tactics indeed extended the time required for the Allies to attain victory – 70 days at Peleliu, 36 at Iwo Jima, 82 at Okinawa – and the cost in killed and wounded for each island soared appallingly. In time, American forces changed their own assault tactics to overcome the enemy's ridge-and-cave defenses by using flame-throwing tanks, armored bulldozers, self-propelled 105mm "siege guns," enhanced naval gunfire and close air support, and special assault teams of infantry and combat engineers to overwhelm and destroy each position. The amphibious battles of 1945 represented war at its most brutal. It was fortunate that no civilians remained on Peleliu and Iwo Jima, but that was not the case in the Philippines or on Okinawa, resulting in grievous collateral losses and widespread devastation.

By the summer of 1945 the Allies were poised to launch Operation *Olympic*, the amphibious assault of the Japanese island of Kyushu by the 600,000-man US Sixth Army, supported by both the Third and Fifth Fleets. D–Day was scheduled for November 1, 1945, and *Olympic* would have been the largest amphibious assault of all time. The soldiers and Marines would have faced an equal number of Japanese troops, and the battle would have raged in the midst of a massive civilian population. Calculations of the potential casualties on both sides in the invasion influenced President Harry S. Truman's decision to drop atomic bombs on Hiroshima and Nagasaki. With Japan's unconditional surrender, the Allies cancelled Operation *Olympic* and the even larger Operation *Coronet*, scheduled to land 25 Allied divisions on the Tokyo plain on March 1, 1946.

As it turned out, the Allied landing in Tokyo Bay was anticlimactic. The Third Fleet launched a joint force of US Marines and sailors, Royal Marines, and Royal Navy seamen who landed unopposed at Yokosuka Naval Base, raised their flags, and set to work rescuing Allied prisoners of war. It was a bloodless yet fitting end to the far-ranging amphibious war in the Pacific.

"The outstanding achievement of this war in the field of joint undertakings," remarked Fleet Admiral Ernest J. King, USN, Commander-in-Chief, US Fleet and Chief of Naval Operations, "was the perfection of amphibious operations, the most difficult of all operations in modern warfare."[10]

# Chapter 12

# The Island Experience
## The battle for Okinawa:
## April 1–June 21, 1945

*Major Bruce Gudmundsson (ret.)*

At the start of 1945, Japan was in a difficult position. Her most powerful warships had been sunk. Her best pilots had been shot down. The fortified islands that formed her first line of defense against the United States had been lost. As a result, her home waters were dominated by American submarines, her communications with the rest of the Japanese Empire were all but cut off, her cities were subject to regular aerial bombardment and her civilian population was on the verge of starvation. To make matters worse, the Americans had returned to the Philippines and the British were on the offensive in Burma.

Difficult as it was, the situation of the Japanese Empire was far from hopeless. The Japanese Imperial Army was still intact. Indeed, that army was not only the undisputed master of Korea and Indo-China, but was still winning significant victories against the Chinese. The nations of the anti-Japanese alliance, moreover, were beginning to tire of the high price of victory. If that price could be raised, they might be willing to negotiate a tolerable end to hostilities. Put more bluntly, Japanese success depended upon the killing of large numbers of American servicemen, for the United States was both the initiator of the demand for unconditional surrender and its chief advocate.

There were few places where the Japanese could fight the sort of battle needed to implement their strategy of attrition. The Philippines provided the attacking Americans with too much room for maneuver. Formosa was too easy to bypass, as were most of the other islands that were still in Japanese hands. Indeed, the only places where the Japanese had the wherewithal to fight a long and bloody battle were the main islands of metropolitan Japan and the substantially smaller island of

Okinawa – the biggest island of the Ryukyu chain. Of these, the one closest to the American-held islands in the Central Pacific – and thus the most likely choice for an American landing – was Okinawa.

The peculiar size, shape and location of Okinawa made it the ideal place for the kind of battle the Japanese needed to fight if their strategy of attrition was to succeed. At 485 square miles, Okinawa was big enough to attract a sizeable American force, yet small enough to prevent the Americans from making full use of their numerical superiority. Because it was a jumble of long, thin peninsulae, Okinawa would severely limit the ability of the Americans to engage in the kind of rapid operational maneuver that was serving them so well in the Philippines. At the same time, the proximity of Okinawa to the island of Kyushu – home to a large number of *kamikaze* squadrons – would make it possible for the suicide planes to play their part in the campaign of attrition.

The advantages of size, shape, and location were greatly enhanced by the character of the Okinawan terrain. The seemingly random interaction of hills and ridgelines, rivers and ravines, fields and villages, small jungles and substantial towns broke the island into a large number of small compartments. Each of these compartments was a one-of-a-kind combination of the various components that made up the Okinawan landscape. Thus, rather than providing the combatants with a small number of large battlefields, Okinawa presented them with hundreds of tiny battlefields, each of which demanded that the tactics of both the attacker and defender be custom-tailored to its peculiarities. At the very least, this terrain would provide the Japanese defenders with a sanctuary that could not be taken from them without a long and bloody struggle.

The most optimistic of the Japanese schemes for killing Americans on Okinawa depended heavily on the *kamikaze*. These called for the Japanese ground troops on the island to allow the largest possible number of Americans to land. Once the Americans were firmly ashore, *kamikaze* planes and suicide boats would attack Allied ships in the waters around Okinawa, destroying as many as possible and driving off the rest. With no fighters overhead, no fighter-bombers on call from nearby carriers, and no gunfire coming from ships off the coast, the Americans' ground troops on Okinawa would be deprived of the weapons the Japanese feared most. They would also be stranded – deprived of supplies, reinforcements, and hope. Once the American landing force had been suitably weakened, 100,000 or more Japanese fighting men on the island would then emerge from their sanctuary and, in a rapid series of bold counterattacks, completely annihilate the invaders.

More realistic proposals also put considerable faith in the ability of the *kamikaze* to inflict damage on Allied ships. The officers who put these plans together, however, were under no illusion about the outcome of the battle. They knew that, no matter what the Japanese did, the Americans would eventually triumph on Okinawa. Their only hope was that the American victory would be a Pyrrhic one – that it would be so costly in American lives that the United States would become extremely reluctant to invade any of the larger home islands. In order to maximize the American losses, the advocates for these less optimistic plans intended to make their stand in the southern third of the island – the home of the vast majority of the residents of Okinawa and the place where the compartmentalization of terrain was most pronounced. Centered on the ancient royal capital of Shuri, this area would become the scene of hundreds of small-scale, close-quarter battles – battles in which the big shells fired by American warships and the bombs dropped by American planes would have relatively little impact.

To enhance their ability to fight in the compartmentalized terrain of Okinawa, the most favored of the Japanese units on that island – the regular army units that were expected to do the bulk of the fighting – were richly supplied with close-range heavy weapons. Antitank companies generally had an official allowance of four 47mm guns; on Okinawa, such units were given six, seven, or eight of these high-velocity weapons. Other weapons were also provided in quantities greater than those called for in standard tables of equipment. Infantry squads, for example, normally went to war with a single light machine gun. On Okinawa, they had two or three light machine guns, as well as one or two of the ubiquitous "knee mortars." (Often described as "grenade launchers" or "grenade dischargers," these handy weapons could fire a standard hand-grenade out to 170 meters, as well as a specially designed projectile out to 670 meters.) Additional close-range firepower came from special heavy weapons units – machine-gun battalions, mortar battalions, and light antiaircraft battalions. These provided rifle-caliber heavy machine guns, medium (81mm and 90mm) mortars, 320mm spigot mortars, and large-caliber (13mm and 20mm) antiaircraft machine guns to reinforce the organic weapons of the Japanese infantry.

The many second-line units on Okinawa – units made up of ground crew from the island's airbases, sailors who found themselves without a ship, and army units of various types that had recently been converted to infantry – were not so well armed. As many of the weapons intended for them had been sent out in ships that had been sunk by American submarines, these units had to make do with a lower-than-normal scale of standard infantry heavy weapons. In many cases, however, they made up for this with skillful improvisation. The units made up of stranded sailors, for example, made extensive use of machine guns and automatic cannon taken from unserviceable aircraft. The mission of many of these second-line units, moreover, was different from that of the first-line units. They were stationed in places other than the main battle area, on the outpost line north of that area and on various outlying peninsulae. The task of these units was to harass and delay the Americans, inflicting losses while buying additional time so that the first-line units could improve their positions. Once this mission had been accomplished, the survivors of the second-line units were to find their way back to the main battle area and join the first-line units fighting there.

Third-line units – labor units and the local home guard ("*Boetai*") – were in the worst position of all when it came to weapons. Those who were issued firearms were given weapons of considerable antiquity and doubtful reliability – some were single-shot weapons that had been in storage for a half-century or more. Those members of the home guard who lacked firearms were issued with improvised spears – bamboo poles tipped with bayonets. Such weapons, however, would play very little role in the fight for Okinawa. Rather than being given sectors of their own to defend, the third-line units were used to provide replacements for men of regular army units who had been killed or wounded. While this policy would create problems of its own, it allowed the Japanese to make full use of their most powerful close-range weapons.

At the heart of the Japanese concept for the use of close-range weapons was the principle of mutual protection. Instead of being concerned with its own survival, the crew of a Japanese heavy weapon was instructed to focus on the task of protecting other weapons in the defensive array. In particular, it was to cover the places that the attacking

Americans would have to occupy in order to attack those other weapons. If every one did as he was supposed to, this system worked very well. Americans attacking one Japanese position would find themselves hit in the flank or rear by fire from other Japanese heavy weapons. If, on the other hand, the crews of machine guns, mortars, antitank or infantry guns failed to keep faith with their comrades, the whole system of martial altruism would break down. Instead of receiving fire from unexpected directions, the Americans would be free to focus their efforts on the Japanese weapons in front of them.

Close-in protection for the heavy weapons that formed the backbone of the Japanese defense came from snipers and men armed with knee mortars. Some of these snipers and mortarmen were co-located with the heavy weapons. Their purpose was to allow the heavy weapons to delay their fire until suitable targets presented themselves. Other snipers and mortarmen were posted outside the firing positions of heavy weapons, protecting them from American scouts that threatened to discover them before they opened fire. These fighters were protected by fighting holes that they called "octopus pots." (The name came from the resemblance of these simple one-man shelters to the cookware used for boiling cuttlefish.)

Substantial reinforcement for the Japanese heavy weapon positions was provided by lighter artillery pieces – 75mm field guns, 105mm field howitzers, and a variety of shipboard, coastal defense and antiaircraft cannon of various sizes. Instead of being kept to the rear of the main battle area as intact batteries, these pieces were distributed in much the same manner as infantry heavy weapons. That is to say, they were hidden in individual firing positions that were sited for mutual support. Thus, just as the fire of one heavy weapon served to protect the firing position of others, the fire of one artillery piece protected the firing positions of other weapons. The great advantage of this system was that it reinforced the network of positions for heavy weapons, ensuring that there were few places within the main battle area that were not covered with effective fire. The great disadvantage was that it was impossible to either mass the fire of several batteries, or shift the fire to hit targets of opportunity. Each artillery piece was aimed at a particular piece of terrain and could not, without enormous effort on the part of its crew, shift its fire to another.

The firing positions of both infantry heavy weapons and light artillery were hard to change because they were, quite literally, set in stone. More precisely, they were located in artificial caves that had been dug into the sides of Okinawa's many hills and ridgelines. Many of these caves were quite elaborate, with multiple entrances, firing positions for a variety of weapons, simple living quarters, observation posts, and storage areas for food and ammunition, as well as provision for drainage and ventilation. The coral rock that most of these terrain features were made of was well suited to the building of these underground fortresses. With the consistency of concrete, it was soft enough to be worked, and yet solid enough to withstand heavy bombardment.

The larger Japanese artillery pieces – the 150mm howitzers, the 105mm guns, and the larger naval and coastal defense weapons – were organized in a more conventional manner. Though also kept in caves, they were brought out into open firing positions whenever they were needed to mass their fire in order to repel a major American attack or support an attack of their own. Because of the threat posed by American ground-attack aircraft, each such use of the Japanese heavy artillery had to be protected by the deployment of a considerable number of antiaircraft guns. Even then, fear of American counter-battery fire – particularly the heavy shells of the American battleships and cruisers – would ensure that each unveiling of the Japanese heavy artillery was a short-lived affair.

The Japanese defenses on Okinawa might well be described as a three-dimensional, multi-layered network of mutually supporting fire-sacks. Americans attempting to engage individual Japanese soldiers – the men armed with rifles or knee mortars – would find themselves surrounded by the fire of several machine guns, mortars, or infantry guns. Infantry units that managed to get close enough to endanger these infantry heavy weapons found themselves exposed to the fire of field pieces and antiaircraft guns. Similarly, tank units that went after the heavy weapons could do so only by exposing themselves to the fire of antitank guns.

Japanese preparations for the defense of Okinawa were greatly hampered by the lack of common vision. A substantial portion of the Japanese leadership – including the senior staff officer on the island, Lieutenant-General Ishama Cho – believed that the key to success on Okinawa lay in vigorous counterattacks conducted on the largest possible scale. For them, the caves were shelters and storage facilities rather than fighting positions. Indeed, a number of unit commanders issued directives forbidding their soldiers to fight from their caves. A second faction believed that the best way to kill large numbers of Americans was to wait patiently for the Americans to attack, to let them walk into the traps that had been set for them, and then destroy them, one squad or platoon at a time, by fire and small-scale counterattacks. The most prominent advocate for this point of view was Colonel Hiromichi Yahara, operations officer of the Thirty-second Army and thus the second-ranking Japanese staff officer on Okinawa.

Because of the lack of a common vision, the Japanese defenses on Okinawa were neither optimized for large-scale counterattacks nor fully prepared for a protracted series of smaller defensive battles. The way that the field artillery was distributed, for example, greatly reduced its ability to mass its fire and thus conduct the kinds of fires best suited to a large-scale counterattack. At the same time, the subordinate commanders who designed the defensive positions for their units often failed to provide for such things as mutual support and surprise. As a result, there were many cases where infantry heavy weapons and light artillery pieces were sited to provide long-range fire over open ground, rather than surprise fire at close range. As such firing positions were predictable, they were vulnerable to the long-range fire of American naval guns, artillery, and tanks, as well as assault by American ground attack aircraft. Likewise, there were many cases where neighboring units failed to harmonize their fire plans, thereby leaving gaps that the Americans could exploit.

The one thing that all Japanese decision-makers on Okinawa agreed upon was that it was pointless to try to defend the place where the Americans were most likely to come ashore. This was a piece of relatively flat land just south of the narrow waist of the island that separated the jungle-covered mountains of northern Okinawa from the densely inhabited south. The west coast of this plain was formed by eight more or less continuous miles of the best landing beaches on Okinawa – the only place where four American divisions could land abreast of one another. Called "Hagushi" by the Americans (for a village located near its center), this landing beach had the additional advantage of being close to two of the four major airfields on the island.

In order to avoid fighting on the beaches, the Japanese all but evacuated the waist of the island. The only unit that remained there was a provisional regiment of laborers and service troops. The Japanese deployed the bulk of their forces – all but two of their infantry battalions, all of their 90 or so tanks, and most of their artillery and heavy weapons – in the southern third of the island. The remainder of the Japanese troops – two infantry battalions and a company of 81mm mortars – were stationed north of the airfields. These were the only Japanese units in the northern two-thirds of the island.

The American attack on Okinawa began March 25, 1945. For seven days, a 1,300-ship armada subjected the southern third of the island to a steady rain of shells, rockets, and bombs. In the course of the seven-day bombardment, the fighter-bombers of 40 aircraft carriers made 3,000 trips to drop bombs on Okinawa. In the same period, the big guns of 10 battleships and nine cruisers fired 13,000 shells against the island. Twenty-three destroyers and 177 landing craft converted into floating mortar and rocket batteries fired millions of smaller projectiles. By the end of this weeklong holocaust, all but one of the buildings in the provincial capital of Naha had been destroyed.

For the Japanese soldiers on Okinawa, the chief effect of the bombardment was to raise morale. While they were building their underground fortresses, they had not been sure whether or not the soft coral rock could withstand the effects of the larger American projectiles – particularly the one-ton shells fired by the mammoth 16-inch (400mm) guns of the newer American battleships. Once it became clear to them that their caves were impervious to everything but a direct hit to an entrance or firing port, the Japanese gained new confidence in their leaders, their tactics, and themselves. The effect of the "Steel Typhoon" on the civilian population, however, was very different. Concentrated in the southern third of the island and *without* the protection of caves, they died by the tens of thousands.

On April 1, 1945 – a day that was both Easter Sunday and April Fools' Day that year – four American divisions landed on the Hagushi beaches. Finding little or no opposition, the men of these divisions moved inland as quickly as they could. Towards the end of the day, they set up a defensive perimeter and prepared for the worst. The many veterans of previous island battles in these divisions were all too familiar with the Japanese fondness for attacking at night, and so took considerable pains to ensure that their units dug fighting positions, set up fields of fire, brought up heavy weapons, and made preparations for the employment of concentrated artillery fire.

When the night attacks failed to materialize, the Americans were greatly relieved. They remained, however, extremely cautious. And so the events of the first day were repeated for three more days – rapid advance to pre-selected points, followed by digging in for the night. What the Americans did not know was that the Japanese decision not to attack was a function of their lack of a common vision for the conduct of operations on Okinawa. Colonel Yahara, the chief proponent of a purely defensive battle, had responded to the American landing on the Hagushi beaches by pointing out the possibility of a second American landing on the southeast coast of the island. Because of this danger, he argued, the Japanese could not afford to launch a large-scale counterattack. When, on April 4, an American amphibious task force appeared off of that coast and began to load Marines into landing craft, his caution was vindicated. For the time being, the influence of the senior advocate of aggressive counterattacks, General Cho, was considerably reduced.

On April 8, the two US Army divisions that had landed on the southern portion of the Hagushi beaches – the 7th Infantry Division and the 96th Infantry Division – ran into the outermost ring of the Japanese defenses. Up to this point, almost all of the Japanese units in the path of the rapidly advancing Americans had been following orders to delay and harass the advancing Americans, but not to try to hold on to any particular piece of ground. Indeed, resistance had been so light that many Americans – including a number of generals – had begun to think that the battle was over. As American tanks fell prey to hidden antitank guns, officers were hit by snipers, and whole squads found themselves caught in sophisticated crossfires at the bottom of ravines, this bit of wishful thinking soon evaporated. For the American fighting men who had landed on Okinawa, the battle had just begun. Unfortunately for them, it was a battle for which they were poorly prepared.

The training of the US Army and Marine divisions that served on Okinawa had focused on three types of tactical enterprise – landings on hostile beaches, patrols through contested jungle, and the seizure of defended hilltops. In the first few days of the operation, the skills associated with the amphibious landings and jungle warfare were of some utility. Among other things, they helped the American infantrymen and Marines to quickly overrun those parts of Okinawa that the Japanese had declined to defend in force. Mastery of the third sort of tactical undertaking, however, was worse than a waste of training time, for it actually increased the vulnerability of the Americans to the traps that the Japanese had set for them.

American tactics for the taking of hills had their origins in the Allied offensives of the last six months of World War I, a time when the Germans were more interested in preserving their own dwindling strength than in holding ground. Because of this desire to avoid decisive engagement, the hard-pressed German infantry tended to withdraw as soon as their positions became untenable. The same consideration kept the German artillery far away from the contested terrain. All of this, in turn, meant that the great challenge faced by the attacking Americans was the conquest of the forward slope of the hill in question. At the bottom of the slope, they were vulnerable to both the heavy weapons of the defending German infantry and the long-range fire of the German artillery. With every step they took up the hill, the Americans increased the likelihood that the Germans infantry would attempt a withdrawal, and decreased the number of German batteries that could effectively target them. As might be expected, the Americans ended the war with a technique for taking hills that emphasized both the need for moving up the forward slope as quickly as possible, and the use of the top of that forward slope as a position of relative safety.

On Okinawa, attempts to rush up forward slopes usually ended in disaster for the American attackers. This was because Japanese heavy weapons were positioned to hit such attacks in the flank or even the rear. Those American soldiers or Marines who managed to reach the top of a forward slope, moreover, quickly discovered that their ordeal was far from over. Just as the bottom parts of the forward slope had been covered by the fire of unseen heavy weapons, the top parts were pre-arranged targets for hidden artillery pieces. Thanks to the Japanese principle of mutual support, the shells from artillery pieces were often hitting the Americans from two or more sides – greatly reducing the chances that an American might find a shelter from the shell fragments flying all about him. Because of this, there were dozens of cases where American units that had captured hills in Japanese territory were driven off of those hills by Japanese artillery fire.

The unsuitability of American "take that hill" tactics led to a great deal of improvisation on the American side. The simplest of these exploited the inherent inflexibility of the Japanese defensive positions –

the fact that the firing positions of most Japanese weapons were fixed. In the highly irregular terrain of Okinawa, this all but guaranteed that there were places that Japanese fire could not reach. As these gaps were necessarily small, only the smallest of American units could make use of them. Once they did, however, they often found themselves able to dismantle a Japanese fire sack one firing position at a time.

William Manchester, who would later achieve fame as an historian, served on Okinawa as a sergeant in a Marine infantry battalion. "To be avoided, and if necessary, ignored," he would write in his memoirs, "were gung-ho platoon leaders who drew enemy fire by ordering spectacular charges. Ground wasn't gained that way; it was won by small groups of men, five or six in a cluster, who moved warily forward in a kind of autohypnosis, advancing in mysterious concert with similar groups on their flanks."[1]

The Japanese inadvertently aided these American infiltration tactics by the way they had organized their divisions. In many cases, battalion commanders who had done a good job of creating networks of tightly integrated fire sacks within their own sectors failed to tie into the networks set up by other battalions. This mistake was a natural result of the ad hoc nature of Japanese formations serving on Okinawa. Of the three infantry divisions of the Thirty-second Army, only one had existed as an intact formation for more than a few months. The 62nd Infantry Division had recently arrived from China, where its 10 infantry battalions had served as widely-dispersed, self-contained anti-guerilla units. Soon after arriving on Okinawa, its fragile inter-unit cohesion was further reduced by the attachment of a variety of service organizations that had recently been formed or assembled into combat units. The 44th Independent Mixed Brigade had been assembled on Okinawa by combining two otherwise unconnected regiments with battalions formed by the conversion of naval construction units. The one formation with components that had had a history of working together – the 24th Infantry Division – also had its inter-unit cohesion reduced by the addition of improvised units of various sorts.

Just as the addition of unfamiliar units reduced the willingness of battalions to cooperate with each other, the Japanese policy of providing a constant supply of unfamiliar men to units in contact tended to degrade cooperation at a lower level. Prior to the battle, the ranks of Japanese battalions on Okinawa had been swelled by large numbers of individual replacements coming from Japan, Okinawans of military age who had been drafted into the army, and members of a wide variety of service units. During the battle, frequent attempts were made to compensate for losses by incorporating impressed civilian laborers, stragglers from units that had been destroyed, members of the local home guard, and young volunteers. Thus, the battle began before many battalions had had the chance to develop the kind of mutual confidence needed to ensure the mutual support that lay at the heart of fire sack tactics. As the battle progressed and the proportion of strangers within a unit increased, both American and Japanese observers noticed a marked decrease in the willingness of Japanese soldiers to betray their own position by firing in support of another. Put more simply, Japanese soldiers were increasingly less willing to take risks to protect their comrades because those comrades were increasingly unknown to them.

The Americans also experienced problems with their replacement system. In keeping with the longstanding American policy of keeping units in combat for as long as possible, divisions often sent individual replacements to join units while the latter were still involved in active combat. This created unnecessary dangers for the replacements, who had to learn a considerable number of essential survival skills in a very short period of time. It also increased casualties among leaders, who were distracted by the need to teach essential skills – or compensate for the lack of them – at a time when they should have been free to focus all of their attention upon the enemy. Some American commanders mitigated the worst aspects of the replacement system by arranging for designated replacements to join units well before landing on Okinawa. This not only improved their chances of getting good individual training, but also gave them an opportunity to become full-fledged members of their squads and platoons. Other commanders reduced the worst effects of the individual replacement system by restricting the assignment of replacements to units that were resting behind the lines. This gave the "old salts" a chance to pass on their hard-earned tactical wisdom to the new arrivals before the latter were introduced to the harsh reality of combat.

Once the Americans discovered a gap in the Japanese defenses, they were usually better able to exploit it than the Japanese were to close it. The American divisions on Okinawa were richly provided with the weapons capable of knocking out a Japanese firing position – Sherman tanks armed with 75mm guns, Sherman tanks armed with flamethrowers, and self-propelled 76mm guns were the favorite choices. All these weapons required were reasonably safe firing positions of their own – places allowing them to bring direct fire to bear upon the tiny openings that served as gun ports and observation slits. In cases where these fighting vehicles were not available or could not be used, American infantrymen and engineers could use portable flamethrowers to drive the Japanese defenders from their caves or explosive charges to turn those caves into tombs.

One of the more innovative of the American cave-busting techniques developed on Okinawa involved the use of fire hoses. When operating in places where their tanks could not get a clear shot at the entrance or firing port of a Japanese cave, the crews of US Army flame tanks would find safe places to hide their vehicles. They would then attach lengths of hose to the high-pressure containers that held the jellied gasoline that fed their turret-mounted flamethrowers. This done, they would creep forward, making full use of the invariable irregularities of the Okinawan terrain as well as the covering fire of American rifles, machine guns, and tanks. Once they reached a position from which they could spray the jellied gasoline on a suspected Japanese position, the dismounted tank men handling the hose would soak the target with hundreds of gallons of unlighted fuel, allowing it to seep into caves and foxholes before igniting the whole with a single burst of flame.

The most accomplished practitioner of this technique was Captain Anthony Niemeyer, a young Texan who commanded a company of flamethrower tanks. On June 11, 1945, his tanks were taking part in an attack against the nearly vertical forward slopes of Hill 95, a piece of high ground that rose some 170 feet (50 meters) above the surrounding countryside. When a heavy artillery barrage aimed at suspected Japanese positions failed to silence the Japanese machine guns, Niemeyer sent his tanks forward to douse the base of the hill with flame. This allowed soldiers of the US Army's 32d Infantry Regiment to move forward and occupy positions from which they could fire on Japanese soldiers who might emerge to contest the next stage of the attack – Niemeyer's attempt to carry a long (200 foot/60 meter) length of hose up to the top of the hill.[2]

Additional support for Captain Niemeyer's ascent came from a number of sources. Heavy projectiles fired by the big guns of cruisers fell onto the area behind the objective, thereby depriving the Japanese of the ability to use the rear slope to bring up reinforcements or shift reserves. Smaller shells fired by field artillery batteries and mortar platoons had the same effect on the top and sides of Hill 95. Machine gun bullets and 75mm shells fired from conventional tanks inhibited Japanese use of firing positions or observation posts on the face of the cliff. A platoon of infantry provided close protection, as well as help in hauling the fuel-filled hose.

Captain Niemeyer and his escorts made slow but steady progress up the cliff, stopping periodically to pour flame into suspected Japanese positions. So that the attackers would be free from worry about running out of jellied gasoline, the tank crews at the bottom of the cliff carefully monitored the expenditure of fuel. As soon as the 300–gallon (1,200-liter) container in one flamethrower tank began to run dry, a fresh tank was brought up and the hose moved from the empty container to a full one. In this way, Niemeyer's single hose was able to pump a great deal of fuel in a relatively small amount of time. Indeed, even when the additional infantry platoons had followed in the wake of the first platoon to the top of the hill and had started to clear larger sections of it, most advances were preceded by bursts of jellied gasoline from Captain Niemeyer's hose.

The ten-week battle for the Japanese-held caves of Okinawa was twice interrupted by Japanese attempts to launch major counterattacks. The first of these, the night attack begun on the evening of April 12, resulted in little damage to the Americans but serious losses to the three Japanese battalions that managed to penetrate the American lines. In little more than 24 hours, one of these was completely destroyed, and the other two deprived of half of their men. The second offensive, which began on May 4, was far more ambitious. It involved the best combat units of all three divisions in a daylight attack, and was preceded by the fiercest bombardment yet to be fired by Japanese artillery in the Pacific War. Notwithstanding the magnitude of the effort, only one Japanese battalion made any significant advance into the American lines. The other units fell prey to the tightly knit American defenses and the enormous firepower at their disposal. Thirty-six hours after the attack began, the commanding general of the Thirty-second Army called off the offensive, ordering the one successful battalion to retreat from the hill that it had captured and leaving some 7,000 dead Japanese soldiers on the battlefield.

The offensive of May 4 greatly reduced the ability of the Japanese Army to resist the American onslaught. More and more of the defenders of fortified caves were second-line and even third-line troops. Conditions in the caves were getting worse. The weather was getting both hotter and wetter. There were fewer opportunities to take breaks above ground for such essential chores as cooking rice or relieving oneself. As a result, many Japanese soldiers decided to launch miniature offensives of their own, preferring to die at a time of their own choosing than to wait for the Americans to burn or blast them out of their caves. These small-scale *Banzai* charges further reduced the strength of many Japanese cave complexes, leaving firing positions unmanned and thereby making it easier for Americans to infiltrate.

As the Japanese grew weaker, the Americans were able to step up the pace of their advance. This was not only a function of Japanese losses, but also of learning on the part of the Americans. Americans learned that infiltration was better than large-scale attack, that going around a hill was better than going over it, and that walking over a piece of ground was not the same thing as controlling it. They also learned that cooperation between tanks and infantry required more than a quick huddle over a map a few minutes before an attack — that dismantling a Japanese defensive position required tank crews and infantry squads that had intimate knowledge of each other, complete confidence in each other, and considerable understanding of the way that the Japanese had assembled their traps.

It took more than two and a half months for the Americans to dismantle, one cave at a time, the Japanese defenses on Okinawa. The task was both arduous and deadly — the source of the vast majority of 8,000 or so Americans killed in the struggle to control the island. The campaign would have been much longer — and the American losses much greater — had it not been for the eagerness of Japanese soldiers of all ranks to fight a very different kind of war. From the two large-scale counterattacks organized by the headquarters of the Thirty-second Army down to the many small-scale *Banzai* charges organized by lieutenants, sergeants, and corporals, these ill-conceived offensives turned out to be a great boon to the Americans. Ultimately, the spirit of dramatic self-sacrifice that had been placed at the center of the Japanese strategy of attrition would prove to be its undoing.

Chapter 13

# Ending the Pacific War
## "No alternative to annihilation"

*Richard B. Frank*

## INTRODUCTION

The most enduring controversy of the Pacific War burst forth at its nuclear climax. For nearly two decades after 1945, the wide US, if not international, consensus accepted that swiftly ending the conflict and saving lives by obviating an invasion justified the use of atomic weapons. By some two decades later, critics had created an alternative canon around three major premises. First, that Japan's strategic situation in 1945 was catastrophically hopeless. Second, that Japan's leaders recognized this and sought to surrender. Third, that American leaders, thanks to decoded Japanese diplomatic messages, knew that the Japanese were near capitulation. Accordingly, the critics charge that American leaders inflicted needless nuclear devastation on Japan in pursuit of some goal beyond the speedy and least costly ending of the war: to justify the enormous expenditure of funds; to satisfy (perverse) intellectual curiosity; to perpetuate the Manhattan Project as a bureaucratic empire; or to intimidate the Soviets.[1]

Over the past two decades or so, however, archives have surrendered a trove of long-held secrets. These disclosures demonstrate that neither of these two entrenched views now serves satisfactorily to describe how the Pacific War ended. The revelations easily exceed either of the prior narratives in twists and surprises. But before we focus the spotlight on this new evidence, it must be borne in mind that the US strategic campaign to force an end to the war by blockade and bombardment forms the backdrop.

## BLOCKADE

American submarines commenced a campaign of blockade against Japan from the first hours of the war.[2] On the day of the Pearl Harbor attack,

Japan possessed 6.3 million tons of merchant vessels. She had captured or built about four million tons through 1944. She started 1945, however, with only 2.5 million tons, and ended the war with 1.4 million tons.[3] American land- and sea-based aircraft became major predators of Japanese shipping in 1944 and 1945. An extremely effective mining campaign by B-29s in 1945 not only sank ships, but also sharply curbed the movement of the remaining vessels. By the late summer of 1945, Japan's shipping situation was approaching collapse. This was not simply a lack of sufficient bottoms to deliver commodities from overseas. Japan's unique economy depended upon a transportation system based on coastal shipping to move raw materials, food, finished products, and military units within the home islands. The collapse of coastal shipping threatened dire consequences for Japan's population.[4]

# THEN BOMBARDMENT

The B-29 Superfortress represented the most advanced heavy bomber of World War II. Army Air Force leaders intended that the Superfortress would defeat Japan and thus clinch the case for an independent air force.

The 58th Wing became the first operational B-29 unit. President Roosevelt's urge to buttress China, combined with the Army Air Force's ambitions for early deployment, merged to send this wing to China in mid-1944 under Brigadier-General Kenneth B. Wolfe. The crews paid a heavy price for rushing the B-29 into combat. More B-29s failed to return for operational reasons, often connected to the fire-prone engines, than because of enemy action. Major-General Curtis LeMay, the supreme airman troubleshooter, replaced Wolfe. LeMay was a realist; he called the whole setup, considering the logistical infrastructure in India, "basically unsound."[5]

The 58th Wing migrated to the Marianas by May 1945. There it joined the 73rd, 313th, and 314th wings. When the 315th Wing arrived, the B-29 force numbered 20 groups, with 1,002 Superfortresses on hand, as of August 1, 1945. LeMay arrived in January to replace the luckless first leader of the XXI Bomber Command, Brigadier-General Haywood Hansell. From November 1944, Hansell had applied the classic creed of the Army Air Force: daylight, high-altitude precision attacks. Weather, not the Japanese, proved Hansell's most obdurate opponent. A paucity of clear days severely restricted opportunities for raids and the phenomenon of the Jet Stream – 130 mile per hour winds – foiled bombing accuracy.

LeMay initially followed Hansell's path, but after two months, he recognized that even he could not make daylight precision bombing work. Consequently, beginning on the night of March 9–10, 1945, LeMay instituted a radical new strategy: night, low-level, mass incendiary attacks on Japanese cities. That first raid burned out 15.8 square miles of Tokyo, and killed as many as 100,000 Japanese. LeMay never wholly abandoned daylight precision attacks, but the main effort remained the relentless pursuit of city burning. By the end of the war, B-29s had torched 66 cities (counting Hiroshima and Nagasaki). Fires consumed about 20 percent of Japan's housing and left about 15 million homeless – about one Japanese in five. Approximately 400,000 Japanese died in air raids, including the atomic attacks.[6]

This campaign was not novel in either its means or its ruthlessness. The precursor was efforts by Japan and Germany to bomb their enemies into submissive terror. The Royal Air Force and the US Army Air Force answered this onslaught in kind in Europe where they gradually discarded every moral scruple (except for the use of poison gas) restraining the employment of massive aerial firepower against urban centers. American leaders considering the use of atomic weapons thus lacked a sense that they were vaulting over any great moral divide, in light of what had gone before both in Europe and against Japan.

| THE STRATEGIC AIR CAMPAIGN AGAINST JAPAN | | |
|---|---|---|
| | XX Bomber Command (From China) | XXI Bomber Command (From the Marianas) |
| Total Sorties | 4,669 | 28,258 |
| Bomb Tonnage | | |
| Total | 12,219 | 167,736 |
| Incendiaries | 3,296 | 103,068 |
| High Explosives | 8,395 | 54,917 |
| Mines | 528 | 9,751 |

The cost was 414 B-29s from all causes. Aircrew casualties totaled 2,897, with 2,148 deaths. Some 334 airmen were listed as captured or interned, of whom 262 survived.[7]

# THE AMERICAN NIGHTMARE

President Franklin Roosevelt fixed the national war aim of unconditional surrender in 1943. By 1945, unconditional surrender represented not a slogan for victory, but a program for peace. It established the legal authority for a radical program of political renovation that would guarantee that Germany and Japan would never again pose a threat to peace.[8]

The Joint Chiefs of Staff bore the duty of devising a military strategy to secure this national war aim. But their appearance of agreement masked an unstable compromise between two diametrically opposite views. General of the Army George C. Marshall identified time as the key impediment to achieving unconditional surrender. Therefore, he placed highest importance on an invasion of the Japanese home islands as the means of swiftly ending the conflict before war-weariness set in. The Commander-in-Chief of the US Navy, Fleet Admiral Ernest King, shared the long-established Navy concept that casualties represented the key menace to achieving American war aims. Blue-uniformed strategists had long since concluded that numberless Japanese warriors, installed in Japan's wet and rugged terrain, rendered an invasion of the Japanese home islands pure folly. Therefore, King advocated the classic Navy strategy for ending the war: blockade and bombardment.

In April or May of 1945, however, King recognized that he could not win a showdown with Marshall over these competing strategies. He therefore agreed that the Joint Chiefs should issue an invasion order to create the option of adding that strategy to the existing strategy of blockade and bombardment. King did expressly advise his colleagues that they would reconsider the need for an invasion in August or September – not because he anticipated the atomic bombs, but because he expected to have the facts on his side by that time.[9]

The overall invasion plan was the two-phase Operation *Downfall*. In Operation *Olympic*, the Sixth Army, backed by the Third and Fifth fleets, would seize essentially the southern third of Kyushu, the southernmost of the home islands. The target date for invasion was November 1.

Southern Kyushu would provide the air and naval bases to support the main effort, Operation *Coronet*, to seize the Tokyo region with the Eighth Army supported by the First Army, which would be transferred from Europe. The tentative date for *Coronet* was March 1, 1946.[10]

The Joint Chiefs formally adopted a policy paper articulating the rationale for this strategy in April 1945. That paper highlighted that no Japanese government had ever surrendered, and that there was no recorded instance of Japanese military units surrendering in the entire war. Therefore, the Joint Chiefs warned that there was no guarantee that a Japanese government would ever surrender or, even if one did, that Japan's armed forces would comply with that surrender. If there was no organized surrender, the Joint Chiefs foresaw "no alternative to annihilation" of the between four and five million Japanese combatants in the home islands, on the Asian continent, and across the Pacific. It is impossible to emphasize sufficiently that the ultimate American nightmare was not Operation *Downfall*, but the prospect of no organized capitulation.[11]

## THE JAPANESE DREAM

Japan's military and political leaders did not stumble through 1945 in a fanatical trance, blinded to their own hopeless situation. On the contrary, Japanese leaders devised a shrewd military and political strategy called *Ketsu Go* (Operation *Decisive*). Its bedrock premise was that American morale was brittle, and could be broken by inflicting enormous bloodletting in the initial invasion of Japan. Even if that invasion succeeded, Japanese leaders believed that American politicians would recoil from the prospect of a vast effusion of blood to continue the conquest of Japan.

In the early days of 1945, Japanese officers displayed their shrewdest appreciation of American capabilities and intentions since the war's opening moves. The key insight was that any American plan must rest upon the ability to project land-based aircraft – especially fighter planes – over the target area. By the summer of 1945, Japanese officers expected their opponents to hold Iwo Jima and Okinawa. The latter, but not the former, could support thousands of planes. Getting out their dividers, they ran an arc from Okinawa representing American fighter plane range. Within that arc fell southern Kyushu and Shikoku. The former, not the latter, offered an excellent set of air and sea bases to support an attack on Tokyo. Elementary analysis of southern Kyushu correctly identified the likely invasion beaches.

Following this analysis, the Imperial Japanese Army devised a new homeland defense scheme featuring two theater commands. Responsibility for guarding most of central and northern Honshu rested with the First General Army (roughly equivalent to an American army group), with headquarters in Tokyo. The Second General Army, with headquarters at Hiroshima, exercised jurisdiction over forces on western Honshu, Shikoku, and Kyushu. Several Area Armies (effectively the equivalent of an American army) answered to each General Army.

Only 12 field divisions celebrated New Year's Day 1945 in Japan proper, far too few to prosecute *Ketsu Go*. Imperial Headquarters embarked on a huge program of homeland reinforcement. From Manchuria came four divisions (two armored and two infantry). But far and away the largest increase in strength sprang from a February 26 order for a gigantic, three-phase mobilization program to create new legions as below.

Once the mobilization was complete, the homeland's defenders would muster 60 divisions (36 field and counterattack, 22 coastal combat, and two armored) and 34 brigades (27 infantry and seven tank). The home defense command rolls would swell by 1.5 million men. The aggregate strength of the homeland armies would reach 2,903,000 men, 292,000 horses and 27,500 motor vehicles.[12]

On April 8, staff officers in Tokyo completed a sprawling master defense plan designed to confront and crush American invaders in one of seven key

|  | General Army Headquarters | Army Headquarters | Coastal Division[a] | Counter Attack Division[b] | Independent Mixed Brigade | Tank Brigade |
|---|---|---|---|---|---|---|
| Phase One: | -- | -- | 13 | -- | 1 | -- |
| Phase Two: | 2 | 8 | -- | 8 | -- | 6 |
| Phase Three: | -- | -- | 9 | 7 | 14 | -- |
| TOTAL: | 2 | 8 | 22 | 15 | 15 | 6 |

a.  The coastal combat division was a static unit, designed to grapple in close-quarter fighting with a landing force a short distance inland from the water's edge.

b.  The counterattack division was a mobile unit, effectively a reduced strength field division, organized to march rapidly from inland positions, and deliver punishing blows against an enemy beachhead.

areas. Emphasis was on Ketsu Number Three (the Kanto-Tokyo Area) and Ketsu Number Six (Kyushu).[13] *Ketsu Go* featured three distinctive aspects. First, Japanese officers recognized the folly of beach defenses in the face of stupendous American bombardments, but they also concluded that waiting until the Americans were fully established ashore would likely preclude successful defense. Therefore, Japanese officers aimed to destroy the lodgments with a counterattack a few days after the landing.

The second distinctive feature of *Ketsu Go* was the comprehensive devotion to *tokko* (special attack or suicide) tactics, not only the now routine air and sea efforts, but also ashore. The incorporation of the civilian population into the defense scheme represented the third highly singular feature of *Ketsu Go*. Under the "National Resistance Program," commanders would summon all able-bodied civilians, regardless of gender, to combat. This involved all males, ages 15 to 60, and all females, ages 17 to 40. These civilians, often drilling with bamboo spears, would perform combat support and later combat roles.[14]

A key premise of *Ketsu Go* was that diplomacy would follow, not precede, the first invasion battle. This was the dominant view in an inner cabinet called the Big Six, comprising Prime Minister Kantaro Suzuki, Foreign Minister Shigenori Togo, Army Minister Korechika Anami, Navy Minister Mitsumasa Yonai, and the chiefs of staff of the Imperial Army and Navy, General Yoshijiro Umezu and Admiral Soemu Toyoda respectively. The Big Six, along with Emperor Hirohito and his confidant, Lord Keeper of the Privy Seal Koichi Kido, were the eight men in Japan who possessed real power to control the nation's fate.[15]

The Emperor confessed after the war that he was an acolyte of *Ketsu Go* until it became clear that Okinawa would be lost. On June 22, he pressed the Big Six to seek Soviet mediation. When the Big Six moved too slowly for his taste, he again tried to enhance this effort with an offer to send Prince Konoye, a former Prime Minister, as a special envoy to Moscow. But Stalin, having been promised at Yalta many profits for entering the war, had his diplomats stall.[16]

## *OLYMPIC* VERSUS *KETSU GO*

General Walter Krueger commanded the US Sixth Army.[17] For *Olympic*, the main combat elements of his army were four corps headquarters, 14 divisions, a separate infantry regimental combat team, and a separate

OPPOSING FORCES FOR *OLYMPIC*[18]

| AMERICAN PLAN | JAPANESE DEFENSES |
|---|---|
| **Preliminary Operations:** 40th Infantry Division and 158th Regiment Combat Team seize islands off the south and southeast coast. | The 40th Infantry Division faces modest resistance. The 158th RCT is heavily outnumbered. |
| **Main Landings:** The American I Corps attacks Miyazaki with the 25th, 33d, and 41st Infantry divisions. | The Fifty-seventh Army defends Miyazaki with the 154th, 156th, and 212th divisions, 5th Tank Brigade. |
| The XI Corps attacks Ariake Bay with the 1st Cavalry, the Americal, and the 43d Infantry Division, plus the separate 112th Cavalry Regiment. | The Fifty-seventh Army defends Ariake with the 86th Division reinforced 98th Independent Mixed Brigade, a separate infantry regiment, three separate infantry battalions, 6th Tank Brigade (minus one regiment). |
| The V Amphibious Corps, comprising the 2d, 3d, and 5th Marine divisions, attacks Kushikino. | The Fortieth Army, with the 77th, 146th, 206th, and 303rd divisions, 125th Independent Mixed Brigade, 37th Tank Regiment defends southwest Kyushu, only 303rd Division at Kushikino. |
| **Reserves** IX Corps of 77th, 81st, and 98th divisions, 11th Airborne Division. | One division and one tank Brigade from the Fifty-sixth Army in Northern Kyushu, 216th Division, and 26 infantry battalions. |

dismounted cavalry regimental combat team. MacArthur retained a strategic reserve of three infantry divisions. Krueger's scheme of maneuver provided for preliminary landings on islands to the south and southeast of Kyushu to seize advanced air warning and sea bases. There were three main landings, each involving a corps, two on the southeastern coast and one on the southwestern coast. Krueger held in reserve a three-division corps and one airborne division.

Airfields on southern Kyushu would host the Far Eastern Air Force elements, including 10 fighter groups, six heavy bomber groups, four medium bomber groups, four light bomber groups, three reconnaissance groups, three night fighter squadrons, and an "air commando" (a hybrid unit of two fighter, one troop carrier and three liaison plane squadrons).[19]

Facing Krueger was Field Marshall Shunroku Hata's Second General Army of two area armies. The Sixteenth Area Army protected Kyushu, and the Fifteenth Area Army defended Shikoku and western Honshu.[20]

The task of making specific dispositions fell to the Sixteenth Area Army. Assessing the American goals (air and sea bases) and means (up to 15 or 16 divisions), the Sixteenth Area Army gradually perceived that multiple landings were probable, targeting Miyazaki, Shibushi (Ariake) Bay, and the Satsuma Peninsula in southern Kyushu.[21]

Although just a single field division defended Kyushu in January 1945, the Imperial Army surged in reinforcements over the next five months, raising the garrison on Kyushu to 14 field divisions, three tank brigades, and eight independent mixed (infantry) brigades. The aggregate forces numbered some 900,000 men.[22]

Comparing the American plan to the dispositions of the Sixteenth Area Army elements reveals the sharp acuity of Japanese assessments.

Feeble naval but formidable air forces backed this ground battle array. The Imperial Navy's handful of cruisers, destroyers, and submarines served mainly as platforms for small suicide weapons. Imperial Headquarters devoted nearly all of Japan's air power to *Ketsu Go*. By the draconian policy of converting training aircraft to suicide planes, declining combat, dispersing and hiding planes, the Japanese swelled their combat aircraft inventory in 1945 to more than 10,000. These they divided almost half and half into *kamikaze* and conventional missions, with the great bulk defending Kyushu.[23]

Japan lacked the weapons and ammunition to fully outfit all of the new formations, but Imperial Headquarters granted primacy to Kyushu.[24] Moreover, Imperial Headquarters distributed ample supplies and arms to Kyushu well in advance.[25]

# RADIO INTELLIGENCE REVELATIONS

Extremely significant new insights on the end of the Pacific War emerged with the release of radio intelligence information beginning in the late 1970s. This evidence provided, for the first time, a complete picture of the diplomatic intercepts. Moreover, the military intercepts unmasked a radical new portrait of American decision making in the summer of 1945.

Each day, a team of editors distilled the tremendous output of intercepted Japanese coded communications into the "Magic" Diplomatic Summary and the "Magic" Far East Summary for a select band of senior American policy makers, starting with the President. The "Magic" Diplomatic Summary demonstrated that the squad of Japanese diplomats in Europe attempting to become peace entrepreneurs lacked any authority from Tokyo for their efforts. It also confirmed that the sole authorized Japanese diplomatic venture aimed not at surrender, but at securing Soviet offices to mediate an end to the war. This enterprise ran from Foreign Minister Togo in Tokyo to Ambassador Naotake Sato in Moscow. In the most significant interchange, Togo answered Sato's insistent demands for concrete terms to present to the Soviets with the statement that Japan was not looking for "anything like an unconditional surrender." Sato then lectured Togo that the best terms Japan could obtain were unconditional surrender, modified only to permit the continuation of the imperial institution – exactly the package that later critics argued would have obtained Japan's surrender without the atomic bombs. But in the "Magic" Diplomatic Summary of July 22, American policy makers read that Togo had rejected this package in the name of the cabinet.[26]

The diplomatic intercepts are, however, a trickle compared to the torrent of military intercepts in the "Magic" Far East Summary. From mid-July to the end of the war, radio intelligence unveiled the huge build-up of Japanese forces in the homeland in general and the even more perturbing evidence of massing Japanese formations at the proposed landing areas on Kyushu. By war's end, intelligence identified 13 of the 14 field divisions (nine in the southern half of the island) and five of the 11 brigades on Kyushu. The final, revised estimate of August 20 credited the Japanese with all 14 field divisions and an aggregate of 625,000 troops on Kyushu.[27]

The portrait of Japanese air power varied only between dark and bleak among the various intelligence centers. By the surrender date, the newly-created Joint Army-Navy Committee on the Japanese Air Forces estimated Japanese air strength in the homeland at 5,911.[28] The intelligence center for the Commander-in-Chief Pacific Fleet (CINCPAC) calculated that by August 13, the Japanese had 10,290 aircraft available for homeland defense.[29] The actual total floated at around 10,700.[30]

The intelligence shattered the basic assumptions for *Olympic*. American officers had anticipated that on X-Day, the Japanese would have only six field divisions on Kyushu and only half of those in the south to confront the Sixth Army's 13 assault divisions. General Marshall explained to President Truman on June 18, 1945 that the Japanese ultimately might commit 350,000 men and eight to ten divisions to oppose *Olympic*. Contemporary planning estimates projected that by November 1945, the Japanese would only be able to muster 2,500 to 3,000 aircraft. Radio intelligence, however, estimated Japanese forces at three to four times stronger on the ground and two to four times stronger in the air.[31]

As Major-General Charles A. Willoughby, General Douglas MacArthur's intelligence chief, declared, further unchecked increase of Japanese strength on Kyushu threatened "to grow to [the] point where we attack on a ratio of one (1) to one (1) which is not the recipe for victory."[32] At the Joint Chiefs of Staff, the secretariat assimilated the radically altered situation and began an agonizing reappraisal of *Olympic*. Planners turned to alternatives, notably a landing on northern Honshu.

While the staff temporized about directly soliciting the views of the theater commanders, Marshall and King did not. On August 7, Marshall asked MacArthur for his personal assessment of the situation. MacArthur replied, essentially, that he did not believe the intelligence and urged that *Olympic* go forward. Admiral King intervened at this point to play his trump card. Since May, King had known, in confidence, that Nimitz had withdrawn his prior support for at least *Olympic*. On August 9, King ordered Nimitz to make his views known to Washington and MacArthur. Nimitz paused before igniting what was sure to be a major confrontation with the Army and MacArthur when, for the first time, evidence appeared that a Japanese surrender might be at hand.[33] In sum, radio intelligence evidence made it virtually certain that *Olympic* would never have gone forward, not because it was unnecessary, but because it had become unthinkable.

# ENTERING THE NUCLEAR AGE

The most unexpected and ultimately controversial legacy of the end of the Pacific War proved to be the advent of nuclear weapons. The nightmare fear that Hitler might be the first to acquire a bomb based upon fission of the atom begat a feverish competition to beat the Germans, first in the United Kingdom and later the United States.[34]

The story of building the bomb fascinates as a sort of modern legend, with scientists in the guise of Arthurian knights grappling with arcane theory (rather than dragons), but the hardest challenge proved to be the mundane issue of manufacturing enough fissionable material. This is to a nuclear weapon what explosive filler is to a conventional bomb. Because engineering, not physics, dominated this phase of development, it was a US Army engineer, Brigadier-General Leslie Groves, who would actually command the project. Ultimately Groves' empire spawned two classes of bomb based on their sources of fissionable material: one of uranium and one of plutonium.[35]

Much writing about the bombs locates the great Rubicon separating the past from the nuclear age as its first use against a city. This is beguiling, but superficial. The real Rubicon was no later than the test of a plutonium weapon in July 1945. More likely it was earlier, when the scientists and engineers agreed that a workable solution to all the theoretical and practical problems was in hand. This was well before July 1945, when the uranium bomb design and manufacturing work was complete.

And the bomb would be used, for the assumption of use existed from practically the first moment President Roosevelt committed the US to the vast project. Everything that occurred in 1945 must be viewed in the context of what historian Barton Bernstein aptly described as the "implementation of an assumption." Some scientists, without knowledge of *Ketsu Go* or the diplomatic intercepts, proposed not to use the bomb, or simply to demonstrate it. The two top scientists, Vannevar Bush and James Conant, recognized that the Rubicon had already been crossed, and were determined to use the bomb on a city, not because they were exceptionally bloodthirsty, but because they believed that only the horror of such an event could induce nations to surrender enough sovereignty to permit effective control.[36]

The *Enola Gay*, a specially modified B-29, dropped the uranium bomb on Hiroshima on August 6. It destroyed the command center for the Second General Army. Urgency to use the second bomb before weather imposed a halt prompted local commanders to release the first plutonium weapon on August 9. Together, the two bombs killed immediately or thereafter some 100,000 to 200,000 Japanese.[37]

## MANCHURIA

Hiroshima electrified Stalin into unleashing his Asian offensive a week early. Marshal Aleksandr M. Vasilevsky commanded a theater with 1.6

million troops, 3,704 tanks, 1,852 self-propelled guns, 16,325 artillery pieces, and 5,058 aircraft.[38] His sophisticated plan aimed to conquer Manchuria with a double envelopment. Marshall Kirill A. Meretskov's First Far Eastern Front would drive westward from eastern Manchuria to meet Marshal Rodion I. Malinovsky's Trans Baikal Front driving from the west. General Maksim A. Purkaev's Second Far Eastern front would deliver a supporting attack from the north. Soviet objectives also included the seizure of the southern half of Sakhalin Island, Korea, the Kurils, and a secret scheme to invade Hokkaido, the northernmost of the Japanese home islands.[39]

General Otozo Yamada commanded Japan's Kwantung Army in Manchuria. His forces numbered 713,000 in 24 divisions, nine infantry, and two tank brigades. About 2,000 aircraft, half of them obsolete, supported Yamada. Because Japan had stripped Manchuria of well-trained units, Japanese staff officers reckoned that the actual combat power of the Kwantung Army was the equivalent of six and two-thirds divisions. Also in the theater were 190,000 men in Korea and about 90,000 in southern Sakhalin and the Kurils.[40]

The Kwantung Army fought hard at those places where its units made stands (and sustained anywhere from 21,000 to about 84,000 killed), but the Soviet offensive simply flowed around and defeated the Japanese by maneuver rather than brute force. Only a narrow margin spared Hokkaido from Soviet seizure with its huge political implications. Japanese resistance on Sakhalin Island stalled Soviet preparations, and President Truman's firm stance on holding previously agreed demarcation lines finally dissuaded Stalin from this measure.[41]

| SOVIET STRENGTHS AND LOSSES IN *AUGUST STORM* [42] | | | | |
|---|---|---|---|---|
| Force | Initial Strength | Killed and Missing | "Medical" | Total |
| Trans-Baikal Front | 638,300 | 2,228 | 6,155 | 8,383 |
| 2nd Far Eastern Front | 334,700 | 2,449 | 3,134 | 5,583 |
| 1st Far Eastern Front | 586,500 | 6,324 | 14,745 | 21,069 |
| Pacific Fleet | 97,500 | 998 | 300 | 1,298 |
| Amur Military Flotilla | 12,500 | 32 | 91 | 123 |
| Total | 1,669,500 | 12,031 | 24,425 | 36,456 |
| Mongolian Army | 16,000 | 72 | 125 | 197 |

# SURRENDER AND COMPLIANCE

The first of the many misconceptions littering the last days of the war is the notion that news of Hiroshima and Nagasaki promptly induced surrender. Japan's militarists, in fact, immediately erected two lines of defense to President Truman's claim that an atomic bomb destroyed Hiroshima. The Japanese atomic bomb program equipped them with no weapon, but it did arm them with knowledge of the incredible difficulty of producing fissionable material. Thus, Japanese officers immediately declared that whatever had struck Hiroshima was not an atomic bomb. Admiral Toyoda advanced the second line of defense: even if the US possessed atomic weapons, it could not have that many, they could not be that powerful, and international opinion would deter their further use.[43] This evidence illustrates the futility of a demonstration of the bomb.

The militarists managed to stall any meeting of the Big Six until news broke of Soviet attacks in Manchuria. Tokyo received a very incomplete picture because the Kwantung Army gained only very partial understanding of the initial scale and success of the Soviet effort.[44] Soviet intervention prompted the Emperor to demand that the government take action. Despite prior emphasis on the vital importance of keeping the Soviets out of the conflict, three of the four senior Imperial Army officers in Tokyo (War Minister Anami, Chief of the Imperial General Staff Umezu, and Vice Chief of the Imperial General Staff Torashiro Kawabe) all believed that Soviet intervention did not invalidate *Ketsu Go*. Further, Kawabe and Anami endorsed a plan to eliminate all vestiges of a separate civilian government and rule Japan from Imperial General Headquarters.[45]

The Big Six deadlocked. Three favored acceptance of the Potsdam Declaration (the proclamation of Truman, Attlee and Chaing Kai-Shek of July 26 setting out terms for Japan's surrender), provided the Allies issued a guarantee about the imperial institution. The other three demanded a trio of additional terms – no occupation, Japanese self-disarmament, and Japanese trials for alleged war criminals – that would have insulated Japan from the US plan for far-reaching reforms.[46] The full cabinet likewise remained split.[47]

A second misconception is that the legal government of Japan ever agreed on its own to surrender. It did not. Further, that government may not have survived had the Imperial Army enjoyed time to execute the scheme to terminate civilian government.

The crisis demanded, and received, extraordinary action. An Imperial Conference of the Big Six, with the Emperor in attendance, convened late on August 9. Prime Minister Suzuki called upon the Emperor to break the deadlock. The Emperor endorsed the single condition. He thus became the legitimate authority that decided Japan must capitulate.[48] Then the extraordinary story lurched into an ominous twist. When the Japanese dispatched a message purporting to accept the Potsdam Declaration, they included a provision that such agreement would not "prejudice the prerogatives of His Majesty as Sovereign Ruler." This opaque language effectively demanded that the US cede powers to the Emperor, in accordance with Japanese law, and guarantee him a veto over the occupation reforms.[49]

Although several cabinet officers urged Truman to accept the Japanese offer, senior State Department officials alerted Secretary of State James Byrnes to the masked significance of the Japanese proposal. Truman sided with Byrnes in rejecting the Japanese ploy, and Byrnes drafted up a response that merely promised that "[f]rom the moment of surrender the authority of the Emperor and the Japanese Government to rule the state shall be subject to the Supreme Commander of the Allied powers."[50] As the US would make clear to Japanese officials in the coming months, this reply made no guarantee whatsoever about the imperial institution.[51] Thus, the notion that the US promised to maintain the imperial institution and the incumbent emperor to obtain Japan's surrender is another myth. The Emperor intervened again and ordered the Japanese government to accept the Byrnes Note.[52]

This still left open the question of whether Japan's armed forces would comply with the surrender. A group of field grade officers organized a *coup d'état* to halt the surrender, and seized the Imperial Palace during the night of August 14–15. The coup ultimately failed, however, primarily because War Minister Anami refused to participate. He chose to commit suicide instead.[53]

Too much has been made of this coup attempt, while too little attention has been paid to a more serious threat. Despite the Emperor's radio broadcast on August 15 of an Imperial Rescript ending the war – he never used the term surrender – senior officers overseas initially refused to comply. The Emperor issued a second Rescript on August 17 to bring these commanders to heel – with which they complied, reluctantly.[54]

Why did the Emperor decide to halt the war? He consistently gave three reasons when asked about his decision. One was his loss of faith in the Imperial Army and *Ketsu Go*. A second was his deep fear that Japan's civil order would crack under blockade and bombardment, and possibly destroy the imperial institution from within. He also specifically cited the atomic bomb.

It is important to emphasize that even the Emperor's intervention was not enough to guarantee that Japan's armed forces would surrender. For the overseas commands, Soviet intervention loomed as the key reason to comply with the order from Tokyo.[55]

Secretary of War Henry Stimson said that the resort to nuclear weapons represented "the least abhorrent choice" before American leaders, thus challenging later critics who argued that surely there must have been a way to end the war without the horror of Hiroshima and Nagasaki.[56] Without the atomic bombs, a new targeting directive to the B-29 force on August 11 would have reoriented the strategic bombing campaign to an attack on the Japanese rail system. This stroke, coupled with the collapse of the internal merchant shipping system and the severe food shortage, would have killed millions by famine in Japan's food deficit areas. Without the atomic bombs, the Soviets would have invaded Hokkaido.[57] On the Asian mainland, the Soviets seized about 2.7 million Japanese nationals, only one-third military personnel. Of this total, some 340,000 to 370,000 perished in Soviet hands. Taking this as a yardstick for the human cost of Soviet occupation of Hokkaido, another 400,000 Japanese noncombatants would have died.[58] Without atomic bombs, it is by no means clear that the Emperor would have intervened to provide the essential first step in the process of an organized capitulation of Japan's government and armed forces. Without an organized capitulation, it is not clear whether the final end of the war would have come in months or years. Thus, Stimson articulated the grim reality of how the Pacific War ended: the atomic bombs were awful, but the alternatives were much worse.

# Endnotes

## CHAPTER 1

1 Louis Morton, *Strategy and Command: The First Two Years*, Washington, DC Office of the Chief of Military History, 1961, p.126.

2 Samuel Eliot Morison, *The Rising Sun in the Pacific 1931–April 1942,* Vol. III of *History of United States Naval Operations in World War II*, Boston: Little, Brown, 1948, p.212.

## CHAPTER 2

1 Emily Rosenberg, "Pearl Harbor," in Chihiro Hosoya, *Kioku to shiteno Pearl Harbor* (Pearl Harbor as memory), Tokyo: Minerva, 2004, pp.27–34.

2 For more information on the battle of Tsushima, see D. Evans and M. Peattie, *Kaigun, Strategy, Tactics and Technology in the Imperial Navy, 1887–1941,* Annapolis: Naval Institute Press, 1997, pp.116–124.

3 Evans and Peattie, *Kaigun,* p.129.

4 National Institute for Defense Studies (NIDS), (eds.), *Hawaii Sakusen* (Hawaii Operation), Tokyo: Asagumo, 1967, p.35.

5 Arthur Marder, *Old Friends, New Enemies*, Oxford: Clarendon Press, 1981, p.297.

6 *Showa Jyu Nen Gunbi Seigen Kenkyu Iinkai Kenkyu Chosa Jiko Dai Rokkan* (Report of the Armament Limitation Research Committee in 1934, vol.6), Boei Kenkyu-jo, NIDS, Japan.

7 NIDS, *Hawaii Sakusen,* pp.45–49.

8 Ibid., p.7.

9 E. King, *US Navy at War 1941–1945,* Washington: US Navy Department, 1946, p.8.

10 Nihoh Kokusai Seiji Gakkai Hen (The Japan Association of International Relations), (eds.), *Taiheiyo Senso Heno Michi,* 7 (The Road to the Pacific War, vol.7), Tokyo: Asahi Shinbun Sha, 1987, p.324.

11 For more information on *Automedon*, see J. W. M. Chapman, "Japanese Intelligence, 1918–1945, A Suitable Case for Treatment," in Christopher Andrew and Jeremy Noakes (eds.), *Intelligence and International Relations 1900–1945*, University Press of Exeter, 1987, pp.160–161; also James Rusbridger, "The Sinking of the *Automedon* and the Capture of the *Nankin*," in *Encounter*, vol.375, No.5, May 1985.

12 COS(40)592, 31 July 1941, CAB66/10, PRO, National Archives, Kew, UK.

13 NIDS, *Hawaii Sakusen,* pp.90–91.

14 Minoru Genda, *Shinjuwan Sakusen Kaikoroku* (The Retrospection of the Pearl Harbor Operation), Tokyo: Yomiuri Shinbunsha, 1972, pp.12–21; Gordon Prange, *At Dawn We Slept,* New York: Penguin Books, 1981, pp.25–26.

15 NIDS, *Hawaii Sakusen,* p.92.

16 Shiryo Chosa Kai (eds.), *Taiheiyou Senso to Tomioka Sadatoshi* (The Pacific War and Sadatoshi Tomioka), Tokyo: Gunji Kenkyusha, 1971, pp.78–80.

17 Hiroyuki Agawa, *Yamamoto Isoroku,* Tokyo: Shinchosha, 1969, p.243.

18 NIDS, *Hawaii Sakusen,* pp.105–108.

19 Nihoh Kokusai Seiji Gakkai Hen, p.336.

20 NIDS, *Hawaii Sakusen,* p.113.

21 Lanchester's Theory was known as "N2 Theory" in the IJN; if five USN battleships and three IJN battleships opened fire on each other, within five minutes four US ships and no Japanese ships would be left. According to this theory, the IJN would never beat the USN in a decisive war without the use of outwitting tactics.

22  Teiji Yabe, *Konoe Fumimaro,* Tokyo: Jijitsushin, 1986, p.162.

23  NIDS, *Hawaii Sakusen,* pp.114–116.

24  NIDS, *Hawaii Sakusen,* p.201.

25  Agawa, *Yamamoto Isoroku,* p.252.

26  NIDS, *Hawaii Sakusen,* p.264.

27  Shigenori Togo, *Togo Shigenori Shuki* (The memoir of Togo Shigenori), Tokyo: Hara Shobo 1989, p.261.

28  Mitsuo Fuchida, *Watashi Ha Shinjyuwan Joku Ni Ita* (I flew over Pearl Harbor), Nara: Yamato Taimusu Sha, 1949, p.7.

29  Prange, *At Dawn We Slept,* p.549.

30  Fuchida, *Watashi Ha Shinjyuwan Joku Ni Ita,* pp.199–200.

31  Agawa, pp. 280–281; Shiryo Chosa Kai, *Taiheiyou Senso to Tomioka Sadatoshi,* pp.87–88.

32  NIDS, *Hawaii Sakusen,* p.475.

33  Asahi newspaper, 19 December 1941.

34  RG-457, National Archives, Washington, DC, US (NARA); HW 12, PRO; Department of Defense, *The "Magic" Background of Pearl Harbor, vol. I–IV,* Washington, DC: US Government Printing Office, 1977.

35  Robert Stinnett, *Day of Deceit,* NY: Free Press, 2000, pp.50–51.

36  Ronald Worth, Jr., *Secret Allies in the Pacific,* North California: McFarland & Company, 2001, p.181; this idea is also supported by Stephen Budiansky, "Too Late for Pearl Harbor," *US Naval Institute Proceedings,* Vol. 125/12/1, 162, Dec. 1998.

37  Laurance Safford (Captain, US Navy), "A Brief History of Communications Intelligence in the United States," SRH-149, declassified per sec, 3 E.0. 12065 by Director NSA/Chief, CSS March 6, 1982.

38  Prange, *At Dawn We Slept,* p.743.

39  Naotoshi Sakonjo, "Tsushin Joho Kara Mita Sinjyuwan Kogeki (Signal Intelligence War and Pearl Harbor Attack)" in Ikuhiko Hata (ed.), *Kensho Sinjyuwan no Nazo to Shinjitsu* (Verifications of the Mystery and the Truth of Pearl Harbor), Tokyo: PHP Kenkyu-jo, 2001, pp.104–108.

40  R. Wohlstetter, *Pearl Harbor: Warning and Decision,* Stanford University Press, 1962.

41  Sakonjo, "Tsushin Joho Kara Mita Sinjyuwan Kogeki", p.202.

## CHAPTER 3

1  R. E. Dupuy and T. N. Dupuy, *The Collins Encyclopedia of Military History,* Fourth Edition, London: BCA, 1993, pp.1232–1235. Despite these significant achievements, the Japanese failed to coordinate their surprise attack properly with diplomatic ultimata to be delivered in Washington, DC. For many historians, this seemingly unprincipled surprise attack was self-defeating to Japan despite its operational success, because it roused the US as few other actions could have.

2  For the Japanese account of the Malaya Campaign, see Bouei Kenshu-jyo Senshi Shitsu (ed.), *Senshi Sousho, Marei Shinkou Sakusen,* Official War History Series, The Malaya Campaign, Tokyo: Asagumo Shinbun-sha, 1966. In visiting Germany in 1940, General Tomoyuki Yamashita, later Commander of the Twenty-fifth Army, had a chance to discuss the feasibility of the Singapore Campaign with Marshal Hermann Goering and officers of German military technical schools. They all told General Yamashita that in the event of war in the Far East, the reduction of Singapore would probably take nearly one and a half years with five Japanese divisions.

3  Masanobu Tsuji, *Singapore 1941–1942: The Japanese Version of the Malayan Campaign of World War II,* Oxford: Oxford University Press, 1988, p.213.

4  There is no doubt, especially after the fall of France in 1940, that in the absence of a fleet available in the Far East the reinforcement of the other two Services, above all the RAF, was essential for the security of Singapore. Britain, however, was not in a position to spare forces for areas where the danger was not imminent. Also, British policy in the

1930s and early 1940s was not to provoke Japan, and to try to avoid war with Japan as long as possible. This meant that Japan retained the initiative and was able to choose the moment of aggression.

5   According to Major Teruto Kunitake, who was in charge of planning both Malaya and Singapore operations, the study for the operation to conquer Malaya was set about in the Operations Section of the Army General Staff in August 1940, and its plan was arranged by the end of October 1941.

6   Tsuji, *Singapore*, p.161.

7   For these military maneuvers, see Masanobu Tsuji, *Japan's Greatest Victory, Britain's Worst Defeat*, New York: Sarpedon, 1993, pp.7–8.

8   S. W. Kirby, *The War against Japan, Volume I: The Loss of Singapore*, London: Her Majesty's Stationery Office, 1957, p.163.

9   For more details, see Kyoichi Tachikawa, "General Yamashita and his style of leadership: the Malaya/Singapore campaign," in Brian Bond and Kyoichi Tachikawa (eds.), *British and Japanese Military Leadership in the Far Eastern War 1941–1945*, Oxon: Frank Cass, 2004.

10   Tsuji, *Singapore*, p.161.

11   Taiwan-gun Kenkyu- bu (ed.), *Koredake-yomeba Ikusa-ni Kateru* (Read This Alone: And the War Can Be Won), Taiwan: Taiwan-gun Kenkyu- bu, 1941, in the Military History Archives of the National Institute for Defense Studies (Bouei Kenkyu-sho). For the English translation of the pamphlet, see Tsuji, *Japan's Greatest Victory, Britain's Worst Defeat*, Appendix 1. This pamphlet was designed to be read quickly by all the officers and other ranks, without strain, in the cramped conditions of a transport vessel. Apart from the preface, there were 18 chapters, including: The Campaign Area in South Asia: What Is It Like?; Why Must We Fight?; What Are You to Do on the Ship?; Scouting and Sentry Duty; and Movement in Special Terrain.

12   The Japanese attacks on Kota Bharu, Pearl Harbor, the Philippines, Guam, Hong Kong, and Wake Island were launched in that order and within a period of seven hours. Since Pearl Harbor lies to the east of the International Date Line, the attack there occurred on the morning of December 7, local time, whereas the attacks on the other places occurred on the morning of December 8, local times. As mentioned before, the landing at Kota Bharu was made one hour and twenty minutes before the attack on Pearl Harbor.

13   See "Tai Bei-Ei-Ran-Shou Senso Shumatsu Sokushin-ni Kansuru Fukuan" (A Plan for Completion of the War Against the United States, Great Britain, the Netherlands, and Chiang Kai-shek), in Takushiro Hattori, *Dai Toa Sensou Zenshi* (A Complete History of the Greater East Asian War), Tokyo: Hara-shobou, 1953, p.283.

14   For Admiral Isoroku Yamamoto's naval plan, see Ikuhiko Hata, "Admiral Yamamoto's Surprise Attack and the Japanese Navy's War Strategy," in Saki Dockrill (ed.), *From Pearl Harbor to Hiroshima: the Second World War in Asia and the Pacific, 1941–45,* New York: Macmillan Press, 1994.

15   Tsuji, *Japan's Greatest Victory, Britain's Worst Defeat*, p.164. Tsuji wrote that "General Yamashita looked as if he was displeased." The real intention of the Southern Army still needs to be examined, but it is likely that it was more interested in the Dutch East Indies, the goal of the first stage of Japan's grand strategy, than Singapore.

16   For Tsuji, see Masanobu Tsuji, *Senkou San-zenri* (Underground Escape), Tokyo: Atou-shobou,1951; Nobutaka Takayama, *Futari-no Sanbou: Hattori Takushirou to Tsuji Masanobu* (Two Staff Officers: Takushirou Hattori and Masanobu Tsuji), Tokyo: Fuyou-Shobou, 1999; Jyo Kojima, *Sanbou* (Staff Officers), Tokyo: Bungei-Shunjyu,1987; Eitaro Tatamiya, *Inbou-ni Tsukareta Sanbou, Tsuji Masanobu* (Masanobu Tsuji: A Man Who Was Obsessed With Conspiracy), Tokyo: Fuyou-Shobou, 1999; Hisahide Sugimori, *Tsuji Masanobu,* Tokyo: Bungei-Shunjyu-Shinsha,1963; Rikusenshi Kenkyu Fukyu-kai, (ed.), *Marei Sakusen* (The Malaya Campaign), Tokyo: Hara-shobou, 1966; Hyoe Murakami, "Jigoku-

karano Shisha – Tsuji Masanobu (The Man from the Hell: Masanobu Tsuji)," *Chuou-Kouron*, May, 1956.

17  To be more specific, operational plans for the Malaya Campaign were made by Major Kunitake, who set about the operational studies in August 1940 in the Operations Section of the Army General Staff. Operational plans for the Singapore Campaign were jointly made, with General Yamashita's strong leadership, by Tsuji and Kunitake in collaboration with Colonel Hanjiro Iketani, another staff officer in the Twenty-fifth Army. However, Kunitake and Iketani's names were rarely mentioned in Tsuji's account of the Malaya/Singapore Campaign. It was his ability and strong determination to execute the operational plans that is to be appreciated in examining Tsuji's role in the Malaya/Singapore Campaign. As staff officer, Tsuji was among the best in the Japanese Army although his style was remarkably different from that of a typical staff officer in the Army. For example, Tsuji always went to the front line to command his soldiers, rather than sitting and waiting in the rear.

18  It is said that when General Yamashita coordinated with the other forces, he advised his counterparts of his intentions regarding his operational plans and of the type of support he hoped for from them, but never inquired into or interfered with how the other forces chose to act.

19  A letter of commendation was usually given to a fighting unit. Although a letter of commendation was in some cases given to individual soldiers, they were war dead being recognized for bravery in battle. It was extraordinary for a living, serving officer to receive one.

20  According to the British official history of the campaign, the total British casualties in Malaya were 138,708, of whom more than 130,000 were prisoners of war. See Kirby, *The War against Japan, Vol. 1*, p.473.

21  For more details, see Ian Ward, *The Killer They Called A God*, Singapore: Media Masters, 1992. See also Tatamiya, *Inbou-ni Tsukareta Sanbou, Tsuji Masanobu* (Masanobu Tsuji: A Man Who Was Obsessed With Conspiracy).

22  For more details, see Murakami, "Jigoku-karano Shisha – Tsuji Masanobu (The Man from the Hell: Masanobu Tsuji)."

23  In Western literature, explanations for the brutal activities by Japanese soldiers can be found in the tradition and social ethos of Japan. There is some truth in it. Most of the Japanese soldiers committed them simply for the sake of their motherland. At the same time, however, it has to be noted that the Japanese soldiers deliberately committed such brutal activities so as to give a sense of "terror" to the local civilians. In so doing, it was not so important who actually were the guerrilla activists. What was important was to execute someone in front of the local civilians. The massacre can be also explained by the strategic considerations of early 1942: Japan had to deploy forces in Singapore to the next places in Southeast Asia, and simply wanted to secure its rear.

24  David Kennedy, *Freedom from Fear: The American People in Depression and War, 1929–1945*, New York, 2000, p.527.

25  Louis Morton, "The Decision to Withdraw to Bataan (1941)" in Kent Roberts Greenfield (ed.), *Command Decisions*, New York, 1959, p.120.

26  Writing a note in 1949/50 to his "Syndicate" of assistants on his war memoirs he was adamant: "The major dispositions were right…if I had known all about it then as I know now, there were no substantial resources which could have been diverted" from the European war. WSC note [undated but 1949/50], Churchill Papers 4/225, ff 118, 123–4; Churchill Archives Centre, Churchill College, Cambridge.

# CHAPTER 5

1  The best account remains Jonathan Utley, *Going to War with Japan*, Knoxville: University of Tennessee Press, 1985.

2  An often overlooked consequence of the "Europe first" grand strategy was to deny the

Pacific theaters large numbers of heavy long-range, large-load bombers until late 1944, with the result that Japanese outposts and the home islands were spared the devastation of strategic bombing until very late in the war. Geography and the absence of strategic bombers imposed a relatively greater burden on the land- and sea-based tactical air forces in the Pacific.

3    R. W. Love, Jr., "Ernest Joseph King," in R. W. Love, Jr. (ed.), *The Chiefs of Naval Operations*, Annapolis: Naval Institute Press, 1980, pp.137–180. The only full-length biography stresses King's personality and is, unfortunately, undocumented, T. B. Buell, *Master of Sea Power: A Biography of Fleet Admiral Ernest J. King*, Boston: Little, Brown, 1980.

4    E. B. Potter, *Nimitz*, Annapolis: Naval Institute Press, 1976.

5    Edward S. Miller, *War Plan Orange: U.S. Strategy to Defeat Japan, 1897–1945*, Annapolis: Naval Institute Press, 1991.

6    David J. Lu, *Agony of Choice: Matsuoka Yosuke and the Rise and Fall of the Japanese Empire, 1880–1946*, Lanham, Maryland: Lexington Books, 2002, p. 201.

7    James William Morley (ed.), *Japan's Road to the Pacific War: The Final Confrontation; Japan's Negotiations with the United States, 1941*, trans. by David A. Titus, New York: Columbia University Press, 1994, p.287.

8    E. B. Potter, *Bull Halsey*, Annapolis: Naval Institute Press, 1985.

9    Jack Sweetman, "Coral Sea," *Naval History*, Vol. 9, No. 3 (May/June 1993), p.25.

10   The most unequivocal codebreaking success of WWII was achieved by a US Army cryptanalyst, who successfully attacked the Japanese diplomatic code, which he entitled *Purple*. Reading *Purple* message traffic in real time and in clear made it possible for American intelligence to eavesdrop not only on all Japanese diplomatic communication with its embassies and consulates everywhere, but also to read reports back to Tokyo from military and naval attachés in other Axis and neutral capitals.

11   Frederick D. Parker, *A Priceless Advantage: US Naval Communications Intelligence and the Battles of Coral Sea, Midway, and the Aleutians*, Fort George Meade, Maryland: Center for Cryptographic History, National Security Agency, 1993; and John Prados, *Combined Fleet Decoded: The Secret History of American Intelligence and the Japanese Navy in World War II*, New York: Random House, 1995, pp.278–335.

12   John Lundstrom, "Frank Jack Fletcher Got a Bum Rap," *Naval History*, Vol. 6, No. 2 (Summer 1992), pp.22–27. Wholly unreliable due to factual errors, the only biography of Fletcher is Stephen D. Regan, *In Bitter Tempest: A Biography of Admiral Frank Jack Fletcher*, Ames: Iowa State University Press, 1994.

13   The dive-bomber pilots who nosed over from 20,000 feet during the attack on Tulagi later complained that their windshields and sights fogged over during the dives. As a result, during the attack by the *Yorktown* dive-bombers on the *Shoho* on the 7th, they dived from 15,000 feet and scored nine direct hits and two near misses. For reasons that are not altogether clear, this was not repeated the following day and was "a serious factor in the poor performance of pilots attacking *Zuikaku* and *Shokaku*" on the 8th. This unique problem was solved by applying new coatings to the glass before the battle of Midway. Harold L. Buell, "Coral Sea Remembered," *Foundation*, Vol. 13, No. 1 (Spring 1992), p.52.

14   A night surface attack by torpedo-bearing destroyers was considered and rejected by the opposing admirals, who were equally reluctant to risk their screening forces.

15   The 217-knot SBD-2 Dauntless dive bomber, which joined the US Fleet in 1940, had the best range of any early American wartime carrier-based plane. It could fly search missions with a 500-pound bomb on the center rack, or strikes with a 1,000-pound bomb and two 100-pound bombs under the wings. The SBD strike group range was limited by the range of escorting fighters and accompanying TBD torpedo-bombers. Although armed for self-defense, SBD pilots preferred to evade opposing fighters.

16   The Mitsubishi A6M2 00 Zero fighter was the first naval aircraft superior to its land-based counterparts. Its two 7.7 cal. machine guns were fired with tracers for ranging

reference and its two 20mm machine guns were used for close-in combat. The Zero first flew in China in 1940 and 1941, when it achieved considerable success, although the plane's lack of armor protection for the pilot and poor Japanese air tactics were soon noted as obvious weaknesses.

17   Buell, "Coral Sea Remembered," p.53.

18   The Nakajima B5N2 Type 97 Kate torpedo bomber was a stable 185-knot plane that carried two 500-pound bombs or one 1,760-pound torpedo. Although the Japanese torpedo was a highly accurate, lethal weapon, the poorly armored Kate was slow and sluggish and, owing to the lack of forward firing guns, effectively defenseless against opposing fighters.

19   John B. Lundstrom, *The First Team: Pacific Naval Air Combat from Pearl Harbor to Midway*, Annapolis: Naval Institute Press, 1984, p.257.

20   The Aichi D3A1 Type 99 Val dive bomber, which entered the Combined Fleet in 1938 and saw combat in China in 1940, suffered by contrast with its American counterpart, the SBD Dauntless. Not only did it have a shorter combat range, but also its fixed landing gear meant that it scarcely made 200 knots. Armed with a single 550-pound bomb under the fuselage and two 60-pound bombs under the wings, the Val was agile, stable during a dive, and reasonably accurate.

21   Lundstrom, *First Team*, p.257.

22   Ibid., p.277.

23   See B. Tillman, "American and Japanese Aircraft at Midway," in R. Cressman et. al., *"A Glorious Page in Our History": The Battle of Midway, 4–6 June 1942*, Missoula, Montana: Pictorial Histories Publishing, 1990, p.206; and B. Tillman, *Wildcat: the F4F in WWII*, 2nd. ed., Annapolis, Maryland: Naval Institute Press, 2000.

24   For a well-informed study of the tactical high command, see R. E. Barde, "The Battle of Midway: A Study in Command," Unpubl. Ph.D. Diss., University of Maryland, 1971. Barde's research is reflected in G. Prange, D. M. Goldstein, and K. V. Dillon, *Miracle at Midway*, New York: McGraw-Hill, 1982, which greatly emphasizes the many "miraculous" events attending the outcome.

25   Morley, *Japan's Road to the Pacific War*, p.287.

26   R. J. Cressman, "'To Retrieve our Initial Disaster'," *Naval History*, Vol. 6, No. 2 (Summer 1992), p.14.

27   Morley, *Japan's Road to the Pacific War*, p.288.

28   For Admiral King's unusual personality, see Robert Love, "Ernest J. King," in Love, ed., *Chiefs of Naval Operations*, p.140. King apparently was unconcerned about being disliked and worked hard not to allow personal relations influence his judgments. For instance, despite a long history of bitter professional rivalry and mutual distrust, King selected Admiral Frederick Horne to be his Vice Chief of Naval Operations in early 1942 owing to Horne's outstanding ability. King's chief of staff, Admiral Charles M. Cooke, who greatly admired his wartime boss, admitted that he was "a strange bird."

29   Not only had the United States accepted responsibility for the defense of Australia, an important political act, but also three divisions of the Australian Army were with the British Eighth Army in the Western Desert defending against a successful Axis offensive in Libya which threatened the Mediterranean Fleet base at Alexandria and the Suez Canal. The first Allied plan to implement the "Europe first" grand strategy, *Gymnast*, envisioned a landing by US Army divisions in North Africa to relieve the pressure on those forces defending Egypt. Although that plan was abandoned and the British had agreed to an American plan to mount a cross-channel invasion of northwestern France in September 1942 – a strategy King loudly advocated, he worried that the exposure of Australia to the Japanese Fleet might result in the withdrawal of the Australian Army from Egypt and inevitable British demands that the United States compensate by reviving *Gymnast* or deploying US Army divisions to Egypt, both of which he and General Marshall strongly opposed.

30 King was unhappy with Fletcher's conduct of the battle of the Coral Sea, but his explanation of his command satisfied Nimitz.

31 Malcolm A. LeCompte, "Radar and the Air Battles of Midway," *Naval History*, Vol. 6, No. 2 (Summer 1992), pp.28–32.

32 G. Prange, D. M. Goldstein, and K. V. Dillon, *Miracle at Midway*, p.103.

33 J. Worthington, "Destroyer at Midway," *Naval History*, Vol. 6, No. 2, p.19.

34 Lundstrom, *First Team*, p.337; and Mitsuo Fuchida and Masatake Okumiya, *Midway: The Battle That Doomed Japan, the Japanese Navy's Story*, trans. by Clark K. Kawakami and Roger Pineau, Annapolis: Naval Institute Press, 1955, p.14.

35 Walter Lord, *Incredible Victory*, New York: Harper and Row, 1967, p.165.

36 Joseph Worthington, "Destroyer at Midway," p.20.

37 Pacific Fleet cruisers embarked four or five Curtis SOC-3 Seagull biplane floatplanes, but they saw limited service during the battle of Midway.

38 John Lundstrom, "Frank Jack Fletcher Got a Bum Rap," p.20.

## CHAPTER 6

1 Field Marshal William Slim, *Defeat into Victory*, London: Cassell, 1956, pp.109–110.

2 WO 172/928 January 1942 PRO.

3 As well as American-British-Dutch-Australian (ABDA) Command.

4 There is much controversy surrounding the Sittang River fighting. The area was supposed to be heavily defended, but the defenses had not been properly sited. There was confusion within senior command regarding the Japanese movements. Two brigades of the 17th were forced to fight towards the bridgehead as the Japanese surrounded them. Smyth was forced to make a difficult decision, allow the Japanese to seize the bridge intact or blow up the bridge before the two brigades had been allowed to fight their way to safety.

5 Smyth was replaced by Brigadier D. T. Cowan as divisional commander on March 1, while Hutton was replaced by General Sir Harold Alexander on March 5. Alexander and his staff arrived with the 7th Armoured and the 63rd Indian Brigades as the last reinforcements.

6 The 18th and 56th divisions were shipped in to support the drive to destroy the Burma Army.

7 The operational command, XV Corps, was not made aware of the plan for weeks.

8 L/WS/1323 Operations in Burma Ciphers, 1 January 1943, OIOC, BL.

9 The HQ was established in Ceylon. SEAC's original mandate was to undertake amphibious attacks against the Japanese in Burma, Malaya, and the Dutch East Indies. When strategic concerns in Europe overshadowed the needs of SEAC, the full development of the amphibious side of the command was delayed until 1945. In principle, however, SEAC was in command of all air, naval, and land forces opposite the Japanese in Burma and Malaya, including American and Chinese air and ground forces in northern Burma, Northern Combat Area Command (NCAC), commanded by Lieutenant-General Stillwell. Eleventh Army Group was the organization that linked India Command and SEAC. The main land organization within SEAC was the Fourteenth Army (formerly Eastern Army), which was placed under the command of Lieutenant-General William Slim. Slim understood that, due to the strategic issues surrounding the amphibious forces, his troops were going to undertake an overland advance into Burma. Under Fourteenth Army was IV Corps (23rd, 17th, and, later, 20th Indian divisions) stationed in Assam and XV Corps (initially 26th Indian Division; by early autumn, the 7th Indian; later in 1943, the 5th Indian Division) stationed in the Arakan region.

10 Slim, *Defeat into Victory*, p. 176.

11 Some of its units, such as the 14/13th Frontier Force Rifles, were so adept at jungle

warfare that they were using flying columns to upset the Japanese lines of
communication and protect the flanks of the withdrawing 20th Indian Division.

12　In April there were more than 148 tons of supplies delivered each day; by June it had
risen to 362 tons.

13　One brigade was sent to Imphal, while the 7th took the 161st under its command.

14　M. A. Lowry, *Fighting Through to Kohima*, Pen and Sword, 2003, p.237.

15　Michael Calvert, *Prisoners of Hope*, Leo Cooper, 1996, p.246.

16　Eleventh Army Group had been renamed in November 1944.

17　By this time the RAF and USAAF had almost complete air superiority over Burma.

18　Slim, *Defeat into Victory*, p.327.

19　A major controversy erupted over the summer. Slim was relieved of command of future
operations in SEAC by ALFSEA commander, General Oliver Leese. However, within days,
Leese himself was relieved of command and Slim was reinstated.

## CHAPTER 7

1　"MacArthur Calls at Adelaide," Adelaide *Advertiser*, March 21, 1942, p.1. Unlike
biographies of MacArthur, which are hazy about the exact time and location at which
MacArthur made this statement, the newspaper states that he made the comment to
reporters while changing trains at Terowie, north of Adelaide, at 2pm on March 20, 1942.

2　D. Clayton James, *The Years of MacArthur: 1941–1945*, Boston: Houghton Mifflin
Company, 1975, p.109.

3　G. H. Brett, "The MacArthur I knew," *True*, October 1947, quoted in D. McCarthy, *South-
West Pacific Area-First Year*, Canberra: Australian War Memorial, 1959, p.20.

4　Richard B. Frank, *Guadalcanal: The Definitive Account of the Landmark Battle*, New York:
Random House, 1990, p.205.

5　Samuel E. Morison, *The Struggle for Guadalcanal August 1942–February 1943*, Boston:
Little, Brown and Company, 1948, p.178.

6　R. L. Eichelberger, *Our Jungle Road to Tokyo*, Nashville: Battery Classics, 1989, p.21.

7　G. Long, *MacArthur as Military Commander*, Sydney: Angus and Robertson, 1969, p.157.

8　Edward J. Drea, *New Guinea; The US Army Campaigns of World War II*, Washington:
US Army Center of Military History, n.d. pp.29–30.

9　Stephen R. Taafe, *MacArthur's Jungle War: The 1944 New Guinea Campaign*, Lawrence,
Kansas: University Press of Kansas, 1998, p.145.

10　James, *The Years of MacArthur*, p.557.

11　Geoffrey Perret, *Old Soldiers Never Die: The Life of Douglas MacArthur*, New York:
Random House, 1996, p.424.

12　S. L. Falk, "The Army in the Southwest Pacific," in William M. Leary (ed.), *MacArthur and
the American Century*, Lincoln: University of Nebraska Press, 2001, p.151.

## CHAPTER 8

1　Dudley McCarthy, *South-West Pacific Area-First Year*, Canberra: Australian War Memorial,
1959, p.592.

2　Quoted in Peter FitzSimons, *Kokoda*, Sydney: Hodder, 2004, p.351.

3　G. C. Kenney, *General Kenney Reports*, Washington: Office of Air Force History, 1987, p.151.

4　John Coates, *Bravery above Blunder: The 9th Australian Division at Finschhafen, Sattelberg,
and Sio*, Melbourne: Oxford University Press, 1999, p.226.

## CHAPTER 9

1　For a detailed account of prewar planning for a war against Japan, see Edward S. Miller,
*War Plan Orange: The U.S. Strategy to Defeat Japan, 1897–1945*, Annapolis, Maryland:
Naval Institute Press, 1991.

2　Yogi Koda, "A Commander's Dilemma: Admiral Yamamoto and the 'Gradual Attrition'

Strategy," *Naval War College Review* 46 (Autumn 1993), p.64.

3   For background on Roosevelt's decision, see Grace Person Hayes, *History of the Joint Chiefs of Staff in World War II: The War Against Japan*, Annapolis, Maryland: Naval Institute Press, 1982, pp.96–103.

4   Ibid., p.100.

5   For a biography of Nimitz, see E. B. Potter, *Nimitz*, Annapolis, Maryland: Naval Institute Press, 1976.

6   The numbered fleet designations resulted from a uniform designation system directed by Admiral King on March 15, 1943. For biographies of Spruance and Halsey, see respectively, Thomas B. Buell, *The Quiet Warrior: A Biography of Raymond A. Spruance*, Boston: Little, Brown and Co., 1974; and E. B. Potter, *Bull Halsey*, Annapolis, Maryland: Naval Institute Press, 1985.

7   For biographies of Turner and Smith, see respectively, George C. Dyer, *The Amphibians Came to Conquer: The Story of Admiral Richmond Kelly Turner*, 2 vols, Washington, DC: Government Printing Office, 1972; and Norman V. Cooper, *A Fighting General: The Biography of Gen Holland M. "Howlin Mad" Smith*, Quantico, Virginia: Marine Corps Association, 1987.

8   Office of Naval Operations, *Landing Operations Doctrine United States Navy 1938*, Washington, DC, 1938, p.151.

9   Philip A. Crowl and Edmund G. Love, *Seizure of the Gilberts and Marshalls*, United States Army in World War II series, Washington, DC: Office of the Chief of Military History, Department of the Army, 1955, p.74.

10   COMCENPACFOR, General Instructions, Oct. 29, 1943, quoted in, Dyer, *The Amphibians Came to Conquer*, vol. 2, p.639.

11   Joseph H. Alexander, *Utmost Savagery: The Three Days of Tarawa*, Annapolis, Maryland: Naval Institute Press, 1995, p.231.

12   Quoted in Joseph H. Alexander, *Utmost Savagery*, p.78.

13   Gordon L. Rottman, *World War II Pacific Island Guide: A Geo-Military Study*, Westport, Connecticut: Greenwood Press, 2002, pp.349–350.

14   United States Strategic Bombing Survey [Pacific] (USSBS), *Interrogations of Japanese Officials*, n.p.: Naval Analysis Division, n.d., vol.1, Interrogation of Commander Chikataka Nakajima, IJN, p.143.

15   Dyer, *The Amphibians Came to Conquer*, vol. 2, p.739.

16   Saburo Hayashi and Alvin D. Coox, *Kogun: The Japanese Army in the Pacific War*, Quantico, Virginia: Marine Corps Assoc., 1959, p.109.

17   Allied Translator and Interpreter Section SWPA No.4 dated May 23, 1944 translation of Combined Fleet Orders Operations No. 73, dated March 8, 1944.

18   For a detailed account of the so-called "Smith vs. Smith" incident, see Harry A. Gailey, *"Howlin' Mad" vs the Army: Conflict in Command, Saipan 1944*, Novato, California: Presidio Press, 1986.

19   Japanese Thirty-first Army, incoming message file, No. 152, captured by US forces. Quoted in Henry I. Shaw, Bernard C. Nalty, and Edwin T. Turnbladh, *Central Pacific Drive*, Washington, DC: Historical Branch, Headquarters Marine Corps, 1966, p.295.

20   Commander in Chief Pacific Fleet serial: 00071 dated June 3, 1944, Outline Campaign Plan – Granite II.

21   CCS 165th Meeting, "Minutes of Meeting Held in Conference Room 'A' War Cabinet Office, London, England on Wednesday, 14 June 1944, at 1430."

22   For a detailed account of the debate, see Robert Ross Smith, "Luzon versus Formosa," in Kent Roberts Greenfield, *Command Decisions*, Washington, DC: Office of the Chief of Military History, Department of the Army, 1960, pp.461–477.

23   Casualty figures from Robert Ross Smith, *The Approach to the Philippines*, United States Army in World War II, The War in the Pacific series, Washington, DC: Office of the Chief of Military History, 1953, p.577.

24  For an account of the evolution of the logistics system in the Central Pacific, see Worrall Reed Carter, *Beans, Bullets, and Black Oil: The Story of Fleet Logistics Afloat in the Pacific during World War II*, Newport, RI: Naval War College Press, 1998.

25  Commander in Chief Pacific Ocean Areas, "Campaign Plan Granite," Jan. 15, 1944.

26  Buell, *The Quiet Warrior*, p.324.

27  R. E. Appleman et al, *Okinawa: The Last Battle*, United States Army in World War II, The War in the Pacific series, Washington, DC: Historical Division, Department of the Army, 1948, p.473.

28  United States Strategic Bombing Survey, *Summary Report* (Pacific War), Washington, DC: 1946, p.10.

## CHAPTER 10

1  Henderson Airfield was named after Major Loften R. Henderson, USMC who was killed on June 4, 1942 off Midway.

## CHAPTER 11

1  CG, 1stMarDiv Final Report on Guadalcanal Operation, Phase V, quoted in George C. Dyer, *The Amphibians Came to Conquer: The Story of Admiral Richmond Kelly Turner*, Washington, 1969, p.541.

2  Saburo Hayashi and Alvin D. Coox, *Kogun: The Japanese Army in the Pacific War*, Quantico, Virginia, 1959, p.110.

3  Definition from Joint Publications 3-02, *Joint Doctrine for Amphibious Operations*, Washington Joint Chiefs of Staff, October 8, 1992, p.GL-6.

4  B. H. Liddell Hart, *The Defense of Britain*, New York, 1939, p.130.

5  The use of military transport helicopters to deliver assault troops well inland from conventional landing beaches did not become standard practice in amphibious operations until after World War II.

6  Admiral Kichisaburo Nomura, interviewed in US Strategic Bombing Survey Interrogation Number 429, volume 2, p.387.

7  Rear Admiral George H. Fort, USN, quoted in Lieutenant-General Merwin H. Silverthorn, USMC oral history interview, 1973, Marine Corps Oral History Collection, Marine Corps Historical Center, Washington, DC, p.316. Silverthorn was Geiger's chief of staff.

8  Nimitz to Vice-Admiral Raymond Spruance, prior to Operation *Galvanic*, quoted in E. B. Potter, *Nimitz*, Annapolis, 1976, p.257.

9  Author interview with former Navy Lieutenant Edward J. Hagan, January 18, 2001. Doctor Hagan landed with the 7th Marines on D-Day at Peleliu as assistant regimental surgeon.

10  Fleet Admiral Ernest J. King, USN, *The War Reports of General of the Army George C. Marshall, Chief of Staff, General of the Army H. H. Arnold, Commanding General, Army Air Forces, Fleet Admiral Ernest J. King, Commander-in-Chief, US Fleet and Chief of Naval Operations*, New York, 1947, p.658.

## CHAPTER 12

1  William Manchester, *Goodbye Darkness*, pp.367–368.

2  Roy Appleman, *Okinawa, The Last Battle*, Washington: US Government Printing Office, 1971, pp.424, 432, and 440–442.

## CHAPTER 13

1  The summary of themes from the postwar critical literature is drawn from J. Samuel Walker, "The Decision to Use the Bomb: A Historiography Update," *Diplomatic History*

14 (winter 1990), and Barton Bernstein, "The Struggle Over History," in Philip Nobile (ed.), *Judgment at the Smithsonian*, New York: Marlowe and Co., 1995.

2 Clay Blair, *Silent Victory: The U.S. Submarine War Against Japan*, Philadelphia: J. B. Lippincott, 1975, is the best account of the US Navy's submarine war.

3 Mark P. Parillo, *The Japanese Merchant Marine in World War II*, Annapolis: Naval Institute Press, 1993, pp.242–243.

4 Joint Army-Navy Assessment Committee (JANAC), *Japanese Naval and Merchant Shipping Losses During World War II by All Causes*, February 1947, Naval History Center, Washington, DC; Statement of Captain Atsushi Oi, 15 Oct 49, Doc. No. 53013, Center of Military History, Washington, DC (CMH); Statement of Lt. Col. Michinori Ureshino, 20 Nov 48, Doc. No. 61341, CMH; United States Strategic Bombing Survey, Report No. 54, Transportation Division, *The War Against Japanese Transportation, 1941–45*, Washington, DC: US Government, 1947, pp.1, 17–18, 27–28.

5 Haywood S. Hansell, *Strategic Air War Against Japan*, Washington, DC: Government Printing Office, 1980, pp.1–17; Kenneth P. Werrell, *Blankets of Fire*, Washington, DC: Smithsonian Institution Press, 1996; Grace P. Hayes, *The History of the Joint Chiefs of Staff in World War II: The War Against Japan*, Annapolis: Naval Institute Press, 1982, pp.343–344, 383–385; Thomas M. Coffey, *Iron Eagle*, New York: Crown Publishers, 1986, pp.113–134, 185–186, 200–213, 215, 244.

6 Richard B. Frank, *Downfall: The End of the Imperial Japanese Empire*, New York: Random House, 1999, pp.52–69, 72–77, 149–154, 333–337.

7 File 760.308.1, United States Air Force Historical Center, Maxwell, Alabama; *Army Battle Casualties and Nonbattle Deaths in World War II, Final Report, 7 December 1941–31 December 1946*.

8 M. D. Pearlman, *Unconditional Surrender, Demobilization and the Atomic Bomb*, Fort Leavenworth, Kansas: Combat Studies Institute, US Army Command and General Staff College, 1966, pp.1–8; R. Dallek, *Franklin Roosevelt and American Foreign Policy, 1932–45*, Oxford: Oxford University Press, 1979, pp.373–376; M. Gilbert, *Winston S. Churchill, vol. 7, Road to Victory, 1941–45*, Boston: Houghton Mifflin, 1986, pp.300–301, 309–310.

9 Frank, *Downfall*, pp.27–37.

10 Downfall, Strategic Plan for Operations in the Japanese Archipelago, OPD 350.05, Sec. 1, Record Group (RG) 165, NARA.

11 Joint Chiefs of Staff 924/15, 25 April 1945, CCS 381 Pacific Ocean Operations (6-10-43), Sec. 11, RG 218, NARA.

12 *Boeicho Boei Kenshujo Senshi Shitsu, No. 57, Hondo Kessen Junbi (2) Kyushu No Boei*, Tokyo, pp.177–182, 211–6, 278–92; Office of the Chief of Military History, Department of the Army, *Japanese Monograph No. 17: Homeland Operations Record* (n.d.), Appendix VII; *Reports of General MacArthur, Japanese Operations in the Southwest Pacific Area, Volume II, Part II*, Washington: Government Printing Office, 1966, pp.591–592, 605–607.

13 April 8 Imperial Headquarters Directive No. 2438: "Outline of Preparations for the Ketsu Go Operation": *Hondo Kessen Junbi (2) Kyushu No Boei*, pp.164–166, 264; *Reports of General MacArthur, Volume II, Part II*, p.601. A complete translated copy of this order is found in *War in Asia and the Pacific, Volume 12: Defense of the Homeland and End of the War*, New York: Garland Publishing, 1980, pp.201–231.

14 Reports of *General MacArthur, Volume II, Part II*, p.612.

15 R. J. C. Butow, *Japan's Decision to Surrender*, Stanford: Stanford University Press, 1954, pp.9–10.

16 Frank, *Downfall*, pp.98–102, 221–232.

17 William M. Leary, ed., *We Shall Return, MacArthur's Commanders and the Defeat of Japan*, Lexington: University of Kentucky Press, 1988, pp.61–62.

18 Sixth Army Field Order 74; *Hondo Kessen Junbi (2) Kyushu No Boei*, pp.305–306, 308–309, 311–315, 318–328, 338–342, 350, 358–365, 458–465, 470–471, 519–521, 522–525, 537–546, 552–556, 565–575, 594–595.

19   Sixth Army Field Order No. 74, 28 July 1945, CMH.

20   *Hondo Kessen Junbi (2) Kyushu No Boei*, pp. 273–6.

21   Ibid., p.294.

22   Ibid., p.444. Contemporaneous plans at IGHQ reflected four reinforcing divisions. The effort to secure a portion of the Thirty-sixth Army from the Tokyo region is covered in "Statement on the Operational Preparations for the Defense of Kyushu," Document 58513, Maj. Gen. Sanada Joichiro, CMH; Statement Concerning Homeland Defense in 1945, Col. Sugita Ichiji, CMH. The Chief of the Imperial Army's intelligence section, Lt. Gen. Arisue, commented after the war that the reason why Imperial Headquarters deferred a decision to dispatch "the decisive battle forces in the Kanto Area to the Kyushu Area" was lack of sound intelligence. Statement of Lt. Gen. Arisue, Doc. No. 61660, CMH.

23   Frank, *Downfall*, pp.204–211.

24   Statement of Lieutenant-Colonel Ohta Kyoshi (Staff Officer in Charge of Transportation and Line of Communications of the 16th Area Army), pp.1–2, CMH. By way of comparison, a staff officer at Imperial Headquarters reported that the First General Army possessed somewhat less than 50 percent of the calculated requirements for provisions, and that this total was far beyond the levels of accumulated arms, ammunition, and fuel. Statement of Lieutenant-Colonel Iwakoshi Shinroku, Doc. No. 62800, CMH. With respect to movement of supplies to Kyushu, the ambitious original scheme called for shipment of all supplies within one week after May 27, from main depots direct to the vicinity of front line divisions. Eighty percent of this goal was completed, but deficiencies and erratic transportation continued to hamper shipments through July.

25   Statement of Lieutenant-Colonel Ohta Kyoshi (Staff Officer in Charge of Transportation and Line of Communications of the 16th Area Army), pp.2–3, CMH. This statement also indicates that by the end of July, the supply stockpiles were distributed equally among caves, schools, and dwellings. For a further discussion of postwar evidence on Japanese logistics see Frank, *Downfall*, pp.176–7.

26   "Magic" Diplomatic Summary, 1 April to 15 August 1945, Entry 9006, RG 457, NARA.

27   "Magic" Far East Summary, 1 April to 15 August 1945, Entry 9001, RG 457, NARA; Joint Intelligence Committee, "Japanese Reaction to an Assault on the Sendai Plain," J.I.C. 218/10, 10 August 1945 (final revision August 20, 1945). The total for Kyushu includes the Tsushima Fortress that was under Fifty-sixth Army. Geographic File 1942–45, CCS 381 Honshu (7-19-44) Section 4, RG 218, NARA.

28   "Magic" Far East Summaries, 19 Jul 45, 9 Aug 45.

29   SRMD-008, p. 266, 16 Jul, p. 297, 13 Aug, RG 457, NARA.

30   United States Strategic Bombing Survey, Report No. 62, Military Analysis Division, *Japanese Air Power*, Washington, DC: US Government, 1946, pp.24–25, 70. For a discussion of the various numbers offered concerning Japanese air strength in the homeland see Frank, *Downfall*, pp.182–183 and notes.

31   The estimate that the initial Japanese capability was to garrison Kyushu with six divisions total, with three in southern part of the island is mentioned repeatedly in planning documents from at least mid-1944 and reiterated in Downfall, Strategic Plans for Operations in the Japanese Archipelago. MacArthur's projection of ultimate Japanese capabilities, including air strength, is from the same Downfall plan. General Marshall's estimate before Truman of ultimate Japanese strength of eight to ten divisions and 350,000 men is found in "Minutes of Meeting Held at White House on Monday, 18 June 1945 at 1530," Xerox 1567, George C. Marshall Library. These minutes make no mention of reference to Japanese air capabilities.

32   General Headquarters, United States Army Forces Pacific, Military Intelligence Section, General Staff, "Amendment No. 1 to G-2 Estimate of the Enemy Situation with Respect to Kyushu," 29 July 1945, p.1, Gen. John J. Tolson Papers, United States Army Military History Institute, Carlisle, Pennsylvania.

33   Frank, *Downfall*, pp.273–277.

34  Richard Rhodes, *The Making of the Atomic Bomb*, New York: Simon and Schuster, 1986.

35  V. C. Jones, *Manhattan: The Army and the Atomic Bomb*, Washington, DC: CMH, 1985.

36  B. Bernstein, "Roosevelt, Truman, and the Atomic Bomb, 1941–45: A Reinterpretation," *Political Science Quarterly*, 90 (Spring 1975), pp.36–37; "The Atomic Bombings Reconsidered," *Foreign Affairs*, 74.1 (Jan.–Feb. 1995); James Hershberg, *James B. Conant: Harvard to Hiroshima and the Naming of the Nuclear Age*, New York: Alfred A. Knopf, 1993, pp.218–219, 226–229; G. P. Zachary, *Endless Frontier: Vannevar Bush, Engineer of the American Century*, New York: Free Press, 1997, pp.214–215, 283.

37  Frank, *Downfall*, pp.261–268, 283–287.

38  David M. Glantz, *The Soviet Strategic Offensive in Manchuria, 1945, "August Storm,"* London: Frank Cass, 2003, pp.29, 40, tables 11, 23.

39  Ibid., pp.141–150, 280–307.

40  Ibid., pp.60–91.

41  Ibid., pp. 301–307.

42  Ibid., table 45, p.340.

43  Statement of Sumihisa Ikeda, 23 Dec 1949, Doc. No. 54479, pp.3–4; Statement of Admiral Soemu Toyoda, 29 August 1949, Doc. No. 61340, p.7, CMH; Statement by Foreign Minister Shigenori Togo, 17 May 1949, p.30, CMH.

44  *Daihon'ei Rikugun-Bu (10)*, p.432; David M. Glantz, *Soviet Operational and Tactical Combat in Manchuria, 1945 "August Storm,"* London: Frank Cass, 2003, p. 31.

45  *Boeicho Boei Kenshujo Senshi Shitsu, No. 82, Daihon'ei Rikugun-Bu (10)*, Tokyo, 1975, pp.430–431, 440; Statement of Col. Saburo Hayashi, 23 December 1949, Doc. No. 54482, p.3, CMH; Memorandum of Admiral Zenshiro Hoshina, Doc. No. 53437 ("Minutes" of the Imperial Conference of August 9–10, 1945); Statement of Sumihisa Ikeda, 27 December 1949, Document No. 54483, CMH.

46  Statement by Foreign Minister Shigenori Togo, 17 May 1949, pp.32–33, CMH; Statement of Former Admiral Soemu Toyoda, 1 Dec. 49, Doc: No. 61340, pp.8–10; Butow, *Japan's Decision to Surrender*, p.161.

47  Butow, *Japan's Decision to Surrender*, pp.164–165.

48  Memorandum of Admiral Zenshiro Hoshina, Doc. No. 53437 ("Minutes" of the Imperial Conference of August 9–10, 1945); Statement of Sumihisa Ikeda, 27 December 1949, Document No. 54483, CMH.

49  H. P. Bix, *Hirohito and the Making of Modern Japan*, New York: Harper Collins, 2000 pp.516–518.

50  B. Bernstein, "Perils and Politics of Surrender," *Pacific Historical Review* 46 (November 1977), p.191; Tsuyoshi Hasegawa, "The Atomic Bombs and Soviet Entry into the War Against Japan: Which Was More Important on Japan's Decision to Surrender in the Pacific War?" in *The End of the Pacific War: Sixty Years*. Harvard University Press, forthcoming.

51  John Dower, *Embracing Defeat: Japan in the Wake of World War II*, New York: W. W. Norton/New Press, 1999, p.81.

52  Bix, *Hirohito and the Making of Modern Japan*, pp.518–519; Frank, *Downfall*, pp.313–315.

53  Frank, *Downfall*, pp.315–321.

54  Ibid., pp.320–322; Richard B. Frank, "Ketsu Go: Japanese Political and Military Strategy in 1945 and the End of the Pacific War," *The End of the Pacific War: Sixty Years*.

55  Frank, *Downfall*, pp.344–346; Frank, "Ketsu Go."

56  Henry L. Stimson, "The Decision to Use the Atomic Bomb," *Harper's*, February 1947.

57  Glantz, *The Soviet Strategic Offensive in Manchuria*, pp.280–307.

58  Robert Nimmo, *Behind a Curtain of Silence: Japanese in Soviet Custody, 1945–1956*, New York: Greenwood Press, 1998, pp.115–117; J. Dower, *War Without Mercy*, New York: Pantheon, 1986, pp.198–199; Dower, *Embracing Defeat*, pp.51–52.

# Select Bibliography

Agawa, Hiroyuki. *Yamamoto Isoroku*. Tokyo: Shinchosha, 1969.

Allen, Louis. *Burma: The Longest War 1941–1945*. London: Dent, 1984.

Alexander, Joseph H. *Utmost Savagery: The Three Days of Tarawa*. Annapolis, 1995.

Alexander, Joseph H. *Storm Landings: Epic Amphibious Landings in the Central Pacific*. Annapolis, 1997.

Appleman, R. & others. *Okinawa: The Last Battle*. Washington DC, 1948.

Baker, A. D. *Allied Landing Craft of World War II*. Annapolis, Maryland, 1985.

Barbey, Daniel E. *MacArthur's Amphibious Navy*. Annapolis, Maryland, 1969.

Bartlett, Merrill L. *Assault from the Sea. Essays on the History of Amphibious Warfare*. Annapolis, Maryland: Naval Institute Press, 1983.

Beard, Charles. *President Roosevelt and the Coming of the War*. Yale University Press, 1948.

Beaumont, Joan (ed.) *Australia's War 1939–1945*. St. Leonard's, Australia, 1996.

Bernstein, B. "Roosevelt, Truman, and the Atomic Bomb, 1941–45: A Reinterpretation," *Political Science Quarterly*, 90 (Spring 1975).

Bernstein, B. "The Atomic Bombings Reconsidered," *Foreign Affairs* 74.1 (Jan–Feb 1995).

Bix, H. *Hirohito and the Making of Modern Japan*. New York, 2000.

Blair, C. *Silent Victory: The U.S. Submarine War Against Japan*. Philadelphia, 1975.

Bond, B. *Chief of Staff: The Diaries of Lieutenant General Sir Henry Pownall, Vol. II*. London, 1974.

Brune, P. *A Bastard of a Place: The Australians in Papua*. Sydney, 2003.

Budiansky, Stephen. *Battle of Wits*. New York: The Free Press, 2000.

Buell, T. *The Quiet Warrior: A Biography of Raymond A. Spruance*. Boston, 1974.

Butler, J. R. M. & Gwyer, J. M. A. *Grand Strategy, Vol. III June 1941–August 1942*. London, 1964.

Butow, R. *Japan's Decision to Surrender*. Stanford, 1954.

Byrd, M. *Chennault: Giving Wings to the Tiger*. Tuscaloosa: University of Alabama University Press, 1987.

Callahan, Raymond. *Burma 1942–1945*. London, Davis-Poynter, 1978.

Callahan, Raymond. "Churchill and Singapore," in Brian Farrell & Sandy Hunter (eds.) *Sixty Years On: The Fall of Singapore Revisited*. Singapore, 2002.

Callahan, Raymond. *The Worst Disaster: The Fall of Singapore*. New edition. Singapore, 2001.

Calvert, Michael. *Prisoners of Hope*. London: Leo Cooper, 1996.

Calvocoressi, R. & Wint, G. *Total War*. London, 1989.

Campbell, Arthur. *The Siege: A Story from Kohima*. London: Allen & Unwin, 1956.

Cannon, M. H. *Leyte: The Return to the Philippines*. Washington, 1954.

Carew, T. *The Longest Retreat: The Burma Campaign 1942*. London: Hamish Hamilton, 1969.

Chosa Kai, Shiryo (eds.). *Taiheiyou Senso to Tomioka Sadatoshi* (The Pacific War and Sadatoshi Tomioka). Tokyo: Gunji Kenkyusha, 1971.

Churchill, W. *The Grand Alliance*. Boston, 1950.

Churchill, W. *The Hinge of Fate*. Boston, 1950.

Clifford, K. J. *Amphibious Warfare Development in Britain and America from 1920 to 1940*. New York, 1983.

Coffey, T. *Iron Eagle*. New York, 1986.

Colvin, J. *Not Ordinary Men: The Story of the Battle of Kohima*. London: Leo Cooper, 1995.

Connell, J. *Wavell: Supreme Commander*. London, 1969.

Cooper, K. W. *The Little Men*. London: Hale, 1985.

Cooper, N. *A Fighting General: The Biography of Gen Holland M. "Howlin Mad" Smith*. Quantico, Va., 1987.

Coubrough, C. R. L. *Memories of a Perpetual Second Lieutenant*. York: Wilton 65, 1999.

Craven, W. & Cate, J. L. *The Army Air Forces in World War II*, vol. 4, *The Pacific: Guadalcanal to Saipan August 1942 to July 1944*. Chicago, 1950.

Crowl, P. & Love, E. *Seizure of the Gilberts and Marshalls*. Washington, DC, 1955.

Cutler, T. J. *The Battle of Leyte Gulf, 23–26 October 1944*. New York, 1994.

Dallek, R. *Franklin Roosevelt and American Foreign Policy, 1932–45*. Oxford, 1979.

Davis, Patrick. *A Child at Arms*. London: Buchan & Enright, 1985.

Dexter, D. *The New Guinea Offensives*. Canberra, 1961.

Dower, J. *Embracing Defeat: Japan in the Wake of World War II*. New York, 1999.

Dower, J. *War Without Mercy*. New York, 1986.

Drea, E. J. *MacArthur's ULTRA: Codebreaking and the War Against Japan, 1942–1945*. Lawrence, KS, 1992.

Dull, Paul S. *A Battle History of the Imperial Japanese Navy, 1941–1945*. Annapolis, 1978.

Dyer, George C. *The Amphibians Came to Conquer*. Quantico, VA, 1989.

Eichelberger, R. L. *Our Jungle Road to Tokyo*. Nashville, TN, 1989.

Evans, David C. & Peattie, Mark R. *Kaigun: Strategy, Tactics and Technology in the Imperial Navy, 1887–1941*. Annapolis, Maryland, 1997.

Evans, Geoffrey. *The Desert and Jungle*. London: Kimber, 1959.

Evans, Geoffrey. *Slim as Military Commander*. London: Batsford, 1969.

Evans, G. & Brett-James, A. *Imphal: A Flower on Lofty Heights*. London: Macmillan, 1962.

Falk, S. L. *Liberation of the Philippines*. New York, 1970.

Farago, Ladislas. *The Broken Seal*. New York: Random House, 1967.

Feifer, George. *Tennozon, The Battle of Okinawa and the Atomic Bomb*. New York: Tickner and Fields, 1992.

Feis, Herbert. *The Road to Pearl Harbor*. Princeton University Press, 1950.

Fergusson, Bernard. *Beyond the Chindwin*. London: Collins, 1945.

Fergusson, Bernard. *The Wild Green Earth*. London: Collins, 1946.

Frank, Benis M. & Shaw, Henry I. *History of US Marine Operations in World War II, Vol. V: Victory and Occupation*. Washington, 1968.

Frank, Richard. *Guadalcanal: The Definitive Account of the Landmark Battle*. New York, 1990.

Frank, Richard. *Downfall: The End of the Imperial Japanese Empire*. New York, 1999.

Gailey, H. *"Howlin' Mad" vs the Army: Conflict in Command, Saipan 1944*. Novato, California, 1986.

Garand, George W. & Strobridge, Truman R. *History of US Marine Operations in World War II, Vol. IV: Western Pacific Operations*. Washington, 1971.

Gatchel, T. M. *At the Water's Edge: Defense against the Modern Amphibious Assault*. Annapolis, 1996.

Gilbert, M. *Winston S. Churchill*, vol. 7, *Road to Victory, 1941–45*. Boston, 1986.

Gill, G. H. *Royal Australian Navy, 1939–1942*. Canberra, 1957.

Gill, G. H. *Royal Australian Navy, 1943–1945*. Canberra, 1968.

Gillespie, O. A. *The Pacific: Official History of New Zealand in the Second World War*. Wellington, 1952.

Gilmore, Scott. *A Connecticut Yankee in the 8th Gurkha Rifles*. Washington: Brassey's, 1995.

Glantz, D. *The Soviet Strategic Offensive in Manchuria, 1945, "August Storm."* London, 2003.

Gow, Ian, *Okinawa 1945, Gateway to Japan*. New York: Doubleday, 1985.

Grant, I. L. *Burma: The Turning Point: The Seven Battles on the Tiddim Road*. London: Zampi Press, 1993.

Grant, I. L. & Tamayama, K. *Burma 1942: The Japanese Invasion*. London: Zampi Press, 1999.

Griffith, T. E. Jr. *MacArthur's Airman: General George Kenney and the War in the Southwest Pacific*. Lawrence, KS, 1998.

Hanley, Gerald. *Monsoon Victory*. London: Collins, 1946.

Hansell, H. *The Strategic Air War against Germany and Japan: A Memoir*. Washington, DC, 1986.

Harries, Mierion & Harries, Susie. *Soldiers of the Sun. The Rise and Fall of the Imperial Japanese Army*. New York: Random House, 1991.

Hayashi, S. & Coox, A. *Kogun: The Japanese Army in the Pacific War*. Quantico, Virginia, 1959.

Hayes, G. *The History of the Joint Chiefs of Staff in World War II: The War Against Japan*. Annapolis, 1982.

Hershberg, J. J. B. *Conant: Harvard to Hiroshima and the Naming of the Nuclear Age*. New York, 1993.

Hill, John. *China Dragons: A Rifle Company at War*. London: Blandford, 1991.

Horn, A. *Wings over the Pacific*. Auckland, 1992.

Horner, D. M. *High Command: Australia and Allied Strategy 1939–1945*. Sydney, 1982.

Horner, D. M. *Blamey: The Commander-in-Chief*. Sydney, 1999.

Hosoya, Chihiro. *Kioku to shiteno Pearl Harbor* (Pearl Harbor as memory). Tokyo: Minerva, 2004.

Hough, F. O., Ludwig, V. E. & Shaw, H. E. *History of the U.S. Marine Corps Operations in World War II: Pearl Harbor to Guadalcanal*. Washington, 1958.

Huber, Thomas M. *Japan's Battle of Okinawa, April–June 1945*. Fort Leavenworth: US Army Command and General Staff College, 1990.

Ienaga, Saburo. *The Pacific War, 1939–1945. A Critical Perspective of Japan's Role in World War II.* NY, 1978.

Isely, Jeter A. & Crowl, Philip A. *The US Marines and Amphibious War.* Princeton, NJ, 1951.

James, D. C. *The Years of MacArthur,* volume II, 1941–1945. Boston, 1975.

Joint Army Navy Assessment Committee. *Japanese Naval and Merchant Shipping Losses During World War II by All Causes.* Washington DC: Naval History Center, February 1947.

Jones, V. *Manhattan: The Army and the Atomic Bomb.* Washington, DC, 1985.

Kennedy, D. *Freedom from Fear: The American People in Depression and War, 1929–1945.* New York, 1999.

Kenney, G. C. *General Kenney Reports: A Personal History of the Pacific War.* Washington, 1949, 1987.

Kirby, S. Woodburn. *War Against Japan,* 5 volumes. London: HMSO, 1956–1969.

Koda, Y. "A Commander's Dilemma: Admiral Yamamoto and the 'Gradual Attrition' Strategy," *Naval War College Review* 46 (Autumn 1993).

Komatsu, Keiichiro. *Origins of the Pacific War and the Importance of "Magic."* Surrey: Japan Library, 1999.

Krueger, W. *From Down Under to Nippon.* Nashville, TN, 1989.

Leary, W. M. (ed.). *We Shall Return! MacArthur's Commanders and the Defeat of Japan 1942–1945.* Lexington, 1988.

Lewin, Ronald. *Slim the Standard Bearer.* London: Leo Cooper, 1976.

Long, G. *MacArthur as Military Commander.* Sydney, 1969.

Lorelli, John A. *To Foreign Shores: US Amphibious Operations in World War II.* Annapolis, 1995.

Lowry, M. A. *Fighting Through to Kohima.* Pen & Sword, 2003.

Long, G. M. *The Final Campaigns.* Canberra, 1963.

Lundstrom, J. B. *The First South Pacific Campaign. Pacific Fleet strategy, December 1941–June 1942.* Annapolis, Md, 1976.

Lundstrom, John B. *The First Team. Naval Air Combat from Pearl Harbor to Midway.* Annapolis, MD, 1984.

Lunt, James. *Hell of a Licking: The Retreat from Burma 1941–1942.* London: Collins, 1986.

MacArthur, D. *Reminiscences.* Greenwich, CT, 1965.

Mains, T. *The Retreat from Burma: An Intelligence Officer's Personal Story.* London: Foulsham, 1973.

Marder, Arthur. *Old Friends, New Enemies.* Oxford: Clarendon Press, 1981.

Marston, Daniel. *Phoenix from the Ashes: The Indian Army in the Burma Campaign.* Westport, CT and London: Praeger, 2003.

Masters, John. *The Road Past Mandalay.* New York: Harper, 1961.

Matthews, G. *The Re-Conquest of Burma 1943–1945.* Aldershot: Gale and Polden, 1966.

Maule, H. *Spearhead General: The Epic Story of General Sir Frank Messervy.* London: Oldhams Press, 1961.

Mayo, L. *Bloody Buna: The gruelling campaign in New Guinea that thwarted the Japanese invasion of Australia.* New York, 1974.

McCarthy, D. *South-West Pacific Area. First Year: Kokoda to Wau.* Canberra, 1959.

Miller, E. G. *Orange: The U.S. Strategy to Defeat Japan, 1897–1945.* Annapolis, Md, 1991.

Miller, J. Jr. *Cartwheel: The Reduction of Rabaul.* Washington, 1959.

Miller, J. Jr. *Guadalcanal: The First Offensive.* Washington, 1949.

Miller, Nathan. *The War at Sea: A Naval History of World War II.* New York, 1995.

Millett, A. R. *Semper Fidelis: The History of the US Marine Corps,* Rev. ed. New York, 1991.

Milner, S. *Victory in Papua.* Washington, 1957.

Mitsuo, Fuchida. *Watashi Ha Shinjyuwan Joku Ni Ita* (I flew over Pearl Harbor). Nara: Yamato Taimusu Sha, 1949.

Morison, S. E. *The Struggle for Guadalcanal, August 1942–February 1943.* Boston, 1948.

Morison, S. E. *Breaking the Bismarcks Barrier, 22 July 1942–1 May 1944.* Boston, 1950.

Morison, S. E. *New Guinea and the Marianas, March 1944–August 1944.* Boston, 1953.

Morison, S. E. *Leyte, June 1944–January 1945.* Boston, 1958.

Morison, S. E. *The Two Ocean War.* Boston, 1963.

Morton, L. "Germany First: The Basic Concept of Allied Strategy in World War II," in Kent Roberts Greenfield (ed.) *Command Decisions.* New York, 1959.

Morton, L. *Strategy and Command: The First Two Years.* Washington, 1962.

Odgers, G. *Air War against Japan, 1943–45.* Canberra, 1957.

Parillo, M. *The Japanese Merchant Marine in World War II.* Annapolis, 1993.

# Select Bibliography

Paull, R. *Retreat from Kokoda*. Melbourne, 1958.

Pearlman, M. *Unconditional Surrender, Demobilization and the Atomic Bomb*. Fort Leavenworth, Kansas, 1966.

Peattie, Mark R. *Sunburst. The Rise of Japanese Naval Air Power, 1909–1941*. Annapolis, Maryland, 2001.

Perret, G. *Old Soldiers Never Die: The Life of Douglas MacArthur*. New York, 1996.

Perrett, Bryan. *Tank Tracks to Rangoon*. London: Robert Hale, 1992.

Perry, F. W. *Commonwealth Armies: Manpower and Organisation in the Two World Wars*. Manchester: Manchester University Press, 1988.

Potter, E. B. *Bull Halsey*. Annapolis, Md, 1985.

Potter, E. B. *Nimitz*. Annapolis, Md, 1976.

Prados, John. *Combined Fleet Decoded. The Secret History of American Intelligence and the Japanese Navy in World War II*. New York, 1995.

Prange, Gordon. *At Dawn We Slept*. New York; Penguin Books, 1981.

Randle, John. *Battle Tales from Burma*. Burnsley, UK: Pen & Sword Books, 2004.

*Reports of General MacArthur, Japanese Operations in the Southwest Pacific Area, Volume II, Part II*. Washington, 1966.

Rhodes, R. *The Making of the Atomic Bomb*. New York, 1986.

Robertson, J. *Australia at War 1939–1945*. Melbourne, 1981.

Rottman, G. *World War II Pacific Island Guide: A Geo-Military Study*. Westport, Ct, 2002.

Ross, J. M. S. *Royal New Zealand Air Force*. Wellington, 1955.

Rusbridger, James & Nave, Eric. *Betrayal at Pearl Harbor*. New York: Summit Press, 1991.

Shaw, Henry I. Jr., Nalty, Bernard C., & Turnbladh, Edwin T. *History of US Marine Operations in World War II, Vol. III: Central Pacific Drive*. Washington, 1966.

Shaw, H. & Kane, D. *History of the U.S. Marine Corps Operations in World War II: Isolation of Rabaul*. Washington, 1964.

Skates, John R. *The Invasion of Japan. The Alternative to the Bomb*. Columbia, 1994.

Slim, Field Marshal the Viscount William. *Defeat into Victory*. London: Cassell, 1956.

Smeeton, Miles. *A Change of Jungles*. London: Hart-Davis, 1962.

Smith, Robert R. *The Approach to the Philippines*. Washington, 1953.

Smith, Robert R. *Triumph in the Philippines*. Washington, 1953.

Smyth, John. *Before the Dawn: a Story of Two Historic Retreats*. London: Cassell, 1957.

Spector, R. H. *Eagle Against the Sun, The American War with Japan*. New York, 1985.

Stephan, John J. *Hawaii under the Rising Sun. Japan's Plans for Conquest after Pearl Harbor*. Honolulu, 1984.

Stimson, H. "The Decision to Use the Atomic Bomb," *Harper's* (February 1947).

Stinnett, Robert. *Day of Deceit*. New York: Free Press, 2000.

Swinson, Arthur. *Kohima*. London: Cassell, 1966.

Taafe, S. R. *MacArthur's Jungle War: The New Guinea Campaigns*. Lawrence, KS, 1998.

Toland, John. *Infamy: Pearl Harbor and its aftermath*. New York: Doubleday, 1982.

US Navy. *Landing Operations Doctrine 1938*, Fleet Training Publication No. 167, with Change Three, August 1, 1943, Washington, 1938, 1943.

Vat, D. van der. *The Pacific Campaign: The US-Japanese Naval War 1941–1945*. New York, 1991.

Walker, J. "The Decision to Use the Bomb: A Historiography Update," *Diplomatic History* 14 (winter 1990).

Warren, A. *Singapore 1942: Britain's Greatest Defeat*. London, 2002.

Werstein, Irving. *Okinawa, The Last Ordeal*. New York: Thomas Y. Crowell, 1968.

Wohlstetter, Roberta. *Pearl Harbor*. Stanford University Press, 1962.

Wigmore, L. *The Japanese Thrust*. Canberra, 1957.

Willmott, H. P. *The War against Japan. The Period of Balance, May 1941–October 1943*. Wilmington, De, 2002.

Willoughby, C. A. & Chamberlain, J. *Reports of General MacArthur, vol. 1; The Campaigns of MacArthur in the Pacific*. Washington, 1966.

Worth, Jr., Ronald. *Secret Allies in the Pacific*. North California: McFarland & Company 2001.

Yahara, Hiromichi. *The Battle for Okinawa*. New York: John Wiley, 1995.

Y'Blood, W. T. *Red Sun Setting. The Battle of the Philippine Sea*. Annapolis, Maryland, 1981.

Zeiler, Thomas W. *Unconditional Defeat. Japan, America and the End of World War II*. Wilmington, Delaware, Scholarly Resources, 2004.

# Index